A KINGDOM FOR US

An Easy Bible Study for People
Who Want to Know What's Going On

KATHY ZUZIAK

CITIOFBOOKS, INC.
3736 Eubank NE Suite A1
Albuquerque, NM 87111-3579
www.citiofbooks.com
Hotline: 1 (877) 389-2759
Fax: 1 (505) 930-7244

Ordering Information:

Quantity sales. Special discounts are available on quantity purchases by corporations, associations, and others. For details, contact the publisher at the address above.

Printed in the United States of America.
ISBN-13:   Softcover   979-8-89391-236-4
            eBook   979-8-89391-237-1

Library of Congress Control Number: 2024916024

CONTENTS

INTRODUCTION

There is a Kingdom and there is a King. Jesus spoke about it. It is a literal kingdom, and He is the King, so when He tells us about it, we can be sure He is speaking from experience and not making things up. Because His Kingdom is not of this world, its boundaries are not earthly. Jesus tells us that the Kingdom is coming and also that the Kingdom is within us. This would not seem to make sense unless you realize that Jesus is speaking of both physical and spiritual kingdoms. The spiritual kingdom is not limited by time or space. Time and space were created by God and, therefore, can be manipulated by Him.

Jesus, as you have probably heard, is not dead. He is very much alive and is seated at the right hand of God in heaven at this present time. The Kingdom of God is a coming world government where Jesus will rule on the earth physically. Unlike the copycat one-world government many power-hungry global politicians are pushing for, the Kingdom of God will solve problems, not create them. King Jesus will protect His citizens, not oppress them for the sake of His own gain. He will solve climate change, end wars and racism, heal the sick, and prosper the global economy like we have never seen before. A one-world government was not the devil's idea. God created Adam to have dominion over the earth. Jesus, the last Adam, will fulfill that destiny. And the Bible tells us the Church will rule with Him at His side. In fact, the Bible says we can consider ourselves to be citizens of that Kingdom even now. The future for a citizen of the

Kingdom is bright. In the meantime, that Kingdom and its resources are available to its citizens now by faith. Why don't we see more evidence of that? Well, you see…

Not everyone is a citizen of the Kingdom of God. Most people are citizens of this world here. The citizens of the Kingdom are those that follow Jesus. It is not a kingdom you can see—yet—but it is a kingdom you can receive by faith and experience in the spirit. And one day very soon, that kingdom will be set up here on the earth and will be seen by everyone, even His enemies. That time is drawing near, and the invisible is now beginning to become visible. In this world, followers of Jesus are called Christians.

Christianity might be known as a religion, but it is way more than that. It is the family of God. His children are at all different levels of growth. God is not only into growing flowers and trees but also into growing people. Looking at the Church is like looking at a school population that ranges from pre-K to college. People who call themselves Christians are at all different levels of maturity. In 1 Corinthians 3:1, Paul says, "Brothers and sisters, I could not address you as people who live by the Spirit but as people who are still worldly— mere infants in Christ." Paul is speaking here to a group of Christian believers that are immature. This is an incredibly important point because it affects other people's perspectives of us. The world (non-believers) assumes Christians are all the same, but there are hundreds of thousands, perhaps millions, of people who are Christians in name only and who have never really been transformed from darkness into light or who are spiritual babies, never having put into practice the principles they have been taught. What the world is seeing now is not a true picture of the mature Church but they will see it soon. The Bible tells us that the whole of creation is waiting for the manifestation or the revealing of the sons of God (Romans 8:19). That means everybody, including living and nonliving things, is waiting to see the Church, the sons of God, grow up, get it together, and start acting like who they were meant to be. The true and living Church, the Body of Christ, is a brilliant diamond that has been hidden in a lump of coal…until now. The Spirit of God is calling, and it's time to grow up and to let our light shine in the darkness. It's time to embrace our citizenship in the Kingdom of Light.

How do we grow up? We need to eat spiritual food. The Bible, the precious and eternal (it will last forever) Word of the Living God, is our food. We need to ingest it, take it in. In order to experience higher levels of maturity, you have to spend time with the Word of God, the Bible. It doesn't make a difference how long you've been a Christian; it makes a difference how much time you spend with Jesus. When we talk about the Word of God, as if He is a person, we are referring to this scripture:

> In the beginning was the Word and the Word was with God and the Word was God. The same was in the beginning with God. In Him was life, and the life was the light of men. And the light shines in the darkness and the darkness did not comprehend it… He was in the world and the world was made through Him and the world did not know Him. He came to His own and His own did not receive Him. But as many as received Him, He gave the right to become children of God, to those who believe in His name, who were born not of blood, nor of the will of the flesh, but of God. And the Word became flesh and dwelt among us, and we beheld His glory,

the glory as of the only begotten of the Father, full of grace and truth. (John 1:1-14)

"The Word became flesh" is talking about Jesus. He is the Son of God, but He is also called the Word of God. He was born as a man with flesh and blood, but He *is* the scriptures personified. When you begin to wrap your head around that, reading the Word—the Bible—makes more sense. This is not a religion or something we do to gain favor from God. This is our bread, our life's sustaining power. It is who we are.

When you read and, yes, study the scriptures, you grow. The word *study* might make you cringe, but all that means is that you don't just read a scripture once and be done with it. You think about it, chew on it, and swallow it until it becomes part of you. You might look up the meaning of the words in a Bible dictionary. You might take notes and draw connections to something else you read in the scriptures and find that it all fits together in an amazing, cohesive way. That's because the words in the Bible are the very own words of God Himself. His words produce life, and when you receive them, they cause you to grow. You can grow like a blade of grass, or you can grow like a beanstalk, it's up to you.

Because of my continued and growing relationship with God, I have seen many miracles in my own life, my children's lives, my friend's lives, and in many others that I have heard about. A believer's life should be filled with miracles. God is alive and active in my life. He wants to be active in yours too. Jesus has not changed. He still teaches, heals people, casts out demons, works miracles, you know, everything He did when He was on the earth because, as you know, He was raised from the dead and is still alive! And because He lives, you can live too. Being a believer can be the richest, most satisfying life you can imagine! That's because we have been translated from the kingdom of darkness (the world) into the Kingdom of Jesus, the Kingdom of Light (Colossians 1:13). Jesus, the King of kings, has provided for us a Kingdom filled with everything we will ever need. He is a wonderful, super great, amazing King!

Of course, it is *His* Kingdom. He is the King. But as you get to know Him, you begin to realize that everything He does is for our benefit. He desires to share His Kingdom with us. Every day in our Kingdom, God does something new and wonderful. It is God's plan that we might experience days of heaven on the earth (Deuteronomy 11:21). Though we struggle and face challenges, God is there to help and to turn our wildernesses into gardens and our failures into victories. He is in the construction business. He makes the crooked places straight, the lame to walk, and the blind to see. My life will never be the same as it was before I knew Jesus, and now that the Light has come, I would never want to go back to being blind, living in the dark, not knowing Him. After reading through this study, I hope you will feel the same.

In this study, I spend quite a bit of time on the devil and his influence. You might never have stopped to think about these things before or heard them talked about very much. Jesus exposed the devil and cast out demons all over the place. He showed us what was going on beneath the surface. The Bible calls the devil the god (little "g") of this world. If we are ever going to get to know the real God while living in this world, we will have to learn to separate what belongs to God and what belongs to the devil.

We know that Jesus is coming back, and sooner than we think. Will He find a beautiful and powerful church fit to rule and reign with Him, or will He find a sad, weak, insipid form of a church fit for nothing but an extreme makeover? Church, it's time to let the Holy Spirit do His work in us now, to change us and make us over into the supernatural body of believers we were meant to be, filled with the glory of God!

This is good stuff, my friend. If you are a regular, non-religious person that just wants to know the truth, even someone who has never read the Bible, this study is for you. If you have some previous knowledge but aren't sure how it all works together, this study is for you too. Perhaps it will help to connect the dots. If you have been asleep, this is your alarm going off. There are a lot of scripture references, but don't stress. You don't have to look up everything at once, but please do look them up for yourselves. For those of us who have a Christian background, think of this study as a chance to go back to the basics to fill in what has been missing and where we got off track. Let's find out what is going on. Happy growing!

"Do not fear, little flock, for it is your Father's good pleasure to give you the kingdom" (Luke 12:32).

LESSON 1

TIME TO WAKE UP AND TIME TO GROW UP

The life of a Christian is not easy, but it is the best thing that could ever happen to us. We are in the world, but we are not *of* this world. We are citizens of a different Kingdom, the Kingdom of Light. We are children of the day, travelling in the midst of a kingdom of darkness. Just look around. The evidence of darkness speaks for itself. Things like cheating, murder, deception, angry mobs, robbing and looting, setting fires to buildings, vulgarity, drugged-up lives are all evidence of darkness. If you are uncomfortable with living in darkness, that is a good sign!

The Church is not a building but a living, breathing entity made up of a diverse group of people like you and me that, all combined, make up what the Bible calls the body of Christ. Jesus went back to heaven, but He left the Church to act in His place. He is the head of the Church, and we are His body, the part that continues to operate in the earth as Jesus did and with His authority, even though He is physically up in heaven, seated at the right hand of God the Father.

Consider these scriptures:

> For as we have many members in one body, but all the members do not have the same function, so we, being many, are one body in Christ, and individually members of one another. (Romans 12:4–5)

Now you are the body of Christ and members individually. (1 Corinthians 12:27)

And He Himself gave some to be apostles, some prophets, some evangelists, and some pastors, and teachers, for the equipping of the saints for the work of ministry, for the edifying (building up of the structure) of the body of Christ, till we all come to the unity of the faith and of the knowledge of the Son of God, to a perfect man, to the measure of the stature of the fulness of Christ; that we should no longer be children, tossed to and fro, and carried about with every wind of doctrine, by the trickery of men, in the cunning craftiness of deceitful plotting, but speaking the truth in love, may all grow up in all things into Him who is the head—Christ. (Ephesians 4:11–15)

Read that last line again. Do you see that it says, "We may all grow up"? There are a lot of ideas, doctrines, ways of thinking that shape us into who we are. If you follow the thinking of the world, you will stay spiritually immature. You will stay in the baby stage. The way of thinking that helps us grow up spiritually is the way that Jesus taught us to think. As we read, listen to, or discuss the scriptures in the Bible, we compare our thinking and acting to God's way of thinking and acting. We want to line ourselves up or match up with how God does it. When we do that, we grow. For instance, in the Ephesians scripture we just read, there are two nuggets we don't want to miss: "but speaking the truth in love, (we) may all grow up in all things into Him…" Speak the truth and speak it in love, it says. When we read that, we might think, *Oh, that's right! I need to be more careful*

to always tell the truth and to be kind when I talk to people.
We will probably have to read that several more times before
our renewed thinking causes our actions to change. When
our actions begin to line up with our thinking, then we have
grown up a little more spiritually. The goal is to become like
Jesus. We may look like ugly ducklings in a world of ducks
now, but we are growing into beautiful swans! We are living
in a natural world, but we are a supernatural people, all at
different levels of growth.

Wait a minute now. Did you say *supernatural?* Yes! Keep
reading. Your life is about to get a whole lot better.

Why Are We So Sleepy?

I remember when my husband worked the night shift.
We lived in a one-bedroom place with a baby, whose crib
was in our bedroom. My husband was gone all night, and
when he got home, I was eating breakfast, and he wanted
to eat dinner. He tried to arrange his sleep time to be able
to do things with us, but it was really difficult. He was not
tired when he just got home, but if he didn't go to sleep right
away, he would sleep all afternoon and wouldn't be able to
get any important things done for the family. He was always
sleepy. I had to try to keep the baby quiet during the day, so
we didn't wake Daddy. We lived in two different worlds for
a long time, the day and the night. We tried to socialize on
the weekends, but he would be so sleepy it was hard for him
to concentrate. He was a night person trying to live in a day
world. This is how it is for us and spiritual things. We are
supernatural "day" people living in a natural "night" world.
We just can't seem to keep our eyes open when it comes to
spiritual things, when the things of God, the family of God,
should be our priority.

"But the path of the just is like the shining sun, that shines ever brighter unto the perfect day. The way of the wicked is like darkness; they do not know what makes them stumble" (Proverbs 4:18–19).

We tend to fall asleep in an atmosphere of darkness. When I have made the long drive from Michigan to Florida, it is really hard for me to keep my eyes open once the sun goes down and the darkness settles in. Some people can drive all night, but not me. I can't continue to drive and have to stop at a hotel and sleep. This same phenomenon is at work in the church that lives in the world today. We live in a time when the darkness is getting darker, there are serious dangers all around us, so what do we do? Instead of rolling up our sleeves and diving into spiritual things, preaching the gospel, doing the works of Jesus, praying for people to be healed, exposing the enemy's lies, our eyelids begin to get heavy, and we "pull over" and take a nap.

Why are we so sleepy? In *The Wizard of Oz* by L. Frank Baum, Dorothy and her friends are trying to get to the Emerald City before the witch stops them. They are almost there, they can see it in the distance, and all they have to do is cross a field of poppies. They begin running excitedly across the field, but something in the poppies makes them drowsy, and even though they want to keep running, they slow down and eventually lie down, close their eyes, and go to sleep. So close to their goal! And who was behind the poppy problem? The wicked witch, not the wizard. Her goal was to stop them from getting to the city. Now we can learn from this story. It makes a good analogy of the Church in these last days. Like the wicked witch, it is the devil's goal to stop us. He makes us drowsy by his repetitive droning on and on about nothing. He talks to our minds and tells us reading the Bible is boring, that we have better things to do than to go to church; you don't have to spend time thinking about God today…do it tomorrow, or better yet, next week, or in the summer when you have more time; after all, you're young and you have your whole life to think about that… You know how he rattles on. We've all listened to his arguments. But should we believe him?

Not if you are aware of his end game. He is lying. Like the wicked witch, the devil (who is the real enemy) has a goal. He is trying to take you out.

Are We Prepared? Or Have You Checked Your Oil?

Jesus is coming back, and the time for choosing, whether we will follow Him or not, will be over. In Matthew 25:1–13, Jesus taught a parable about what happens when you fall asleep and are not prepared. In this parable of the ten virgins or bridesmaids, He is the bridegroom, and the Church is the ten bridesmaids. The story is that the bridesmaids all went out to wait for the bridegroom to come. All of the ladies brought lamps with them because it was night and they needed light. Five of the ladies were wise and brought extra oil for their lamps, while five were foolish and did not bring any extra. As the bridegroom delayed his coming, the bridesmaids all fell asleep because remember, it was dark out. At some point, a cry went out, "He's coming! He's coming!" Everyone woke up and found their lamps were burning low. The five wise bridesmaids that had brought extra oil were able to trim their lamps and get them to light back up. The five foolish bridesmaids had to go back to town to buy more oil. In the parable, while those ladies were gone back to town, the bridegroom came, opened the door to the marriage feast, and the five wise bridesmaids went in. Then, interestingly, later when the others came back, the door to the marriage celebration *remained* closed to them. They were really surprised. The door was totally closed! They had been sleepy and not been paying attention. They hadn't prepared for that possibility—not just that they would be late but that they might not get in at all. Think of the marriage feast representing heaven, and you have the idea. This might be more serious than you thought.

In the dark, we tend to get sleepy, right? We need to be wise and take that into consideration when we are making our plans in this life. Jesus called those five people who hadn't planned ahead *foolish*! The New Testament tells us again and again that Jesus, the bridegroom, will return and that his coming will be a surprise. It tells us we will be living in dark times. Jesus said if you knew that a thief was coming to break into your house in the middle of the night, you would prepare, make sure the doors and windows were locked, put in an alarm system, call the police, or something! Jesus was warning us, be ready *ahead* of time, before He comes. You won't have time once He gets here. The door will be shut. If you are on the outside, you will not be happy. Now is the time to buy your *oil*! We know the bridegroom is coming. Just like when we hear about a crisis, we rush to the stores and stock up on water and flashlights and toilet paper. Shouldn't we be stocking up on spiritual things? Especially since this life, we are told by Jesus, is just temporary, an introduction to the real and permanent life that begins *after* this one. Don't be foolish. Check your engine light!

"Do not store up for yourselves treasures on earth, where moths and vermin destroy, and where thieves break in and steal. But store up for yourselves treasures in heaven, where moths and vermin do not destroy, and where thieves do not break in and steal" (Matthew 6:19–20).

In that parable, there were only five bridesmaids who stored up ahead of time. The door opened for them, and they were able to go into the marriage feast. Many people believe that Jesus was referring to the time when the Church will be raptured, protected, and delivered from the end-time tribulation period. Are we prepared, or are we in that 50 percent that missed it? Fifty percent is a lot of church members! Does that surprise you? Where is our wisdom? Where is the storing up? Some of our storage containers are embarrassingly bare. Go get some oil, *extra* oil!

Waking Up

How do we wake ourselves up? In the C. S. Lewis story, *The Silver Chair*, there is a group of travelers that has gone underground to a dark kingdom, where they are attempting to rescue a prince from an evil queen. The evil queen confronts them trying to escape and begins to lie to them, telling them that there is no land above the ground and that the dark kingdom is the only reality. She sprinkles some sleep-inducing substance in the air and keeps talking to them in a soft, soothing, monotone voice, saying that there are no trees, there is no sun, no sky, etc. The fire in the fireplace is warm, and the characters all eventually begin to get drowsy and let down their guards. They start to hypnotically mimic her words until one of them realizes what's happening and sticks his foot deliberately into the fire. God bless that marsh-wiggle character! Immediately, the pain wakes him up, and he begins to shout, helping the others to shake off their sleepiness! As soon as they are awake and realize what the evil queen was doing, they band together to defeat her and save the prince! Once you are aware of the plan of the enemy, you can defeat him.

We can learn something else from this story too. Our world is growing darker. The media, news shows, comedy shows are telling us that there is no right and wrong, that God is a fable. Lying, stealing, cheating, even murder is okay as long as it helps you get what you want. They tell us up is down and dark is light over and over and over again until we are in a hypnotic trance. Somebody needs to stick his foot in the fire or pinch himself and shout to the others to wake up! There is an opposing force at work here, and it is trying to keep us from realizing there is a real sun and a real sky, a real Jesus! The enemy is trying to keep us from making it to the Emerald City. The game is on, and our opponent is playing for keeps. He has set traps along the way, mine fields, ambushes, detours, and deceptions to keep us from succeeding. He talks to us in our minds with that soothing, monotone, hypnotic voice that we assume is our own thought voice. He lies, lies, lies, and we accept it as the truth. How can we know it is the wrong voice we are listening to? How do we tell the lies from the truth? This is how, my friend—we get familiar with what the Bible says about things. The Bible tells us the truth.

Two Roads

Our life here on this earth is a dangerous journey. The good news is that God did not leave us defenseless. He has given us a roadmap, the Bible. Like Dorothy on her way to Oz, we are on a journey, the yellow brick road, a growth process, heading toward the real reality of a glorious city and Kingdom called in the Book of Revelation the New Jerusalem. Then it's on to whatever else God has imagined. However, like in the classic book *Pilgrim's Progress* by John Bunyan, the devil, our enemy, has built another road. Let's call it the red brick road. It looks like the yellow brick road and is even made with similar-looking bricks. It appears to be moving in the same direction as the yellow brick road, but at some point, it begins to veer just slightly to the left. By the time you have walked a distance, you have clearly moved *way* to the left of your original direction, and you never noticed it. The yellow brick road is a growth process toward God. On the yellow road, God is involved with you, and you are involved with Him. It is the road to heaven and eternal joy because He is there. The red brick road is the way of the world.

The red brick road is a road that operates in a worldly, Godless realm, where the devil is in charge. This world and all its glitz and glamor, celebrities, media, social media, sports games, online shopping, the world, the long work hours, family and friend obligations, the world, endless bills, poor health, stress and exhaustion, you know what I mean—the busyness of the world, all the distractions, is like the red brick road, and it is heading in the wrong direction if that destination is all without God. It is not necessarily those things themselves. We all live in the world and have to deal with those things, but it is the avoidance of God that is the problem. The world insistently whispers, "You don't need God, you can live this life all by yourself, you don't need God." In its hypnotic way, it drones on and on. "There is no real God, and even if there was, He doesn't have time to think about you. You don't need Him, you can live this life by yourself." The world turns us around and around slowly, like twisting us on a swing, and then lets us go, spinning out of control. We are so busy with our everyday lives that we have no time left for the one thing that will save us. Do you think that is an accident?

Once you know an enemy is involved, smart people begin to open one eye and ask, "What is going on here?"

This is what is going on. The red brick road seems to be okay for a while, but it leads only to stress, fear, destruction, and eventually hell. Jesus said a lot of people go that way, but seemingly few find the good road that leads to life. We want to find and stay on the right road, the *yellow* brick road that leads to life.

A Roadmap to the Kingdom

The Bible is our playbook, roadmap, GPS, or instruction manual, and when we read it and study it, with the help of the Holy Spirit, we can understand not only where we are but who and why and when as well. If we use our roadmap wisely, we will avoid dangerous pitfalls, construction traffic, and detours and arrive at our destination, which is life everlasting and the glory of the great and powerful God, Jehovah the Good. Not only that, but we will find the blessings, the beautiful views, the waterfalls, all of those special gifts that God has prepared for those that walk along His road.

So how does one utilize this roadmap? It is a thick book and rather daunting, right? The way to read the Bible is a little bit every day. Leave it open on the kitchen table or on your nightstand so when you go to bed and when you wake up, you will see it and read. Many people nowadays have the Bible downloaded on their phones or iPads. The format doesn't matter, the reading it and hearing it do. Growth for a Christian is found in consistency. It is the same with praying or talking to God. It's not that you pray two hours but that you pray every day. Paul said in 1 Thessalonians 5:17 to "pray without ceasing." We work up to it. Soon we are talking to God throughout the day. The same with the Bible. You don't have to read the whole thing at one time, not even a whole chapter, just a verse or two. You think about that verse throughout the day, meditating on it, imagining how it applies to situations in life, seeing things from God's perspective. Then you begin to see how that verse connects to a verse you read a few days ago. And one verse leads to another…the Bible is so amazing! You will probably not want to put it down. There are no rules. Sometimes you read more, sometimes less, but the main thing is that you are consistently reading, learning about the God who created you. And the more you learn about Him, the better He gets (He was that good all along, you just didn't realize it). Talk about Him with someone else. Discuss what you read. Set aside a time of day that you always read the Bible, such as while you eat breakfast, before you go to bed at night, first thing when you wake up, when you get home from school, right before you do your homework, etc. If you miss a day or two, make up for it the next time by reading extra. This is how we learn about who Jesus is and who *we* are. This is how we learn about the Kingdom of Light and how it conquers the kingdom of darkness. This is how we begin to wake up and become who we are supposed to be.

To make sure we are staying awake, we hang out with other Christians. We help each other, give each other a poke if we begin to look sleepy—not literally. We go to church services, attend a Bible study (look at you! You're doing it!) or a home group, volunteer to help in one of the ministries at church where you can meet people and make friends. If you have a responsibility at church, you will make sure you get there every week, right? That's wisdom. Store up that extra oil! It's all about consistency. You will find yourself learning and growing and helping others at the same time. Win-win! Keep the words of God in front of your eyes. Write them on your refrigerator. Teach them to your children. The more time you spend with *those words*, the more you will grow. The more you grow, the better this life gets!

Deuteronomy 11:18–21 tells us,

> Therefore you shall lay up these words of mine in
> your heart and in your soul, and bind them as a
> sign on your hand, and they shall be as frontlets
> between your eyes. You shall teach them to your
> children, speaking of them when you sit in your
> house, when you walk by the way, when you lie
> down, and when you rise up. And you shall write
> them on the doorposts of your house and on
> your gates, that your days and the days of your
> children may be multiplied in the land of which
> the Lord swore to your fathers to give them, like
> the days of heaven above the earth.

He has given us the playbook. This is how God says we win the game.

It's daytime in the Kingdom of Light. Time to rise and shine!

> Arise shine:
> For your light has come!
> And the glory of the Lord
> Is risen upon you
> For behold the darkness
> Shall cover the earth
> And deep darkness the people;
> But the Lord will arise over you,
> And His glory will be seen upon you.
> The Gentiles shall come to your light,
> And kings to the brightness of your rising.
> (Isaiah 60:1–3)

Discussion Questions

1. Have you ever started to feel sleepy when the subject of God or church or the Bible comes up?

2. Many people wonder why they are here, what their purpose is, and where they are going. How does knowing about our journey to the Kingdom of God change your perspective of the importance of your life?

3. We are all in a stage of growing to become more like Jesus. What stage would you say you are closest to: infant, toddler, elementary school, middle school, high school, college, mature adult? Why? How do you know?

LESSON 2

Why Do We Need the Bible?

We are living in challenging times. On one hand, life is increasingly getting easier with new inventions and technology. (What would we do without cellphones?) On the other hand, life is getting increasingly more dangerous with terrorism, lawlessness, wars, earthquakes, threats of climate changes, new virus outbreaks, and even asteroid collisions! If you are paying attention, you might wonder where all this is heading. Will the world as we know it last another century? Will we have to travel to the stars to save our people from extinction? There have been lots of thoughts and debates on the subject, books written, movies produced. Even for those who believe in some sort of higher power, there are conflicting views. So what do Christians believe and where do they get their information from?

Have you ever heard someone say that one can never understand or know God? Have you ever heard someone say that the Bible is too hard to understand? Usually the people who make statements like these have never tried to read the Bible, or at least never tried very hard. They probably don't go to church, so they wouldn't be learning anything there either. Many years ago, I heard a man say, "Nobody can read the whole Bible!" That was pretty funny to me because by that time I had read through the entire Bible at least three times. Yes, people are funny. I used to think that if God was so big, it would be impossible for him to care about me because I am so small. In the same way, I used to think I could never have a relationship with my neighbors until one day I said hi, and it changed everything. Do you think it could be that way with God?

Getting to Know the Real God

Human beings have great imaginations. When we think about God, we can imagine all kinds of ways that God could be. We have imagined Greek gods and Roman gods, gods of agriculture, gods of fertility, gods of war, gods of the weather, etc. We have used our imaginations to create hundreds of different gods with hundreds of different personalities. Aren't we clever? But these gods are always disappointing us. They are too much like us, and we have faults. In order to get to know what the *real* God is like, we need more information. Just relying on what we *think* He should be like is sketchy at best and dangerous at worst. And since God wants us to know Him, too, He came up with a plan. It's called the Bible.

The Bible was given to us by God as a manual for how to connect with Him and how to live on this earth successfully. It was written by different men over several hundreds of years as the Holy Spirit (God) inspired them. As you read it, you pick up strongly on God's personality with a hint of the flavor of the individual who actually wrote the words down.

As we read it, we take into consideration the culture and the times of the individual people who wrote the words God inspired them to write, but the cultural context is secondary to the overall words of wisdom themselves. The words transcend the time in which they were written. The words themselves are living and are, in a real sense, eternal. They were timely for people who lived a thousand years ago and are timely for us today. How is that even possible given all the variety of cultures and circumstances we find ourselves in?

The answer to that is found in the nature of who God is. He is eternal, no beginning, no end. His words come from His thoughts, just like ours do (we are made in His image and are an expression of Him). Because He is eternal, His words are also eternal. They don't change because He doesn't change, and that's why His words are important to us. They are a solid rock that is constant. But in addition to that, His words express His personality and His mannerisms, His hopes and desires and affections, the things He likes. And they identify those things that bug Him and even those things He detests. If you want to get to know God, then get to know what He said about things. And since he created you, if you want to get to know yourself, read what He said about you!

We can learn things about God as He reveals Himself by what He has chosen to say and not to say. We can learn a lot from what specific events in history He has chosen to spotlight for us. He doesn't record only positive examples but also negative so that we can see both sides. He records people with weaknesses and people with strengths, people that liked Him and people that didn't. All the stories and all the letters are written to us and for us so that we can get to know Him and so that we can be successful in our lives here on the earth. This life on earth, even though temporary, is important. We know we are eternal beings and that there is a life after this, but there is also a plan for your life now, and God wants to show you what it is.

Some people say you can never really know God. He is too big and too far away, like an alien presence that interferes in our lives every once in a while. But we have the Bible, which tells us clearly the opposite. God wants to be known. He wants to be close. He loves us!

Discussion Questions

1. Why do we need the Bible?
2. Who wrote the Bible?
3. If you were writing about yourself, what is one thing you would want people to know?

What about All Those Translations?

But you may ask, there are so many different translations of the Bible, how do we know which one to believe? Have you ever wondered about that? The answer is that each translation is taken from the original words written in the Hebrew and Greek languages. The Old Testament was written in the Hebrew language, and the New Testament was written in Greek. Those languages are not always translatable word for word in English. The Hebrew language uses 45,000 words and about 35,000 word combinations, while English uses 170,000 words. One word in Hebrew might have three or more descriptive word meanings in English. One translator might choose a different word description from another translator, but basically, the sentence will mean the same thing. So different translations are all saying the same thing, just in slightly different ways. Another thing that happens in translation, according to *One Bible, Many Versions* by Dave Braun, is thought-for-thought, rather than word-for-word, translations. For instance, one translation might say, "If I have found favor in your eyes…," and another might say, "If it pleases you…" In any case, the meaning of the thought is the same.

Someone who wants to study a Bible passage to get the exact word translation (which is not as dry and scholarly as it seems and can be very helpful) can easily use a reference tool of the original language to help him. There are all kinds of resources available to anyone who wants to know. One resource is called a concordance dictionary to look up original word meanings. It's a good thing to have on hand. It lists every single word in the Bible and gives the original language definition. Don't worry about having the *right* translation, just read any of them. (Having said that, there are a few types of Bibles that have been rewritten to support the claims of non-Christian leaders. These are not true translations because they have been altered in original content, so don't read those.)

Some of the main translations are the King James Version (KJV), New King James (NKJV), New International (NIV), Amplified (AMP), New Revised Standard (NRSV), English Standard (ESV), New Living Translation (NLT), and many more. Most of them are available online and easily accessible.

Discussion Questions

1. Which translation do you have?
2. Which other translations have you seen?
3. If you were writing about yourself, what is one thing you would want people to know?

The Bible is divided into two main sections, the Old Testament and the New Testament, or Old Covenant (agreement/contract) and New Covenant. The Old Testament contains thirty-nine books, and the New contains twenty-seven books, each divided into chapters and verses. This helps us to organize things. Don't worry if you have to use the table of contents. That's what it's there for! The chapters and verses were not in the original texts but were added later.

The Old Testament is the same scripture that has been carefully and meticulously handed down for centuries by the Jewish people. It contains the history of the Jewish nation from the beginning of creation until the Book of Malachi (written about four hundred years before Jesus came). Stories about Noah, David and Goliath, Daniel and the lions' den, all the psalms and proverbs, and books of prophecies are all in the Old Testament. Christians and Jews both use the Old Testament, but only Christians use the New Testament—these books are the scriptures that talk about Jesus.

The New Testament starts with the Gospels of Matthew, Mark, Luke, and John, which are accounts of the life and ministry of Jesus, written from four different perspectives. The books following the Gospels are the Book of Acts (a history of how the Church got started) and then letters addressed to certain early church groups, like the Romans (the Christians in Rome), and letters written by prominent church leaders to the Church at large, like 1 Peter and 2 Peter. The last book of the New Testament is the Book of Revelation, which is a prophetic look at the end of the age and the return of Jesus to set up His Kingdom on the earth. Some people tell you to stay away from reading that one, but I say go for it! In fact, that was the first book of the Bible I ever read because I wanted to see what happens at the end of the story. Spoilers—He wins!

Now it's your turn. Here are some scriptures to look up. Take your time and read them carefully. Remember, these things were written for us to help us. They are not somebody's imagination but the real deal. Use the table of contents.

These scriptures are all found in the New Testament:

- Luke 1:1–4—This is from the Gospel of Luke, who also wrote the Book of Acts.

- 1 John 1:1–4—There is a Gospel of John and also three letters written by John. This is from the first letter. It's in the back of the book, close to Revelation.

- 2 Timothy 3:16–17—There are two letters written by Paul to his protégé, Timothy. This scripture is from the second letter.

- 2 Peter 1:20–21—There are two letters written by Peter. This is found in the second letter.

Discussion Questions

1. How many total books are in the Bible, both in the Old and New Testaments?

2. In which Testament, Old or New, would you find these books? Circle the answer.

Acts	OLD NEW	Psalms	OLD NEW
Genesis	OLD NEW	Luke	OLD NEW
Revelation	OLD NEW	Proverbs	OLD NEW
Isaiah	OLD NEW	Matthew	OLD NEW
John	OLD NEW	Daniel	OLD NEW

LESSON 3

What Do We Know about the Real God?

To help us learn our way around the Bible, we are going to focus on some of the things we know about God and where to find that information. Get a pen or a pencil. As you look up the scriptures, feel free to underline sentences, phrases, or words that stand out to you. You might want to find that reference again sometime. The Bible is like a workbook. Take notes, circle things, mark certain passages. If you don't feel like you can write in your Bible, put that one back on the shelf and go get another one you can write in. When you study the Bible, it is not necessary to read all the way through from beginning to end each time. Some of the time you might be reading through one of the books, but many times you might be following a theme and bounce back and forth all over the place. For this lesson, we will be looking up scriptures from both the Old Testament and the New. Before long, you will be an expert at knowing the location of all the books.

Science and God

We know, or most of us know, that there is a higher power because the order of the universe is too intelligent to have been an accident. The media and the education system present belief in God as superstition and unscientific, but many renowned scientists believe in God. Sir Francis Bacon, the founder of the scientific method of observation, said, "God never wrought miracles to convince atheism (or unbelievers) because his ordinary works convince it. It is true that a little philosophy inclineth man's mind to atheism; but depth in philosophy bringeth men's minds about to religion. For while the mind of man looketh upon second causes scattered, it may sometimes rest in them, and go no further; but when it beholdeth the chain of them, confederate and linked together, it must needs fly to Providence and Deity."

Basically, Sir Francis was saying (in 1620 English) that when you scientifically observe all the so-called coincidences in nature together, the "chain of them," you come up with a universe designer, or God, as the only plausible scientific explanation. The first and second law of thermodynamics are examples of a scientific approach to the state of the universe. The first law, called the Law of Conservation of Energy, basically declares that energy cannot be created or destroyed. Once God has made it, it can change states, but nobody is going to uncreate it. The second law of thermodynamics says that the entropy or disorder of any system always increases. This means that the universe tends toward disorder, not order. This law does not support the evolutionists' theory that the universe grew from randomness into an ordered system. As someone said, evolution theory is like saying if you throw the letters of the alphabet into the air, they will come down forming a dictionary. The theory of evolution to explain life on our planet is basically about as unscientific as it gets. Here is an excerpt taken from a Lumen Learning Biology course. You will probably feel really smart after you read it.

An important concept in physical systems is that of order and disorder (also known as randomness). The more energy that is lost by a system to its surroundings, the less ordered and more random the system is. Scientists refer to the measure of randomness or disorder within a system as entropy. High entropy means high disorder and low energy. To better understand entropy, think of a student's bedroom. If no energy or work were put into it, the room would quickly become messy. It would exist in a very disordered state, one of high entropy. Energy must be put into the system, in the form of the student doing work and putting everything away, in order to bring the room back to a state of cleanliness and order. This state is one of low entropy. Similarly, a car or house must be constantly maintained with work in order to keep it in an ordered state. Left alone, the entropy of the house or car gradually increases through rust and degradation. Molecules and chemical reactions have varying amounts of entropy as well. For example, as chemical reactions reach a state of equilibrium, entropy increases, and as molecules at a high concentration in one place diffuse and spread out, entropy also increases.

All physical systems can be thought of in this way: Living things are highly ordered, requiring constant energy input to be maintained in a state of low entropy. As living systems take in energy-storing molecules and transform them through chemical reactions, they lose some amount of usable energy in the process, because no reaction is completely efficient.

They also produce waste and by-products that aren't useful energy sources. This process increases the entropy of the system's surroundings. Since all energy transfers result in the loss of some usable energy, the second law of thermodynamics states that every energy transfer or transformation increases the entropy of the universe. Even though living things are highly ordered and maintain a state of low entropy, the entropy of the universe in total is constantly increasing due to the loss of usable energy with each energy transfer that occurs. Essentially, living things are in a continuous uphill battle against this constant increase in universal entropy. (https://courses.lumenlearning. com/suny-wmopen-biology1/chapter/ thermodynamics/)

Do you know how the universe is kept in constant and perfect order, even though it wants to break apart all the time? God holds it all together! In fact, Hebrews 1:3, describing Jesus, says, "Who being the brightness of *His* (God's) glory and the express image of His person, and *upholding all things by the word of His power...*" The word *upholding* means "to bear" or "to carry." Colossians 1: 16-17 (NIV) says about Jesus, "For in Him all things were created, things in heaven and on earth, visible and invisible, whether thrones or dominions or rulers or authorities. All things were created through Him and for Him. He is before all things, and in Him all things hold together." If God, even for one nanosecond, took His eye off any part of the universe, stopped caring about it, and just let it go, it would completely collapse into randomness.

Real science and God always agree. You don't have to leave your brain behind when you believe in God. Just because you can't see Him doesn't mean He doesn't exist.

That's silly. There are many things in this world that we don't see, yet we know they are there. Jesus used the example of wind. (John 3:8). He said you can't see it, but you can hear it. We know the wind is there because we can see its effects, like the leaves are moving. So it is with God.

Although many of us believe in a higher power, we don't all believe in the same one. Our imaginations have concocted hundreds of different types of godlike personas, just like Marvel Comics have created Spiderman and Captain America. Buddhists have one god, Hindus have many gods, Muslims have Allah. Just because we all use the same word to describe a higher power, calling it "god," doesn't mean we are all believing in the same actual being. The fact that so many people and countries and cultures have taken the time to invent gods for themselves tells us that there is a need to know who is behind all this. There are questions people have. Who are we? Why are we on this planet? How did we get here? Who's in charge? Have you ever wondered these things? Well, the Bible has the answers. Keep going and you'll probably find out.

In the Book of Acts, Paul tells of his travels to Athens and about the Greeks having idols and altars for many different gods. He found a monument labeled, "To the Unknown God," and began to preach and teach them about the *real* God. The thing is, we don't have to make Him up. He's real, and He gave us the Bible to show us what He's like. Discovering who the real God is in the midst of all the rumors and fake identities is like finding the missing piece of the puzzle of your life. Let's find out what we know about the real God.

The Real God

What is God like? He is amazing! He is strong and mighty, an all-powerful, all-knowing, loving, fair, holy, creative being that is everywhere at all times, past, present, and future. So He's big, really big! Or He can be present in something small, like a burning bush. If you put all the superpowers from all the superheroes we ever made up into one big super guy, God would be better! Get your Bibles ready. Here are some things we know and where you can find them in the scriptures. There are other places as well. These are just examples. Look them up!

- *God is a spirit.* He is not flesh and bones like us, so He is not limited by space or distance. That doesn't mean He doesn't have a body. It's just made of something other than flesh and bones. We will have to have a spirit body when we go to heaven. You can find this in John 4:24 (one of the four Gospels in the New Testament).

- *God looks like us, or rather, we look like Him.* He has arms, legs, hands, feet, eyes, ears, etc. He has a body, just not a flesh body like ours (Ezekiel 1:26, 8:2–3 in the Old Testament).

- *God is always referred to in the scriptures as "He,"* no matter who the inspired writer was, even in the midst of various cultures of pagan goddess worship. Jesus revealed Him as the Father (Matthew 6:9 in the New Testament).

- *God lives in heaven and has created angels to serve Him.* Read Isaiah 66:1 and Psalm 103:20 in the Old

Testament. Angels also help us (Hebrews 1:13–14 in the New Testament).

- *God has emotions like we do.* Actually, we have emotions because God has them. We were created in His image (Genesis 1:27 and 6:6, and Nehemiah 8:10).

- *God is light, not has light but He is light.* First John 1:5 tells us in Him there is no darkness at all. There is no bad, no evil, just good. God is good all the time. When He spoke out into the universe, "Let there be light!" He was directing His presence to fill the atmosphere. He created the sun later on (Genesis 1:16–19). The sun is not as bright as God.

- *God is holy and has a code of conduct.* To be holy means you are set apart as sacred or precious from everything else. God is uniquely Himself, totally pure, totally good, no contamination from things or beings that are not. God's perfectness is expressed as holiness. He is, therefore, worthy of all honor, glory, praise, and even worship. There is no one like Him anywhere (Isaiah 6:3, 1 Peter 1:15–16).

- *He is righteous.* Righteous means "rightness." He is always right about everything. To be righteous is the opposite of being sinful. There is no sin (error, mistake, treachery) in God (Psalm 97:2, 98:2).

- *God is love.* There are different definitions or kinds of love in our culture. God's kind of love is unconditional. It is active and moving always outward to express itself. God's love caused Him to create the world and make people so He could share His love with them. God's love is so powerful it can change people. His love is healing to our hearts and lives, like drinking hot chocolate on a cold day. It warms our insides (1 John 4:7–8).

- *God loves us* (1 John 3:1, 4:19; John 3:16).

Okay, that's a lot of scripture to look up. Hope you underlined a few things so you can go back and find them again.

Discussion Questions

1. Why do you think it is important to look up the scriptures and see them for yourself?
2. Why do you think people tend to disassociate science from belief in God?

The Trinity

Now here's something fascinating about our God…it is the concept of the Trinity.

The word *trinity* itself is not found in the Bible, but it is a word we use to describe the magnitude of God. In a way, it is like a book or movie trilogy. There are three parts to the whole story. With God, however, it is not a chronological trilogy; it is all three happening at the same time.

God displays His personality and character through three separate functions or ministries (jobs): the Father, the Son, and the Holy Spirit. Each person of the Trinity is the same God but with a different hat on. Similarly, I might be a wife, a mom, a daughter, a teacher, or you might be a father, a brother, a son, or a mechanic. We are multifaceted persons because we are just like Him with the difference being that He actually *is* three separate persons in one.

God the Father is the one who sits on the throne in heaven. God the Son (Jesus) is the person of the Trinity who became flesh and blood like us and the one who leads us to the Father. He took off His "God clothes," so to speak, at a point in time to put on humanity clothes and identify with us. He is the part of God we can touch. "Who, though he was in the form of God, did not count equality with God a thing to be grasped, but emptied himself, by taking the form of a servant, being born in the likeness of men" (Philippians 2:6–7 ESV). How amazing is that!

God the Holy Spirit is the power and creativity behind everything God does. He knows all the inside parts of God, His personality. He points the way to Jesus, who points the way to the Father. There are not three gods; there is one God but three persons. It is said that St. Patrick explained the Trinity by using a clover. There are three leaves but only one stem. An interesting fact is that the word translated *God* right in the first verse of Genesis 1 comes from the word *Elohim*, which is a plural word. Here are some scripture references about the Trinity: 2 Corinthians 13:14, John 1:14, John 10:30, Luke 1:35, and Matthew 28:19.

Don't worry if you don't completely understand the concept yet. God is bigger than us. If we could understand everything about Him, then He wouldn't be God, we would!

The Father—God the Father desires a family. He is a protector and a provider for His children. He wants us to come to Him with every need and has planned an eternity of joy for us. If you have children, you know how important they are to you. You want them to be safe, to be well, to be successful, and to be happy. God feels this way, too, but even more so. He is better at it.

If you had a father who made mistakes, remember, people make mistakes. God is the perfect good father and doesn't make those mistakes. His love for you is not selfish. It is perfect!

The Son—Jesus came to reveal to us the heart of the Father, to show us that God wants a close family relationship with us, not just a creator-creation or master-servant type relationship. Jesus came down to earth to show us how to do our lives successfully. Without God to show us, we come up short of the perfection that He desires for us in every area of our lives. We may think we're doing fine, but that's because we don't know how great it could be. Not only did Jesus come to show us the right way to live, but He came to show us the right way to love. Because of His great love for us, He laid His precious life down as a sacrifice so that we could live, so that we could know the love of the Father, and so that we could live together with Him forever (more on that later).

The other really important thing about Jesus is that He is called the Word of God, which means, if you think about it, when God speaks, Jesus comes forth. When God said, "Let there be light!" Jesus *was* those words. God so intensely and intimately connects Himself to His Word that He calls it His Son. His Son is a part of Him, His own expression of His own thoughts. Mind-boggling, isn't it? But how precious! God loves His Word like a Father loves a Son. This is why God can never lie. The integrity of His Word is in His own identity. He *is* the truth. So coming back down to where our brains can wrap around it, we know we can always trust what God says to be true. Every time. If it is Monday and God says it is Tuesday, it will become Tuesday.

No matter what we see or feel to the contrary, God's Word is always, forever true.

The Holy Spirit—When people become Christian believers, the Holy Spirit comes to live in them. God in us—that's as close as it gets. God the Holy Spirit is the creative force that powerfully created the universe, yet He is the same Spirit that came rushing in to fill Jesus's disciples on the Day of Pentecost (Acts 2). He was excited about it! Because He lives in us, His power is readily accessible to help us overcome the world and live in victory. The Holy Spirit helps us develop our character to be more like God. He comforts us when we are sad or lonely, and He warns us when we are close to danger. He interprets the scriptures for us and helps us to understand things about God. He gives us special gifts of supernatural power at times so that we can help the Church and those around us. When we don't know what to say or which direction to go, He is right there inside us, like a compass or GPS, pointing the way. He is our ultimate best friend. What a God!

God Is a King

One more cool thing about the real God: He is a king! He is the King of kings and Lord of lords! That's where we got the idea of royalty from. His majesty is unquestioned in heaven. Angels worship him 24-7. Living in the USA, we don't deal with royalty very often, like some other countries do, although we have seen something of it occasionally in the media. There is a certain conduct required of royalty that is not required of commoners. In public, it would be rare to see a guy give the king a big bear hug or high five. Things are, of course, more relaxed at home for the king with his own children. But word to the wise, there are protocols to follow surrounding kings and kingdoms. As you read the scriptures, keep in mind that the Father, the Son, and the Holy Spirit are to be honored as the most high, the almighty, the everlasting King of glory!

Discussion Questions

1. List ten things you know about God.
2. What are some of the "hats" that you wear?
3. We know the Bible states that the Word of God is the same as Jesus, His Son. How does that help you to be able to trust what He says? How does that make the Bible different from every other book?

LESSON 4

THE PROBLEM

In the last lesson, we learned that God wants to get close to us and wants us to get to know Him. He gave us the Bible to help us learn about Him. This lesson contains a lot of scriptures to look up. That's a good thing. But if you so desire, you can read through the lesson and then go back and look up the scriptures later. You'll eventually want to look them up for yourselves. Remember, the Bible is a book of truth, the living Word of God—Jesus Himself. The more you read it, the closer you will get to Him and the more your life will be changed for the better.

So if God wants to be known and wants to be near and involved in our lives, what's stopping Him? If He's a good God, why are all these bad things happening in the earth? Isn't He in control? Without knowledge of the backstory, people can get confused. They are hesitant to get to know a God who seems…erratic. He's supposed to be loving, but maybe His idea of loving is not the same as ours. Is He sometimes good and sometimes bad? How can we trust Him?

The problem of what to do about God is not going away. But instead of reaching out to get to know God better, people tend to busy themselves in their everyday lives, putting off thinking about it. That strategy works until there is a crisis or someone dies, reminding them of how short this life on earth really is. They think about God for a few days, never finding an answer to their unspoken questions, and then it is back to being busy, busy, busy again. I'm reminded of the proverbial ostrich with his head in the sand, pulling his head out when he hears an alarm and then sticking his head back in the sand, hoping the problem of figuring God out will go away. But it doesn't.

Option 1 and Option 2

Suppose you had a choice between option 1—living your life relying on the mighty God, the Creator of the universe who happens to love you, who is on your side, who wants to help you and prosper you, heal you, take care of you and your family—or option 2—just living your life in this crazy world by yourself with no help—which would you choose? No-brainer! Pick option 1, which is God. And suppose you had a choice between option 1—living out your eternity forever in joy, peace, light, and amazing, overflowing love in the Kingdom of God as a son or daughter of the Most High King of all the universe—or option 2— living out your eternity forever alone in a place of torment with burning flames and darkness, where worms crawl in and out, which are punishments created for the devil, who hates you. Which would you choose? No-brainer again! You'd pick the first one, right? So would I!

Choosing Life

The truth is, you *do* have a choice. God does not randomly pick people for heaven and send the other people to hell. You are the one who chooses your future. Option 1 (life) is the good one, and option 2 (death) is the bad one. Contrary to what you may have heard, there is no third option. Those of us who want to cling to the notion that it doesn't matter or that there is a third option of not choosing have already chosen option 2. That would be the ostrich strategy (it is not effective). Would you like to go on record as choosing option 1 today? Good for you! The key to obtaining access to option 1—the Kingdom of God— is in our relationship with the King Himself. You have to know Him, and He has to know you in order for you to gain entrance into the Kingdom. It's all in who you know (more on this later).

Believe it or not, some people choose option 2… I know, I don't understand it either. Seriously, who wouldn't want to have a relationship with the King of kings? He's awesome! Deuteronomy 30:19–20 says,

> I call heaven and earth as witnesses today against you, that I have set before you life and death, blessing and cursing; therefore choose life, that both you and your descendants may live; that you may love the Lord your God, that you may obey His voice, and that you may cling to Him, for He is your life and the length of your days…

Okay, we get it. We want to choose life and choose God. We'd be foolish not to. Really, the only thing standing in the way of us having a personal relationship with God, the King, from our end, goes back to the trust issue. We believe there is a God, but can we believe He is good all the time? Can we safely put our trust in Him? The answer to this question is profoundly yes!

And…oh yeah, somewhere in the back of our minds is a nagging little hunch that *we* might not be good enough for *Him*.

Could I Be the Problem?

The issue for *us* may be trust, but the issue for Him is *purity*. He is 100 percent pure goodness and righteousness, 100 percent holy and perfect, pure, pure, pure! There has never been a time when God made even one tiny mistake or had one unkind or selfish thought. He is all light, all good, and is perfect in all His ways. This presents a problem for us in that even though God *wants* to get close to us, He cannot. We are not 100 percent pure like him even though some of us like to think we are. We make mistakes. We mess up.

You can't say you're 50 percent pure or even 99.9 percent pure because once something is tainted or poisoned even a little, it's just not pure anymore. Imagine if the cook dropped your food on the floor before serving it to you.

Would you eat it? What if he put just one poison mushroom in the stew? What if the nurse wanted to put a used Band-Aid on your cut? No way! We are either pure, 100 percent clean, or we're not. God is pure; we are not.

The purity and holiness of God radiates strength and power, so for us to come close to Him, it would be like getting too close to the sun. We love the warmth and light of the sun as long as it stays far away and doesn't burn us up. But God is not content to stay far away from us. He loves us and wants to draw us close.

You might be thinking way in the back of your mind, *How could a God so perfect even want to get close to someone who messes up as much as I have? Doesn't He know what I've done? He loves everyone, but I am not very good at loving everyone. Doesn't He know the things I've said? I wish I could take back some of those things now. If I'm being honest, I'm mostly out for* number one—me. *I have wanted to be my own god. And if God knows everything, He probably knows all my thoughts. Good grief! That seals it. I will never be able to measure up, unless... maybe if I do some good things... How does this judgment thing work? How many good things do I have to actually do to make up for my sketchy life? How do I get to heaven or get into the Kingdom or whatever the place is you're talking about?* This is the question *everyone* should be asking! If you are thinking something along those lines, you are actually making great progress. If you see yourself as perfect (I wonder what mirror you're looking into), you will have a hard time understanding your need for a savior.

The "Good Person" Defense

Many people see themselves through "rose-colored glasses." That means they project a rosy (healthy, normal, or better than normal) hue on what is deadly pale and corrupt. They tend to overlook what they consider to be minor infractions of morality like little "white" lies and selfish decisions. They have convenient amnesia about their faults. They cut themselves slack and live by "the end justifies the means" philosophy. They judge themselves by their intentions (although others are judged by actions). They think of themselves for the most part as "good" people. That means basically that they have never killed anybody. I know, I used to think like that too. Of course, if you watch much TV, you will soon begin to realize that even murderers usually think of themselves as good people. Our definition of good is one thing, and God's definition of good is another. Clearly there is a discrepancy.

Some denominational churches have categorized sins into the bad ones and the not-so-bad ones. I know, I went to one of those denominational churches for many years. Unfortunately, Jesus did not agree with that idea. In fact, He showed us that sin is sin and is all in the bad group, the terribly bad poison mushroom group. If you take out the idea that some sins are not so bad and put *every* sin in the terribly evil category, we are all in trouble. I don't know anybody who has never made a mistake, so the good person theory doesn't hold up with God. It is a delusion. For instance, taking a paper clip home from the office that you have no intention of returning is stealing. Telling a fib is lying. We all like to cling to the "at least I've never murdered anyone" defense, but Jesus said if you are angry with someone without cause, it is the same as murdering them (Matthew 5:21–22). And His stance on adultery was, "You have heard that it was said to those of old, 'You shall not commit adultery.' But I say to you that whoever looks at a woman to lust for her has already committed adultery with her in his heart" (Matthew 5:27–28). Wow! See what I mean? God is 100 percent pure, and we are not. That's a problem. Even if our *actions* don't condemn us, our *thoughts* will. There are not enough good things that you could ever do to cancel out all that sin. And remember, because God is holy, *no* sin, no impure thing can get close to His presence.

How Do We Bridge the Gap?

So the issue becomes, how can we get good enough to get close to God? *What can we do?*

Some other religions have tackled the problem from that way—that is, what can man do to get good enough to attain eternal life (heaven, paradise, the kingdom, etc.)? They have their own books similar to the Bible, but they are full of words of man's ideas, not God's, and directions about how to do "good" things to make their god, whoever it is, happy with them. And it seems like those gods are never happy for long. Some of those "holy books" command men to kill other people that don't agree with them. Well, we know *that's* not right. Some of those books command men to live in a simple way, denying themselves any pleasure or beauty. We know *that* can't be right either. God created beautiful things for us to enjoy. (Remember the Garden of Eden, filled with abundance and beauty?) Some of those books command men to pray certain prayers over again and sacrifice various things to gods that can't talk back. Even with all that working and trying, huffing and puffing, the result is that the people subscribing to those religions never have any real assurance that their gods have been satisfied. Proverbs 14:12 says, "There is a way that seems right to a man, but its end is the way of death." After all is said and done, those people still don't know for sure if they're going to heaven when they die.

The Bible is *radically* different! Christianity is *radically* different. Christianity takes the problem from the opposite way. This way shows us what God has done for *us*. It says that man can do nothing to save himself. But because our God is so wonderful and loves us so much, He did all the work. Doesn't that sound more like our God? Because of what Jesus did, the gates of heaven have been opened to us, and we can know *for sure* that we are qualified to go there when we leave this world. What did Jesus do? Read on, my friend.

Knowing the backstory on how and why this all came about is crucial. It explains how the God we so easily take for granted came to rescue us even when we were enemies. The story is found in the Bible, our new best friend.

Discussion Questions

1. Feeling far away from God feels like being far away from "home," the place where everything makes sense. Have you ever felt really far away from God?

2. Have you ever tried to rationalize your behavior by saying to yourself you meant well or that you're okay because another person was worse than you?

The History of Everything

God is perfect. He is wonderful! "In Him is light and there is no darkness at all" (1 John 1:5). He is righteous, which basically means He is always right and fair. He is holy, which means He has never done anything wrong or messed up in any way. He is so pure that if something unclean just comes near Him, it will be destroyed. He is like the sun burning a million degrees.

Whatever gets too close to the sun is consumed. When God's light comes into contact with darkness, the darkness is thoroughly destroyed. Just like when you walk into a dark room and turn on the light, the dark disappears. God created man to be like Himself, filled with light. But as you will see in the backstory, one day, man "chose" darkness instead of light, and He was changed. Sadly, it became impossible for God to get close to us anymore. If He got close, the darkness would be destroyed, but then so would the man. However, God is also very, very smart, and He made a plan to help change us back. As you will see, it involves another choice.

Here's the history. When Adam, the first human man, was created, God breathed life into him, and he became a living soul. Eve was created from a rib from Adam's side, the perfect complement to him. In God's eyes, Adam was both male and female. He placed Adam and Eve in a beautiful, lush garden on the earth. He gave them dominion over the garden and over all the earth, to rule over the animals and fish and birds and every other creature (read Genesis 1:26–29 and all of chapter 2). God Himself would come down and walk with Adam and Eve in the garden in the cool of the day.

God loved Adam and Eve. They had been created in the very image of God himself, little gods of the earth. We look just like Him, just as our children look like us. The angels, who were other created beings, were very interested and watched to see what God would do with the man.
(Job 38:4–7, 1 Peter 1:12).

We know that one of the angels (Lucifer, also known as Satan and the devil) was a traitor. Lucifer was created as a very beautiful and powerful angel, but his beauty and power were his downfall. He desired to be like God, to take His place on the throne of the universe, and led a third of the angels to his side. He attempted to overthrow God, the King (read Isaiah 14:12–15). Seriously, how dumb was that? Jesus calls the devil a liar and a murderer from the beginning (John 8:44) and says that he only comes to steal, kill, and destroy (John 10:10). He is *not* a nice guy! When his coup failed, Lucifer, or Satan, as he became known from then on, came down to the earth and messed with God's precious new creation, man.

Entering a serpent's body, he met Eve and Adam in the garden and pressured them into committing a treasonous act against God. The story is found in Genesis 3:1–7.

Read it for yourself. I'm paraphrasing.

God said to Adam, "I have given you all the trees in the garden to eat from. There are all kinds of varieties out here. Try them all, especially the tree of life. That's a good one! But be careful not to eat the fruit off the tree of the knowledge of good and evil. If you do, *you will surely die*." Satan said to Eve, *"You will* not *surely die*. You will become like God! Go on, take a bite. He just doesn't want you to have any fun!"

Who was it again that really wanted to become like God? You guessed it! Satan did. It was his own desire. Adam and Eve were already like God, but Satan made it sound like they were missing out on something. He is a liar. He twists and perverts the truth. The devil tricked Eve and then Adam, who was with her, and they each took a bite of the fruit of the forbidden tree. *They had a choice*. Should they believe God and do what *He* said, or should they believe the devil and do what *he* said? The Bible says that when you obey someone, you become their servant (Romans 6:16). Which master did they obey? The wrong one!

Satan was a traitor and the enemy of the King. Adam and Eve, instead of obeying the commandment of the King, changed masters and obeyed Satan, His enemy. They committed treason. They chose an alliance with the wrong kingdom!

Of course, they were sorry, but it was too late. The damage had been done. Because God is a King who is righteous and just, His kingdom is subject to laws. One of those laws is that His Word is to be obeyed. Once He has said something, it is established. He couldn't take it back.

Sadly, by this one sin, one act of treachery, Adam and Eve had become enemies of the King. It was a terrible tragedy! The penalty that had been decreed for this treasonous act was *death*. In an instant, the darkness of the devil's nature flooded into them and replaced the light of God's nature. This *first death* was a cut off from their relationship with God. They immediately lost their covering, the presence and glory of the life-giving God, and felt naked. Up until then, they had been protected, shielded by the Spirit of God, and destined to live forever, even in their flesh and blood bodies. But *death* entered into the picture, and they began to slowly degenerate. Even so, it took them over 900 years of physical decline before death was possible for their amazing bodies! (Adam lived to be 930 years old, see Genesis 5:5).

And remember the dominion that Adam had been given in the earth? By his alliance with the devil, Adam had unwittingly given the keys of that dominion over to him (Luke 4:6). Now the devil was the god or ruler of this world (John 12:31, 16:11), and the King's plans for good were replaced with the devil's plans for evil. The ground was cursed. Destructive hurricanes, tornados, tsunamis, droughts, volcanic eruptions, and ice storms began to happen in the world. Bacteria and viruses attacked creatures and plants. Plants meant for food turned poisonous.

Even the animals began killing and eating each other. This was a death, too, a *death* for the world and all of creation (Romans 8:19–23).

But the worst death of all was the death after death, the *second death* (Revelation 2:11). This was the eternal death. Once a man's flesh body has died, he himself, the eternal spirit, must reside somewhere. Unfortunately, with sin still a part of him, that place cannot be with God. The only other option is to spend eternity with the father of sin, the devil. And the future of Satan is already determined. He is to be thrown into the lake of fire, away from God, to burn forever (Revelation 20:10). He is being thrown in the garbage dump, heaven's incinerator.

The Tragedy of Unbelief

Imagine how God must have felt to see His best creation, made in His own image, become the captives of His enemy! It gives us the idea of what sin is to God. It is terrible, the worst sort of tragedy! God had warned them, saying death would follow sin, but they didn't listen. They didn't believe Him. And that, my friends, was the real sin. *Unbelief.* God didn't really care about that fruit, whatever it was. The Bible doesn't even specify what kind of fruit it was. The real problem was that Adam didn't believe what God said, God who cannot lie! Instead, he believed what the snake said, the devil whom Jesus declared is a liar and the father of lies (John 8:44). And because of that one sin of unbelief (believing a lie instead of the truth), death now had permission to enter the world, and it opened a Pandora's box of trouble (Genesis 3:8–24).

Discussion Questions

1. What are some of the ways that people try to make themselves good enough to please God?

2. Should a judge overlook the crimes of his children? Why or why not?

3. The devil is the ruler of this world. What are some evidence that you see of this?

4. How do you think the world would look if God was in control?

LESSON 5

THE SOLUTION

To recap, Adam and Eve had sinned and lost their connection with God. And to make matters worse, God had placed Adam and Eve in charge of the earth and had given them dominion over everything, but by that one sin of obeying the devil, they had given over control of the whole world to him. It was like God had given Adam a big shiny, expensive sports car, but then Adam gave the car keys to the devil. The devil was now driving the car. He had taken over the driver's seat, if you will. Whether we realize it or not, the devil is the ruler of the world now. Because of that one sin of Adam's, just one, the world became subject to the devil's nature, which is darkness and death. Satan moved in, bringing all his belongings. It was like a big box of his stuff was delivered to his new home—earth. Destruction, sickness and disease, poverty, famine, war, hatred, evil, you name it, anything that sounds uncomfortable and not such a good idea is coming from that box of death. This world we live in is *not* the same world that God had in mind when He created it. We live in an upside-down, bizzarro world of the devil's creation. That is why there are bad things happening. *God is not doing it!*

Oh, the devil is not getting away with anything. God has already judged and sentenced him. The end of the story for the devil is burning and torment forever, which he clearly deserves. There will come an end to all this, and God will toss that guy into the eternal lake of fire. The trouble is that all his servants, the angels that followed him in the rebellion, *and* all of the people who are part of his kingdom in this world and that have his sin nature (all of mankind) will go down with him. That is bad news for us. The lake of fire is a sentence to be carried out in the future. In the meantime, when people die now, they go to be where their king dwells. We call it hell. The Bible tells us that hell was created for the devil and his angels (Matthew 25:41). Going from hell to the lake of fire is the true meaning of the saying, "Out of the frying pan and into the fire." Very bad news.

Now you may say, "I don't want to go down with the devil! I don't even like him! What if I try to show God that I'm a good person and I keep all the Ten Commandments and I never sin anymore? Do I still have to go to hell? Can't good people go to heaven?" Well, according to James 2:10 (NIV), "For whoever keeps the whole law and yet stumbles at just one point is guilty of breaking all of it." If you sinned only one time in your life or broke only one commandment, like Adam and Eve, you are guilty of breaking the whole law and, thus, will be sentenced to hell. Remember, one poison mushroom ruins the whole stew. God is not happy about that, but He is just. It is the law. Think about it. Have you ever told a lie? Even a "white" lie? Have you ever stolen anything or borrowed and not returned something? Have you ever lusted? Have you ever hated anyone or done something unkind? Have you ever wished you had something that someone else has? Have you ever put anything or anyone ahead of God in your life? If you have done or even thought about doing any of these things, you have broken the law… the whole law.

Well, when you put it like that…yes. We all have. It's not just you. We are all doomed. But keep reading. This is not the end of the story.

The Nature of God vs. the Nature of the Devil

God is good—all the time. The devil is bad—all the time. Here is a list of some of their qualities or, as the Bible puts it, their "fruit" (Galatians 5:19–23):

Fruit of the Holy Spirit	Fruit of the Flesh	
Love	Sexual immorality	Division
Joy	Selfish ambition	Dissention
Peace	Impurity	Lustful pleasures
Patience	Idolatry	Heresies
Kindness	Sorcery	Envy
Goodness	Hostility/Hatred	Murder
Faithfulness	Quarreling	Jealousy
Gentleness	Drunkenness	Deception
Self-Control	Wild parties	Outbursts of anger

We may not have done or even *wanted* to do all those things on the flesh list, but the thing is, we are all growing on the devil's nature "tree." Our fruit ripens into that stuff. The fruit of the Spirit is hard to do or get because it is not our natural tree, but the fruit of the flesh comes easy to us. It is our natural fruit. We know it's not good, but what can we do?

The scripture says there is not one man, not one of us who has not sinned. "For all have sinned and come short of the glory of God" (Romans 3:23). There isn't any of us that God considers a "good" person. We have all contracted the sin virus, and whether we are showing symptoms or not, we are death waiting to happen, dead men walking.

The Problem of DNA

It may be commendable that you want to do good deeds. It certainly seems commendable that you want to get out of the devil's realm. Unfortunately, even if you want to back out of his syndicate, it's not that easy. Adam and Eve have passed down their sin nature to *everybody*! It's in our spiritual DNA.

If you try to do good things all day, you will probably mess up tomorrow. We are all sin*ners* now, thanks to Adam, not because of *what we do* but because of *who we are.* We sin because we are sinners. That's what we do. We can't help it. We are filled with darkness. Yes, we are doomed if no one comes to save us. Even if we sometimes do good things, our hearts are still corrupted with sin. And God is absolutely pure. He cannot mix with sin even if He wanted to. This is a huge problem—for Him and for us!

That is the bad news. But hang in there, we are coming to the good news! Someone *did* come to rescue us. His name is Jesus! Read on, fellow travelers.

The Sacrificial System

What we find out from reading the Bible is that from the very beginning, even before Adam sinned, God had a plan to save us. He was not ambushed by the actions of the devil. Even from the foundation of the world, Jesus was the savior

(Revelation 13:8). Now that I know a little more about God, that doesn't surprise me. He knows everything. Thank God He had a plan!

Remember that the penalty for Adam's sin (or any sin) was death. Genesis 2:17 tells us that God said, "But of the tree of the knowledge of good and evil you shall not eat, for in the day that you eat of it you shall surely die." That decree started the whole thing. The cycle of sin and death just kept going around and around. Mankind was helpless against it, but God wasn't. The Old Testament tells us that God set up a system of sacrifices to temporarily cover sins, to *hide* them from Himself. The whole business of sacrifice, one thing representing and substituting for another, was His idea. The system of sacrifice worked like this. A person would bring an animal (like a lamb) that cost him something to the temple and lay his hands on it to symbolize his identifying with the animal, and the priest would then kill the animal, sprinkling the blood on the altar. The sin symbolically transferred to the animal as the person's representative, and the man would walk away free and clean, less the price of one lamb. The animal was sacrificed and died in the man's place. The blood (or death) of the animal satisfied God's justice temporarily.

Was a blood sacrifice really necessary, all those poor animals? The answer to that is found in Leviticus 17:11, "For the life of the flesh is in the blood, and I have given it to you upon the altar to make atonement for your souls; for it is the blood that makes atonement for the soul." God's answer is yes, it was and is really necessary. If you go back to the story in the Book of Genesis, you can see that God must have conducted the first sacrifice Himself when He covered Adam and Eve with animal skins (Genesis 3:21). The sin problem is extremely serious to God, a life-and-death matter.

It requires blood (meaning life) as payment, either man's or an animal substitute. Even today, the law has not changed. Remember, God is the High King, and *His definition of sin is treason.* Some people treat the idea of sin lightly, but they are misinformed.

This sacrificial system worked pretty well, but people don't just commit one sin; they sin all the time, right? That's a lot of lambs. Even though the people tried really hard not to sin, offering sacrifices became a full-time job for the Jewish priests, and it was only a temporary fix. The blood of bulls and goats and lambs could only postpone judgment. It was like paying interest only on a credit card. You never pay it off. The bill keeps coming every month. To get rid of the problem of sin permanently for everyone forever, a massive debt, it would require a massive sacrifice.

No animal was valuable enough, no blood was expensive enough—that is, until Jesus, the Son of God and second person of the Trinity, offered to shed His own hundred-percent pure, holy, and perfect God-blood for us.

As much as He might want to, God couldn't just say, "I forgive everybody!" The law, established by God Himself, had to be obeyed and the sentence of death carried out on a human. Animal sacrifices could cover sins temporarily, but they were not enough to get rid of the sins once and for all. Because the transgression or sin was committed by a human being, a human death was required to fulfill the demand of God's justice. A human would have to pay the penalty. But God had thought it all out.

Here was the plan: Jesus would become a human! Because God had previously established the system of representation and sacrifice, something representing something or someone else, it was legally acceptable to Him that Jesus represent all of humanity. That is why Jesus left His glory in heaven and became a man, born as a baby in this world. He came not only to represent God to all the people but also to represent all the people to God. He is the perfect mediator!

The mission of Jesus was to come to earth in a human body and die as a once-and-for-all sacrifice for all the people in the whole world forever. (This would include you and me.) He is called the Lamb slain from the foundation of the world. John the Baptist even called Him the Lamb of God right from the beginning of His ministry (John 1:29–36).

All of our sins were transferred to Jesus on the cross, all of our sicknesses and diseases, all of our failures and mistakes, our selfishness, our hatred, our grief, our rejection, our fear, all of our pain, every kind of death. And when that last bit of our darkness went into Him, when He had on purpose received all of the sins we would ever commit, Jesus died with all that on Him, taking it with Him to the grave. Unlike animal sacrifices, which temporarily covered sin, Jesus's sacrifice was so *powerful* that it didn't just cover sins but totally obliterated them, wiped them away forever. It completely paid the penalty for all the sin anywhere, everywhere, for all time, past, present, and future! It was like a nuclear blast aimed at that Pandora's box of death the devil brought in. After all, the blood of Jesus is the blood of God! There is nothing more valuable than that! The very definition of God is everlasting life. Death is the absolute opposite of what He is all about. It must have been an excruciatingly hard thing for Him to accept death in His own body. We may never fully understand what His sacrifice cost Him, the price of God's Lamb!

"As far as the east is from the west, so far hath he removed our transgressions from us" (Psalm 103:12).

Discussion Questions

1. Why does blood have to be shed to atone for sin?

Jesus, while on the cross, right before He gave up His Spirit, cried, "It is finished!" Then He died in our place, carrying out our sentence and fulfilling the justice of the law. But how would we know the sacrifice had worked? How would we know that God was satisfied and that we would no longer be held responsible for a sin nature handed down from Adam? This is how we know: *death was defeated!* Jesus was raised from the dead! His resurrection *proved* that debt of sin has been completely paid for! He came back to life representing *us*, free and clean, as if we had never sinned. He showed Himself to His disciples so they would know His sacrifice was successful. We can now come into the presence of the living God free and clean from all sin and begin our relationship with Him again. No more darkness. We are back in the light, baby! Our sin natures have been changed back to God natures. This is the basis for the New Covenant or New Testament. This, my friend, is good news. It is very, very good news! The word *gospel* means good news!

To help us understand more fully how Jesus's blood paid for our sins, think of it like you owed a mortgage of $100,000 and were so behind in your payments that the bank was ready to foreclose. But right in the nick of time, the bank president comes to your house, shakes your hand, and declares that not only was your mortgage paid off but also that you now have a hundred billion dollars in your checking account! He is overjoyed and you are now his best friend. The fact is, the precious blood of Jesus actually way *overpaid* for our sins! God is not just satisfied with the payment; He is superbly *over*-satisfied! He is now your best friend.

Discussion Questions

1. Why was the resurrection of Jesus so important?

It's a Free Gift!

The sacrifice of Jesus for us was an incredibly generous gift. God did not have to give His Son; He did it out of love for us. That is how important we are to Him. Never think God doesn't care about you. He more than proved that He does. Romans 8:32 says, "He who did not spare His own Son, but delivered Him up for us all, how shall He not with Him also freely give us all things?" God truly loves us, more than we know!

So how come everything didn't go back to the way it was in the Garden of Eden? If Jesus defeated death and the devil for us, why are bad things still happening? Why is the evidence of the devil still all around us? God, the great High Judge, has set up a legal process, much like the "reading of the will (testament)" event that happens when people are told of their inheritance when a family member dies. Many people do not know about the reading of the will. They are still living in the devil's world. To take advantage of this marvelous gift of life, we have to legally or purposefully *receive the gift* of forgiveness and eternal life. Take it, sign for it, so to speak. "For the wages of sin is death, but the gift of God is eternal life in Christ Jesus, our Lord" (Romans 6:23). Once we hear the good news of our inheritance, the good news that Jesus has paid for our sins, we are required to personally receive it for ourselves by faith, like we are signing a receipt. Yes, Jesus died for the whole world, but it's more personal than that. He loved *you* and He died for *you*. God is handing *you* the gift. Will you receive it?

How does one "receive" the gift? Good question! It is super easy. In Mark 1:15, Jesus said, "The time is fulfilled, and the kingdom of God is at hand; repent and believe in the gospel." The Greek word for *repent* means to change your mind, how you think about things. In this case, it means to change from seeing this life like everybody *else* does and the way the world is in your mind to seeing reality as *God* sees it. Repentance includes realizing you have not measured up and that only Jesus can save you. Repentance can happen in the blink of an eye. Once you have made up your mind to believe the Gospel (the good news of the free gift of eternal life), then you can receive it by your faith. You accept it for yourself. This can all happen very quickly. For some, it might take a little longer because they haven't completely made up their minds to change the way they think. For some people, it's just a little step into the Kingdom, but for others, the step seems like a giant leap. The devil also gets into the mix and causes confusion and distraction. He tries desperately to blind us and stop us from finding the truth.

In some churches, new believers are asked to say the Sinner's Prayer, although that is certainly subjective and not mandated in the Bible. There are no particular words, but saying something is good. "I believe Jesus died on the cross in my place and paid for all my sins. He's my savior and He is my King! From now on, I will believe His Word over any other word. Jesus is my Lord, and I will not serve the devil." If you say (or pray) something like that, you have announced to God and the spiritual world that you have changed kingdoms. You have confessed that Jesus is officially your Lord. Awesome! It's so easy! "If you confess with your mouth the Lord Jesus and believe in your heart that God has raised Him from the dead, you will be saved. For with the heart one believes unto righteousness, and with the mouth confession is made unto salvation" (Romans 10:9–10).

This is such good news, right? The word *gospel* means... you got it, good news! If you have never said anything like that, about Jesus being your own personal savior, now is a good time to do it. When you believe and receive the free gift of "salvation" that God offers (being saved from association with the devil and going to his hell), you are what the Bible calls *born again*, changed from sin nature to God nature, and that changes everything.

Here are some scriptures that talk about God's solution to the problem of sin:

> For God so loved the world that He gave His only begotten Son, that whosoever believes in Him should not perish but have everlasting life. (John 3:16)

> He who believes in the Son has everlasting life and he who does not believe the Son shall not see life, but the wrath of God abides on him. (John 3:36)

> Therefore, as through one man's (Adam) offense judgment came to all men, resulting in condemnation, even so through one Man's (Jesus) righteous act the free gift came to all men, resulting in justification of life. For as one

man's disobedience many were made sinners, so also by one Man's obedience many will be made righteous. (Romans 5:18–19)

I have written these things to you that you may know that you have eternal life. (1 John 5:13)

By scriptures like these, we can know for sure that we are saved from hell and have access to heaven and everlasting life. If you believe Jesus died for your sins and you have accepted Him as your savior and as your King, you are saved. It is finished. We are safe and we are free.

We Are Free!

God has done his part. God has done everything He is going to do to free us from the captivity of the devil's kingdom. He has unlocked the prison door. But many people who don't know they are free continue to live in their prison, even though they could walk out at any time.

They continue with their "normal" lives, eating prison food, working for the warden, as if Jesus had never been raised from the dead. What happens to those people when they die? If they have never legally and officially accepted Jesus as the sacrifice for their sins, they will never be able to enter heaven or the Kingdom of God. Their sin will still be there, causing separation, darkness. They will be dispelled by light, like a magnet repels another magnet from the same pole. The two—God and them—will never be able to get together. Unbelievers have not ratified the contract by believing, so they have not entered into the agreement of the New Covenant. That is sad because God has offered the free gift to everyone.

And that is why we preach the Gospel! In other words, that is why it is so important to tell people what Jesus has done for them so they can believe too! It's so easy that a child can do it. You don't have to have a degree in divinity. You don't have to have a degree in anything! God made it so available for everyone that there is no excuse for them not to *receive the gift* of life. So go tell someone you love!

Paul is speaking here in Romans 10:10–17 (ICB):

> We believe with our hearts, and so we are made right with God. And we declare with our mouths to say that we believe, and so we are saved. As the Scripture says, "Anyone who trusts in Him will never be disappointed." That Scripture says "anyone" because there is no difference between Jew and non-Jew. The same Lord is the Lord of all and gives many blessings to all who trust in Him. The Scripture says, "Anyone who asks the Lord for help will be saved."
>
> But before people can trust in the Lord for help, they must believe in Him. And before they can believe in the Lord, they must hear about Him. And for them to hear about the Lord, someone must tell them. And before someone can go and tell them, He must be sent. It is written, "How beautiful is the person who comes to bring good news."
>
> But not all the Jews accepted the good news. Isaiah said, "Lord, who believed what we told them?" So faith comes from hearing the Good

News. And people hear the Good News when someone tells them about Christ.

Hiroo Onoda

During World War II, a Japanese soldier named Hiroo Onoda was sent by the Japanese army to the remote Philippine island of Lubang. His mission was to conduct guerrilla warfare during World War II. Unfortunately, he was never officially told the war had ended, so for twenty-nine years, Onoda continued to live in the jungle, ready for when his country would again need his services and information. He ate coconuts and bananas and deftly evaded searching parties he believed were enemy scouts. Onoda hid in the jungle until he finally emerged from the dark recesses of the island on March 19, 1972, when his former commanding officer contacted him and personally told him to come out because the war was over.

Hiroo Onoda lived for twenty-nine years hiding, fighting, surviving, not realizing the war was over. Many people still believe that God is mad at them. They don't know He has set them free from bondage to the world that the devil has created and from judgment and hell to come. They stay in their prisons and decorate them and tell themselves what a wonderful life they have. They don't know their lives could be so much more! The cry of Christian evangelists is, "Come out! Come out of the confined life you have made for yourself! Be free! Let Jesus be your sacrifice and be reconciled to the Father who loves you."

God is not trying to make your life harder! He wants to help you, heal you, prosper you, show you how to really live. And He has made a home for you for eternity with Him. In John 14:2–3, Jesus says, "In My Father's house are many mansions; if it were not so I would have told you. I go to prepare a place for you. And if I go and prepare a place for you, I will come again and receive you to Myself, that where I am, there you may be also."

A believer's eternal future is secure and a sure thing! You are safe.

And now the fun begins…

We begin the process of learning who we are.

Discussion Questions

1. The free gift was free for us, but it was not free for God. Have you ever bought something for someone else? It was free to them, but not to you.

2. What is the most expensive gift you have ever given to anyone?

3. How does giving someone a free gift make you feel?

LESSON 6

What Is a Covenant?

This lesson is looking into the problem and solution from a slightly different perspective. Some of the information is the same but goes a little deeper. We know that the Bible contains the Old and New Testaments. A testament is a will and, in some cases, the evidence of certain facts. The Testaments of the Bible have also been called the Old and New Covenants. The Bible, therefore, is God's statement to us about what is going on, how He feels about it, what He has done about it, and what He expects us to do about it.

A covenant is a solemn agreement between two parties, either groups or individuals, where each party makes vows or states what they are willing to do in order to make a treaty, a lasting bond, or connection with each other. It is a serious, binding contract, and in the Old Testament days, covenants were often made by mixing the blood of the two parties, signifying a unity lasting until death. Practically speaking, if you broke your part of the agreement, you could be sentenced to death. That's about as serious as it gets. To "cut a covenant" is still a common phrase in some cultures. Each party would cut themselves on the finger, hand, wrist, or forearm, shedding blood. Then they would put their arms or fingers together or signify the mingling of blood together to show that they were now brothers or family, unified by sharing blood with a commitment to protect and help each other. The scars from the wounds would remind both of them of the bond they shared. Why would people do this? *Because we are stronger together than when we are alone.* Usually vows were said signifying that the resources of each party were now available to both of them, such as one tribe sharing their weapons and the other tribe sharing their food source. The tribal groups, families, or individuals became stronger against other common enemies because of the alliance of the covenant. Using blood pacts, blood covenants, or becoming blood brothers is a system found in cultures all over the world.

Jesus made a covenant with us. He shed His blood and has the scars to remind Him. God's covenant with us is not for His own protection but for ours. We are stronger with Him. He used the covenant system to help us to see that His agreement to protect us is serious and lasting, a legal promise that cannot be broken.

The Marriage Covenant

Marriage is also a covenant. Both parties say vows, what they are willing to do to make the bond, to unify, or to become one blood with each other. These words are said, "Till death do we part," or "As long as we both shall live." The wife takes the husband's family name, blending the two families. There is blood shed when the two become intimate for the first time. Their resources are shared with each other. Jesus said in Mark 10:6–9, "From the beginning of creation, God made them male and female. For this reason a man shall leave his father and mother and be joined to his wife, and the two shall become one flesh, so then *they are no longer two, but one* flesh. Therefore, what God has joined together, let not man separate."

Two becoming one is the whole point of making a covenant. We are stronger together. You can see how the stability of such a solid agreement would produce a safe and secure environment in which to raise a family. God sees the promises made as binding until death. We should too. The marriage covenant is also symbolic of the relationship between Jesus and the Church. The Church is called the bride of Christ.

> So husbands ought to love their own wives as their own bodies; he who loves his wife loves himself. For no one ever hated his own flesh, but nourishes and cherishes it, just as the Lord does the church. For we are members of His body, of His flesh and of His bones. "For this reason a man shall leave his father and mother and be joined to his wife, and the two shall become one flesh." This is a great mystery, but I speak concerning Christ and the church. (Ephesians 5:28–32)

We want God's promises to us to be secure and lasting. He expects the same from us. This is what a covenant is all about.

Romans 1:31 (KVJ) tells us that in the last days, people will be "without understanding, *covenant breakers,* without natural affection, implacable, unmerciful." Many people in this generation have not understood what it means to make a covenant with another person. They conveniently forget the vows of the covenant and walk away from their promises. They break contracts, agreements, and promises right and left. Our society used to frown on such behavior, but now, due to the desensitizing and numbing effects of the media, it not only accepts it as normal but also often encourages it. We have allowed the unbelievers shaping our media resources to dictate the rules of our society. This may be okay with unbelievers because they don't know any better, but it should not be okay with us. People like to recite the media's shallow definition of marriage as "it's just a piece of paper," referring to the signed contract. But most of us know it is much more than that. The broken marriage system has caused many people in this generation to choose to live together without making a covenant with each other at all. They think they can avoid the mess of divorce that way, but this strategy usually leads to trouble too. It is very challenging to have a lasting relationship where there is an absence of trust. Where there is no promise of a secure bond from either party, although many times one or both of the people involved have naively assumed there to be one, trust can become very fragile. Breakups from live-together relationships can be just as hurtful and complicated as a divorce. Either way, God's plan of a secure family environment is weakened.

High Standards / Better Results

When we are faced with a high standard like that, immediately our thoughts go to a situation where that didn't happen. We know of couples that lived together happily all their lives without being married. We know divorced couples who are much better off now than when they were married. The devil loves to provide excuses for why we don't have to live up to God's standards. But after we are born again, and if we continue to renew our minds with the Word of God, we begin to respond to higher standards differently. We know God is trying to help us, not hurt us. His ways are higher than ours and better than ours. We begin to want to do things His way. When we realize He is not mad at us for messing up, we are no longer afraid to try it His way, and we begin to see the good results.

Sometimes we forget that the devil also has a plan. He attacks marriages and families because we are stronger together. So we don't condemn people that have gone through divorce; divorces are tragic for everyone involved, but we sure don't encourage it either! If two people are willing, marriages can be healed, just like bodies can be healed. We will be able to resist the devil better if we stand together to counter his attacks against us. The scripture gives us a picture of how two is better than one. "One can chase a thousand, and two put ten thousand to flight" (Deuteronomy 32:30). "Again I say to you that if two of you agree on earth concerning anything that they ask, it will be done for them by My Father in heaven" (Matthew 18:19). Two believers in covenant together can be a powerful force against the enemy. *Jesus and the Church together in covenant are unstoppable.*

The Old Covenant (Testament)

In the Old Testament, God made a covenant with the Jewish people. Why the Jews? Why does God refer to them as His chosen people? The Jewish people are special because they are descendants of the man called Abraham, God's friend (James 2:23).

Abraham, friend of God

In the Book of Genesis, the book of beginnings, God tells us about a man called Abram. Abram was born from the lineage of Noah's son Shem, only nine generations after the flood and only forty years after the death of Noah. (Noah had three sons: Shem, Ham, and Japheth.) The significance of that is simply that these people were still around for a long time, having personally witnessed the flood, which was a judgment of God on sin, so it was quite possible that Abram's family knew all about that, and perhaps even talked to Noah or one of his sons. Isn't that interesting?

God said to Abram, "Get out of your country, from your family and from your father's house to a land that I will show you. I will make you a great nation. I will bless you and make your name great; and you shall be a blessing. I will bless those who bless you and I will curse him who curses you, and in you all the families of the earth shall be blessed." (Genesis 12:1-3). God led Abram to the land where Canaan, the son of Noah's son Ham, had settled after the flood. The land of Canaan was populated by many different tribes of people by that time, and idol worship was a part of their culture. The giving of this land to Abram was part of a fulfillment of Genesis 9:25–26 when Noah prophesied over his children: "'Cursed be Canaan; a servant of servants he shall be to his brethren.' And he said, 'Blessed be the Lord, the God of Shem, and may Canaan be his servant…'"

God made a covenant with Abram, changing his name to Abraham and saying,

> And I will establish my covenant between Me and you and your descendants after you in their generations, for an everlasting covenant, to be a God to you and your descendants after you. Also, I give to you and your descendants after you the land in which you are a stranger, all the land of Canaan, as an everlasting possession; and I will be their God. And as for you, you shall keep My covenant, you and your descendants

after you throughout their generations. This is My covenant which you shall keep, between Me and you and your descendants after you: Every male child among you shall be circumcised..." (Genesis 17:7–10).

This covenant was passed down generationally through the descendants of Abraham's son, Isaac. Isaac had two sons, Jacob and Esau. Before Isaac died, he blessed his son Jacob and passed down the blessing of the covenant to him. This is important for us as Gentile Christians, too, because the scriptures have included us retroactively. "Those who are of faith are sons of Abraham" (Galatians 3:7). "If you are Christ's, then you are Abraham's seed and heirs according to the promise"(Galatians 3:29).

When God delivered the Jews from slavery in Egypt and they had travelled to the wilderness of Sinai, He spoke to them through His prophet Moses. This is what He said:

Thus, you shall say to the house of Jacob and tell the children of Israel: You have seen what I did to the Egyptians, and how I bore you on eagle's wings and brought you to myself. Now therefore, if you will indeed obey My voice and keep My covenant, then you shall be a special treasure to Me above all people; for the earth is Mine. And you shall be to Me a kingdom of priests and a holy nation. These are the words which you shall speak to the children of Israel. (Exodus 19:3–6)

God said what He was willing to do. He would make them a kingdom of priests with Him as their king. A priest represents the people to God and God to the people. They would be a nation that represented God to the rest of the world. He said they would be a treasure to Him and inferred that the blessings of the whole earth would be shared with them. He also said what He required from them. They were to obey His voice and keep His covenant. Moses spoke all of God's words to the people. Then it was their turn.

"Then all the people answered together and said, 'All that the Lord has spoken we will do'" (Exodus 19:8). They meant well, but they had no idea how hard it would be to do what God required. Next, in Exodus 20 to 23, God laid out the rules for "keeping His covenant." They are the Ten Commandments and some other guidelines on how to live as a free people. In Exodus 24, after hearing all of God's requirements, the people again replied, "All the words which the Lord has said, we will do." It must have sounded simple enough, and they were caught up in the moment. God was speaking to them, and they must have been thrilled! But did they stop to consider what He was asking of them? In hindsight, I don't think so. They didn't realize how far away from God's holiness they really were. Many of us are in the same boat.

Moses wrote down all the rules and details. They made an altar. There were animal sacrifices and offerings made. Moses sprinkled the blood on the altar.

> Then he took the Book of the Covenant (all the things he had written down) and read in the hearing of the people. And they said, "All that the Lord has said we will do and be obedient." And Moses took the blood and sprinkled it on the people, and said, This is the blood of the

covenant which the Lord has made with you according to all these words. (Exodus 24:5–8)

Okay, so that all sounds good, right? God tells them what He is willing to do, and the people tell God what they are willing to do. God was faithful; He is always faithful to His Word. No trouble on His side. The trouble with this covenant was that the *people* were not faithful. They did **not** do what they said they would do. Even though they said three times that they would do everything the Lord required of them, they could not actually keep the commandments of the Lord. Look at what happened. Moses went up the mountain to receive further instructions from God about setting up the priesthood (remember, He had said He would make them a kingdom of priests). From Exodus 25 to 31, Moses was receiving instructions from their faithful God and was up on the mountain for forty days. In Exodus 32, the next chapter, we find that the people got tired of waiting for Him to return. They went to Aaron, Moses's brother and assistant, and asked him to make them a golden calf to be a god for them. It took them less than forty days to prove that they could not keep their end of the bargain. They immediately broke the first two commandments—to love and worship only God alone and make no graven images of other gods.

The Old Covenant Was Impossible to Keep

Because of the sin nature (devil's nature) of man, nobody could actually do all the things God required of them. They may have wanted to. They may actually have done some of them, but nobody could consistently keep all of them. The standard was higher than they could reach. James 2:10 explains, "For whoever shall keep the whole law, and yet stumble in one point, he is guilty of all." In order to keep God's covenant, they had to keep *all* of the Ten Commandments, not just some of them.

Below is the list. I used to pat myself on the back because I thought I could keep number 6.

Ten Commandments (Exodus 20)

1. I am the Lord, your God. You shall have no other gods before Me.
2. You shall make no graven or carved images, no idols.
3. You shall not take the name of the Lord your God in vain.
4. Remember to keep the Sabbath day holy. (Do not work on this day.)
5. Honor your father and mother.
6. You shall not murder.
7. You shall not commit adultery.
8. You shall not steal.
9. You shall not bear false witness against your neighbor.
10. You shall not covet.

When I was young, I was not taught to think about the meaning or heart behind the laws. I memorized the strict letter of the law. This is how the Jews were looking at it. But when Jesus came, He taught the people to look more at the meaning. "Do not murder" should be understood as do not be angry with your brother without cause (Matthew 5:22). "You shall have no other gods before Me" should be understood as to love the Lord your God with your whole heart and soul and mind and strength (Luke 10:27). So if you go through all the ten and really think about what they mean, you start to realize how far we have all strayed from the perfection of God.

The Ten Commandments Somewhat Defined

As you go through these, the idea is to see where you have missed it, not that other Christians are so much better than you or that you are better than them. Use the commandments as a standard to measure yourself to. And God knows there are sometimes special circumstances. The Jews considered plucking ears of corn off their stalks to be harvesting, which was "work" and, therefore, against the fourth commandment. One time, Jesus allowed His disciples to pick corn and eat it on the Sabbath because they were hungry. He said the Sabbath was made for man, not man for the Sabbath. God judges the heart, the intentions, not just the actions of a person.

1. *Have no other gods*—Of course, we shouldn't worship Buddha, but this commandment also means there is nothing ever higher or more important in your thoughts than God. We are to love the Lord our God with all of our heart, soul, mind, and strength. This leaves no room to put anything else first, even ourselves or our families.

2. *Make no idols*—Lots of things can be idols besides images of Hari Krishna. There are physically carved images, like little statues, and there are mentally carved images that we make for ourselves and lift up to the highest place in our lives, where God should be. TV can be an idol, money can be an idol, football

can be an idol—anything that takes the place of God in our eyes and our hearts, anything we sacrifice our time, money, and relationships for. Oh yes, and those little statues of Mary and various saints that people have in their cars and on their lawns are just as much idols as the statues of Buddha and Hari Krishna.

3. *Do not take the name of the Lord in vain*—This means cursing or swearing using the name of Jesus Christ or God or anything that belongs to God. His name is sacred and powerful. When God speaks, His Word expresses His thoughts, and they create good. He is a great king. We are created in His image to be like Him. What does using any kind of vulgar language to express our thoughts say about us? We shouldn't use the Lord's name in any evil, destructive, or useless way or for any purpose other than to bring glory to God. You wouldn't want someone to say your name in a vulgar way every time things go wrong. Neither does God.

4. *Keep the Sabbath day holy*—God provided a day of rest, a day to focus on Him. The Sabbath day for Jews is Saturday. Christians use Sunday because it was the day Jesus rose from the dead. Church services are usually held on Sunday. God said to do no work on the Sabbath. The Jews were good at this one. Jesus got in trouble because He healed people on the Sabbath. His message was to do good on the Sabbath. God rested on the seventh day of creation. He wants us to rest, too, and take a break from the world.

5. *Honor your parents*—Take care of them, don't belittle them. Jesus took care of Mary even when He was on the cross. If your parents made mistakes, God says we should still honor them. He didn't say we have to agree with them. Honoring your parents brings the blessing of long life.

6. *Don't murder*—This is not talking about war. It means don't take another life for your own interests. Cain slew his brother Abel because he was jealous. Not a good reason. God loves people. It would not be right to kill your baby because you don't want to take care of it. That is serving your own interests. Let someone adopt it. "Whoever hates his brother is a murderer" (1 John 3:15). The devil was a murderer from the beginning (John 8:44). Don't be like him. Love people.

7. *Don't commit adultery*—This is stepping on someone's blood covenant with someone else. Not cool and never appropriate. A marriage covenant is between two people, not three, and God takes covenants seriously. Sleeping with random people is never a good idea, but if you do, that is called fornication, not adultery. Adultery means one of you is married. Jesus said that if you lust after someone, even just fantasizing in your mind, it is the same as actually committing adultery. First Corinthians 6:16 says, "Or do you not know that he who is joined to a harlot is one body with her? For 'the two,' He says, 'shall become one flesh.'" The scripture goes on to say, "Flee fornication (sexual immorality). Every sin that a man does is outside the body, but he who

commits sexual immorality sins against his own body."

8. *Don't steal*—You don't need to take someone else's blessing, not even a big company's blessing. God has enough for you too. Just ask Him, and He will give you what you desire, (Mark 11:24). The devil comes to steal, kill, and destroy. He is a thief. Don't be like him.

9. *Don't bear false witness against your neighbor*—Tell the truth in a court of law and out of court. Don't lie about someone else. Better yet, don't lie about anything! When we lie, we are often involving someone else. God wasn't saying it was okay to lie if it just affects you and not your neighbor; He was saying don't take someone else down with you. The devil is a liar and the father of it (John 8:44). Don't be like him. Jesus is the way, the *truth*, and the life. Truth is always the best option. It will all come out in the end anyway.

10. *Don't covet or desire other people's stuff, including their spouses*—Get your own. Don't be jealous or envious because someone else has what you want. God will give you whatever you need. Just ask Him.

God knew these things were going to be too hard for us to keep up, especially with our sin natures. He is not surprised when we miss it. It is in our nature to sin, just like it is in a dog's nature to bark or a bird's nature to sing. The problem was in our spiritual DNA. The Old Covenant or "the law" was impossible for man to keep. God saw that the only way to fix it was to make a whole new covenant, one that was fail-safe, where He could make sure it would succeed. But in the meantime, He left the people this set of guidelines, given through Moses, written by the finger of God Himself, supernaturally, on two stone tablets (Exodus 31:18).

The New Covenant

God had a plan all along. The Bible tells us that this plan was devised from the foundation of the world or, in other words, even before Adam and Eve sinned. God knew right from the beginning what would happen. He knew He had an enemy and that that enemy would try to wreck everything. But just because He knew doesn't mean he would stop it from happening. He made it work for Him, instead. He took lemons and made lemonade right from the beginning, and no one knew, not even the angels, that God had wanted lemonade all along.

God knew we couldn't keep the Old Covenant. He gave us the Ten Commandments to help us realize, in case we were not getting it, that we needed help. Romans 7:7 (CSB) says, "I would not have known sin if it were not for the law. For example, I would not have known what it is to covet if the law had not said, Do not covet." The purpose of the law was to show us how much we had gotten off track, how far away from "pure" we were, and how badly we needed God's support to help us. Man continued to sin because of his fallen nature. We proved ourselves over and over to be "lemons." Then when the time was right, God sent Jesus to make the New Covenant, the lemonade.

God had given man a free will to choose to love and obey Him. He actually used the enemy to give them the option to choose something else. He didn't want to force people to love Him like robots. He didn't create man to serve Him like the angels. He had made man in His own royal image in order to have a family, and it was important to God that we were free to choose. A free will is an honor and a privilege, and God didn't change after Adam's poor choice. He still loved His creation. Man, even in his fallen state and sinful nature, was doing all kinds of things that were not good. They were sinning against God and His Word all the time without even realizing it. So He gave us the law, the Ten Commandments, to guide us in the right direction.

Galatians 3:24 (NLT) tells us, "The law was our guardian (or tutor) until Christ came; it protected us until we could be made right with God through faith." He let people try for a long time, giving them the system of animal sacrifices to cover their sins, but all those animal sacrifices could never change their nature. Every child born into this world is born with the devil's nature. Something else had to be done. So God set up a final sacrifice that would pay for every sinful action, every sinful thought, and, in addition, also made a way that by believing His Word (reversing what Adam and Eve had done), we can be born again spiritually, made holy with brand-new spiritual DNA, translating us out of the kingdom of darkness and back into the Kingdom of Light! Seriously, God is brilliant!

> But now Jesus, our High Priest, has been given a ministry that is far superior to the old priesthood, for He is the one who mediates for us a far better covenant with God, based on better promises. For if the first covenant had been faultless, there would have been no need for a second covenant to replace it. (Hebrews 8:6–7)

With the New Covenant, the law of God is not written on stones but on our hearts. We *want* to do it now. He has given us the Holy Spirit to help us succeed. Ezekiel 36:26–27 prophesies about the New Covenant, "I will give you a new heart and put a new spirit within you; I will take the heart of stone out of your flesh and give you a heart of flesh. I will put My Spirit within you and cause you to walk in My statutes, and you will keep My judgments and do them." The Ten Commandments was given as a temporary guide to show us how to live. *But now we are no longer trying to keep the Ten Commandments, we are simply relying on the Holy Spirit to guide us and show us what to do every day.*

How to Ratify the Contract (Covenant)

Jesus sacrificed Himself for us all. His blood was precious enough to pay for the sins of everyone in the world and then some. This remedy is in the form of a blood covenant, which requires both parties to "sign" or participate. In order for us to ratify the covenant (contract) so that it takes effect for us personally, there is one action on our part we must take. *We need to believe.* That's it! Just believe that Jesus paid for our awful sins. When we believe God's Word instead of the devil's, acknowledging and repenting of our sinful past, having a sincere faith that Jesus died in our place, paying our debt with His own life, we are changed back from darkness to light again. The curse is reversed! Our spiritual signature is written right next to God's on the contract. And God's name is signed in blood. This is called being *born again.* It isn't necessary for us to shed blood with animal sacrifices. It's already been done for us. Jesus was our Lamb. He shed His *own* blood and He was the mediator between God and man. We don't need a priest or a minister to mediate for us. Jesus's blood represented both us and God in this transaction. Jesus did all the hard part. We just have to agree with Him. It isn't necessary to feel anything or say any particular words. Just believing will do it. It is a free gift, but it is not automatic. The faith or believing part is crucial.

Born Again?

Just because someone goes to church does not make them a believer, just like walking into a garage does not make you a car. Just because your parents were Christians doesn't make you a Christian by default. Being American doesn't make you a Christian. Taking Communion, following the golden rule, and even trying to follow the Ten Commandments don't make you a Christian. Only your faith, your belief in what Jesus has done, makes you one.

When Jesus said, "You must be born again" (John 3:3), He meant you must change your spiritual DNA. Man was created with a spirit, a soul that lives in a body, a three-part being, kind of like the Trinity. God likes things in threes. Mankind, as we learned, was created in the image of God, with His nature, personality, and character. When Adam and Eve chose to believe the devil instead of God, they were "born again" into the devil's nature and became sinners in their spirits, the inside part of them. It was after that choice, that *belief* in the words of the serpent (who, of course, was really the devil), that Eve took the first bite and Adam followed her. Sinning by thinking with their minds and then taking action with their bodies was a *result* of the sin nature in their spirits.

When we choose to believe God and receive Jesus's sacrifice for our sins, we receive His forgiveness, declaring

Him to be our Savior and Lord, and we are "born again"—
again—back to the holy nature of God Himself. We become
holy again on the inside! We are no longer sinners in our
spirits. Our souls and bodies remain the same, still corrupted
by our old sin natures, old habits, etc. Our thought life and
our flesh still may mess up and sin sometimes, but it doesn't
change who we are inside. Our spirits are remade in the
image of God. The Holy Spirit then takes up residence in our
brand-new, squeaky clean, and holy spirits. The Holy Spirit
could not possibly live inside us if we still had our old sin
natures. Think about it, God is so pure! When the scripture
says, "For He made Him who knew no sin to be sin for us,
that we might become the righteousness of God in Him" (2
Corinthians 5:21), it is telling us we have been made as pure
as God on the inside.

New Creatures / New DNA

When we were sinners, we sometimes did good things,
but that didn't change our natures, who we were inside.
Now that we are born again, it is our nature to do good, but
occasionally, our flesh flares up and sins. Our good deeds
did not change our bad spiritual DNA before, and our not-
so-good deeds cannot change our good spiritual DNA now.
Being born again means literally we are born as a new creature,
a new spirit that did not exist before. "Therefore, if anyone is
in Christ, he is a new creation; old things have passed away;
behold, all things have become new" (2 Corinthians 5:17).
The Amplified Bible puts it this way, "Therefore if anyone is
in Christ [that is, grafted in, joined to Him by faith in Him
as Savior], *he is a new creature* [reborn and renewed by the
Holy Spirit]; the old things [the previous moral and spiritual
condition] have passed away. Behold, new things have come
[because spiritual awakening brings a new life]."

The Holy Spirit, together with the Word of God, produces a son or daughter of God through our faith. Just like the Holy Spirit overshadowed Mary and she became pregnant with the Son of God, so the Holy Spirit over-shadows us when we believe God's Word, and He reproduces Himself in us. Our spirits are reborn and made in His image. In an instant, we are changed from darkness to light, from the nature of the devil to the nature of God, from death to life. It is a miraculous "every man for himself" kind of thing. You have to believe for yourself. God begets children. He doesn't have any grandchildren. Each person needs to be born again through their own faith and become a new creature in Christ. Your parents can't do it for you.

New Spirit / Old Flesh

The challenge for us as believers, after we are born again, is to train our souls (our minds, will, and emotions), which have not been regenerated, to become like Jesus. Romans 12:2 says, "And do not be conformed to this world, but *be transformed by the renewing of your mind*, that you may prove what is that good and acceptable and perfect will of God." Our spirits are born again and made perfect, but our souls and bodies are still operating like before. They need to be retrained and renewed as well, but this transformation is not automatic or instant. To change them to be like Jesus takes effort on behalf of the believer. God instantly transformed our spirits, but renewing our minds and emotions is the responsibility of each believer. The only way for that to happen is to consistently realign ourselves up with what the Word of God says we should be. The scriptures function like our very own personal trainer. Just like people are at different levels of physical fitness, Christians are at all different levels of mind and soul transformation. Some people don't work out at all, some work out occasionally, and some work out daily. The results of our spiritual workouts will show in our souls, our personalities, just like our physical workouts show the results in our bodies. Ephesians 4:22–24 tells us, "You were taught, with regard to your former way of life, to *put off your old self,* which is being corrupted by its deceitful desires; to be made new in the attitude of your minds; and to *put on the new self,* created to be like God in true righteousness and holiness." We are told to be "dead" to the old man, the old us, and "alive" to the new man, which is patterned after Jesus. "I have been crucified with Christ: nevertheless, I live; yet not I, but Christ lives in me: and the life which I now live in the flesh, I live by the faith of the Son of God, who loved me, and gave Himself for me" (Galatians 2:20).

This takes practice. It takes faith. Every day we get another chance to try again, and it does get easier as we do it. But this is where many Christians miss out. They don't realize they have a part to play. We learn by reading the Word or listening to preaching how we are supposed to act, and then we train ourselves to modify our behavior. The Holy Spirit helps us. God is not mad at us when we make mistakes. We are like little children learning to walk all over again.

The New Testament, especially the letters written to the Church, is where we find out what we should be like after we have been born again and how we should be living. It is like learning how to live in a foreign country. You have to learn the new rules and the new culture. We are new creatures learning to live like citizens of heaven while still living here in this world. We need the Bible to show us and train us how to be.

Living Examples of Jesus

To be a Christian means that you are a disciple of Christ Jesus. The word *Christ* comes from the Greek word *christos*, which means "anointed one." It was translated from the Hebrew word for the Messiah, the anointed king. Christ is not Jesus's last name; it is His ministry. Being a disciple of Christ means you have made a decision to follow and emulate Him and…His ministry. Jesus is our role model for living. What did Jesus do? He preached about the Kingdom, healed the sick, and cast out demons that are causing trouble for people. Since He is not physically here, His disciples have become His living representatives on the earth, the examples of what He would be like if He was here. Just like being an American means you represent America to the rest of the world, both who we are and what we do here in the land of America, being a Christian means you show the world what it is like to be Jesus the King and to do what He would do. Sometimes we forget that we are representing Him and just represent ourselves. No wonder the world is confused!

Some people misunderstand what being born again means. They have the idea that it is some sort of elitist group, Christians who think too highly of themselves, a group that judges others harshly while not living up to Christian ideals themselves. Some people who identify or claim to identify as born-again Christians have done weird, wacky, and foolish things, which have caused others to mock and slander authentic believers. These examples are poor representations of true disciples and, in fact, do not represent us all. We need to be careful and realize people are watching us. They are looking for authenticity, not a pretense or show. Trying to look holy on the outside when there's no transformation on the inside is what the Pharisees did and what Jesus didn't like. You don't need to wear a big cross or carry a three-foot-high Bible around to prove you are a better believer than someone else. Born-again Christians are not better than anyone; they are new creatures that have realized they are forgiven. They are free. Let's use our freedom to help others, not accuse them. That's the devil's angle. Let's not give cause for him to use our words and actions against us to try to tear down the Kingdom. Let's help build it up!

Discussion Questions

1. Why is it important to tell people about the Gospel (good news)?

LESSON 7

TRADITIONS—MAN'S OR GOD'S?

Traditions can be helpful, and traditions can hold you back from God's best. Traditions are usually set by the culture. The traditions of celebrating our holidays, like Christmas and Thanksgiving, can be a wonderful and joyful cultural experience. It all depends on what we are used to. I remember visiting some people at Christmastime and participating with them while we opened presents. Everyone ripped open their presents all at the same time. I was shocked and appalled. In my family, we all waited patiently for each person to open their presents one at a time so that we could all see the surprise and enjoy the moment with each loved one. Were we right and they were wrong? No, not at all. Family traditions are made up by each family. If we think of our churches as being different branches of the family, we can see that they may, and do, differ in how they want to "open the presents." For most of us, the holidays, birthday parties, and wedding ceremonies are a happy part of our family life. There are lots of traditions in our everyday lives that are positive, such as shaking hands when you meet someone or hugging a loved one. We want to keep those. Other traditions may not be so helpful.

Have you ever heard the phrase "set in their ways"? A lot of times this refers to an older person but not always. Many people are waiting longer these days to get married and have children. Because they are already used to a certain lifestyle, this makes it harder for them to adjust and to compromise the "ways" they have set in place for themselves. They are used to certain ways of doing things, like working out or hanging out with their friends or traveling. These "ways" of life are cultural traditions they have established for themselves. It is not easy for them to give up those things or even to compromise and to make the adjustments needed in order to establish a new lifestyle, such as marriage or having a family. Do you know anyone like that?

Traditions are not bad things, but if the traditions get in the way of progress toward a more important goal, then they might need to change. If a couple desires to have a family, then they may have to adjust their ways or lifestyle to focus on what they consider to be the more important goal of raising children. They don't have to give up everything, just move it around a bit. Traditions are subject to change. Before I was married, I celebrated my family Christmas on Christmas Eve. That had been my family's tradition for all my life. My husband's family also celebrated on Christmas Eve. This was a problem. After I was married, we had to choose which family tradition we would change. It ended up that I celebrated with his family on Christmas Eve, and we started a new tradition to celebrate with my family on Christmas Day. My relationships with my husband and my new in-laws were more important to me than my tradition, and as uncomfortable as it was for me to adjust, making progress toward the greater goal was my priority.

The Church has this same problem. It has traditions that, uncomfortable as it may be, require adjustment and change from time to time. Believe it or not, many of our religious traditions are based on culture or what some guy or group thought was a good idea at the time. They are not always based on scripture or might be loosely based on scripture in a vague way. Some of the traditions that people assume have always been there are just ways that worked at the time for that situation, and we have continued to carry them on without knowing or caring why. But tradition is not the same as the Word of God in most cases. Tradition is most often manmade and a cultural thing. Even the Jews during Jesus's time had trouble with traditions.

God gave Moses the Ten Commandments to follow, but by the time Jesus came on the scene, the Jews had developed hundreds of additional rules and regulations that they added to the law. Their "oral tradition" took on an equal importance to the actual law given by God, and it became a stumbling block for the people. People needed the priests, Pharisees, scribes, and lawyers to interpret all these man-made laws for them, and it was all very complicated. Jesus said, "Woe to you, teachers of the law and Pharisees, you hypocrites! You shut the door of the kingdom of heaven in people's faces. You yourselves do not enter, nor will you let those enter who are trying to" (Matthew 23:13). He was saying that they were getting all tangled up in their traditional, man-made, cultural (and sometimes wrong) interpretations of the Bible and not seeing the simple truth of God's Word. They were making it impossible for themselves to connect with God and His Kingdom. Worst of all, they were taking everyone else down with them!

Jesus told the religious leaders, "You nullify the word of God by your tradition that you have handed down. And you do many things like that" (Mark 7:13). It is the Word of God that we need to follow. The *Word* brings *life*. You would think that religious leaders would know what they are doing. Sadly, many people in leadership positions in the Church today are in the same rut as the Pharisees during Jesus's time. And sadly, many people hang on tightly to Church traditions as if they *were* scripture, and this has caused a lot of confusion, division, and the "nullifying" of the Word of God, which is not helpful, to say the least.

Church Traditions

Traditions comfort people, but they can also prevent them from discovering the blessings that God has for them as they move forward. In the Old Testament, the Israelites, after they had been rescued from Egypt, had to follow the cloud of God's presence by day and the pillar of fire by night. The cloud protected them against the hot sun, and the fire protected them against the cold night. They weren't allowed to get too used to being in one place. When the cloud moved, they had to pack up camp and move on. God doesn't want us to get so comfortable that we stop growing. Many of us have become so comfortable with our church traditions that if anyone suggests making the smallest change, like the color of the altar cloth or the way we collect the offering or someone sits in "my" seat, we have a big fit and threaten to leave the church! Woah, let's settle down everybody! What is our focus here?

Church dress code

The tradition of dressing up for church services wasn't part of the early Church, since most regular people had only one or two outfits. Some reports say that as Christianity unified the poor and rich classes, people began to wear their best clothes because certain rich folks came to the same services, and nobody wanted to look bad in front of them. They weren't dressing up for God. And it wasn't until at least the mid-1800s that a variety of clothing became available to the new rising middle class anyway. Dressing up for church is a *cultural tradition*. Some people think it is not "right" for a preacher to wear jeans and sneakers. Most likely, God doesn't care that much. He's more concerned with what is happening on the inside of people. "Your beauty should *not* come from outward adornment, such as elaborate hairstyles and the wearing of gold jewelry or *fine clothes*. Rather, it should be that of your inner self, the unfading beauty of a gentle and quiet spirit, which is of great worth in God's sight" (1 Peter 3:3–4).

There are no scriptures that talk about the Church having to dress in any certain way. If anything, that scripture seems to support *not* dressing up! Many folks believe that they are honoring God, showing respect by dressing up, and that is fine. But let's not confuse what you think is fitting, what *you* require, with what God requires or even cares about. The Church is a body of believers, not a building. You are just as much "in church" on Monday when you meet a Christian friend for coffee in your shorts as you are on Sunday when you dress up to go to a service. So relax and be you. If you want to dress up, go for it. If you don't, that's okay too. Let's not judge the heart of someone by their outfit. That said, let's be reasonable. Wear something!

Church liturgy

Traditions of liturgy are *cultural*. Liturgy is the order of service, the responses, the prescribed readings, the hymns, etc. The scripture says, "And let us not neglect our meeting together, as some people do, but encourage one another, especially now that the day of his return is drawing near" (Hebrews 10: 25). We know we need to meet together, but there is no scripture stating a preferred order of service for the Church. There are no prescribed prayers other than the Lord's Prayer, in which He said to pray "in this manner," not necessarily those words every time. And He didn't say to pray it every time you get together. When people take things out of context and build a shrine around it, the thing that was once so precious becomes mere religious tradition and ineffective, according to Jesus. When I was young and learning the traditions of my church, I took a kind of pride in being able to say the Lord's Prayer really fast to get it over with. It was just words to me, a tradition I was forced to follow with no meaning behind it. Is this what we want our children to learn about God and how to talk to Him?

There are other prayers quoted in the Bible, but none of these is mandated to be recited constantly by the Church assembly. How would we like it if every time we met with our children they only read or, more likely, recited the same letter over again? Or how would we like it if every time we met with our friends they read from a script that someone else wrote for them to say? Prayer is our communication with our heavenly Father. It is our own thoughts and our own words that He loves to hear, not someone else's, eloquent as they may be.

There are no seasonal readings, and there are no prescribed hymns in the New Testament. In other words, liturgies of various churches are man-made and, therefore, subject to change. In the early church days, people met from house to house. There wasn't even a church building. Nowadays, the church building has traditionally become known as "the church," which it is not. It is only a building that houses the Church, which is the people. This problem of what is the real thing and what is not is the same problem the Jews found themselves in, promoting tradition over the real thing. Jesus admonished the Pharisees, "Well, did Isaiah prophesy of you hypocrites, as it is written: 'This people honor Me with their lips, but their heart is far from Me. And in vain they worship Me, teaching as doctrines the commandments of men.' For laying aside the commandment of God, you hold the tradition of men… All too well," Jesus said, "you reject the commandment of God, that you may keep your tradition" (Mark 7:6–9).

Sitting, standing, kneeling are all postures that people do in church services. Why and when is up to the people.

Should we stand to sing? We probably should because our posture will most likely help us to sing better. Did God say to do that? No, that is up to us. God never recommended standing for the reading of the "gospel" and sitting for the reading of the other scriptures. Scripture is *all* the Word of God. Some people kneel for the distribution of Communion, some people stand, and some people sit. These are things made up by people and not mandated by God. I guess if there was room enough, you could even lie down, although that may be counterproductive.

Church music

Church music is purely *cultural*. There are no special songs or hymns that Jesus identified to be sung in every service. The scripture says He "sang a hymn" on the way to the Garden of Gethsemane. It was not specific. One generation's cutting-edge worship songs will be the next generation's oldies. So if you are clinging to the old hymns because you think they are more spiritual than the new stuff, you are just fooling yourself. The older hymns have a historical connection, which some folks like, but other than that, music in the local church is just about that group's personal taste.

Many people love to sing certain songs in a church service because they have good memories associated with that particular song. Maybe it was sung at a funeral of a close family member, and every time they hear it sung, they think of that loved one. Maybe a certain song at one time stirred up someone's strong emotions. They felt closer to God, and so they like to try to get those feelings back. Maybe they remember singing that song as a child. Maybe it was their grandmother's favorite hymn, or their parents' favorite. This is personal taste, which is not a bad thing, but it is also not a scripture-based thing, nor is it mandated by God.

As far as the historical connection goes, the oldest hymns, even Gregorian chant, are not really connected with Jesus or the early church in any way, or at least not in the way we like to think. King David made up lots of different songs, as recorded in the Book of Psalms, but we have no idea what any of them sounded like. The oldest known hymn of the early church was discovered in 1918 and is dated AD 260. There is no evidence that Jesus or the apostles sang it. They didn't sing it in 1918, and we don't sing it now. Martin Luther wrote "A Mighty Fortress Is Our God" somewhere between 1527 and 1529. That is 1,500 years after Jesus. So is the historical connection that we long for actually with the church in the Middle Ages? The Middle Ages is when the church started becoming really corrupt, so I don't think so.

There is nothing wrong with history, but let's not confuse history with spirituality. In Luke chapter 9, when Peter, James, and John saw Jesus transfigured on the mountain, they saw Him standing and talking to Moses and Elijah, who were alive and well. Peter wanted to build a tabernacle for Moses and one for Elijah, both historical figures of the Jewish faith, and one for Jesus, as if they were all equally important. God spoke audibly from a cloud to the men, saying, "This is my beloved Son. Hear *Him*!" (Luke 9:35).

God did not elevate history over the eternally present, living Spirit of God residing in His Son Jesus. When critiquing music in the church, we should keep in mind that God lives in the present, not just in the past, and can move easily through many different styles and genres. What is important is the spirit behind the music. If the spirit is godly and lifts up Jesus, don't knock it. If the spirit is worldly or the lyrics are full of unbelief, get rid of it!

The oldest hymns sung in the churches today have probably been around for only the last few hundred years. The same goes for musical instruments. King David did not play the organ, but he did play some kind of stringed instrument, which is more like a guitar, and when he played, the evil spirit left King Saul. Are we saying old hymns are bad and that we should all be singing new songs and playing guitars? No way! It is up to the local church and the people that attend there as to what style of music they want to sing. We just want to keep an open mind when it comes to music, both ours and that other church down the street. Are you a little bit country or are you a little bit rock and roll? It is purely cultural taste.

Tradition?

What pew or chair you sit in, what the robes of the pastor look like or if he wears jeans, should he preach from a pulpit high above the people or down on the floor, near to them, whether there is an altar at the front, where the choir stands, if there is a crucifix hanging, should you be quiet or loud, should you sit still or dance, should you sing one song or five songs, should the words be on a screen, or in a bulletin or in a hymn book, should the announcements be made at the beginning or the end, should we go up to give an offering or pass a basket, etc.—all these seemingly important parts of our services are simply man-made, cultural traditions and not established by God. Again, they are not bad; they are just not mandated by God, as many people would lead you to believe. Traditions and cultural decisions are based on what seems best at the time. It's okay to change them. It will not hurt God's feelings. We don't want to teach traditions as if they are doctrine (basic foundational beliefs), like the Pharisees were doing.

While the purpose here is to rethink some of our ideas of what is absolutely necessary in the church service, we don't want to just bust in and overthrow the tables, so to speak. Most people tied to traditions are trying to do the right thing. Our position is to think right ourselves, make gentle suggestions when given the chance, and pray that the church be set free from bondage to cultural things that don't matter. Jesus is what matters. Jesus is not tied to one culture or the other. He taught the people from a boat in the water. Today we use microphones. Jesus in our churches is what matters!

That said, there are a couple of traditions that Jesus did set up. These are not man-made but God-made, and therefore, we want to keep those no matter what.

Discussion Questions

1. What are some man-made traditions you have seen in church?

2. Why do you think some churches provide written responses for people to say?

3. Do you think it is important to dress up for church? Do you think the people in a church should judge a person by the clothes he wears to church?

4. What style of music seems to draw you closer to God?

Two Important Traditions Set Up by Jesus

Water baptism

After you become a believer and you have declared, at least to yourself but hopefully to anyone who will listen, that you are a follower of Christ, a Christian, there should be some sort of feeling of relief. There is new peace with God, and with our conscience, that makes us feel safe. We are saved and we are safe. Death no longer has us in its fear grip. We know that we are going to be with Jesus when we leave this world and transition to the next, glory to God! It's okay to celebrate this momentous occasion. The angels in heaven rejoice over us! Jesus said, "I tell you there is joy in the presence of the angels over one sinner who repents" (Luke 15:10). After this momentous occasion, we find out that the next thing to do is to be baptized in water. This is an outward sign for the life change that has *already* taken place in your spirit. Baptism does not substitute for a personal faith in Jesus, but it is a celebration of it.

Jesus Himself was baptized and He encouraged it. He said in Mark 16:16, "He who believes and is baptized will be saved; but he who does not believe will be condemned." And in Matthew 28:19, He says, "Go therefore and make disciples of all nations, baptizing them in the name of the Father, and of the Son, and of the Holy Spirit…" The Church has continued this tradition. For instance, the scripture tells us that "those who gladly received his (Peter's) word were baptized; and that day about three thousand souls were added to them" (Acts 2:41). That's a lot of baptizing in one day!

The scripture explains this tradition, "Do you not know that as many of us as were baptized into Christ Jesus were baptized into His death? Therefore, we were buried with Him through baptism into death, that just as Christ was raised from the dead by the glory of the Father, even so we also should walk in newness of life" (Romans 6:3-4).

We are showing through baptism our connection with Jesus not only in His death but also in His resurrection. The idea is that, as Jesus said, he who believes and then gets baptized, which is an act of obedience and declaration of what has been done on the inside, will be saved. "He who believes and is baptized will be saved; but he who does not believe will be condemned" (Mark 16:16).

But somewhere along the way, people began to think of the act of baptism as being more important than the "he who believes" part. Maybe it was easier. They started baptizing people of all ages without requiring them to believe.

Most likely, they thought they were doing a good thing, protecting them through an act that had become synonymous with believing. If someone was dying, they would baptize them no matter what spiritual decisions had been made. It got to be so twisted and turned around that *baptism* became the qualification for becoming a Christian, and actual *faith* was not even part of the discussion. Baptizing infants became a tradition in many churches with the idea that when the child grows up, he will *become* a believer. That was wishful thinking. You can imagine what a motley crew the so-called Christian Church became! It really became more like a club with baptism as the initiation ritual. It added many people as members that were never actual believers. Without believers and without God, the Church eventually became powerless and ineffectual. When Martin Luther came along and reminded everyone that the "just shall live by faith" (Romans 1:17), he was called a heretic! What a mess! Thank God for the Word, which straightens us out.

Do you have to be baptized to go to heaven?

So how important is baptism? Well, it is very important because Jesus said to do it. But on the other hand, the thief that was crucified next to Jesus believed in Him, calling Him Lord, and that was enough for Jesus to receive him into the Kingdom (Luke 23:42–43). Jesus said to him, "This day you will be with Me in Paradise." Was it necessary for the thief to be baptized first? Apparently not. So this tells us that the act of baptism does not save us, *faith in Jesus saves us.*

Baptism is like getting the membership card saying you are an official member of the Church. Getting baptized doesn't make you a member, but it is like the "card" with your name on it. If you don't have the card, you are still on record as being a member, but we all want to have the card, so let's get baptized. If a believer dies and has not been baptized, will he still go to heaven? Yes, because he has *believed* in Jesus and "signed the contract" by receiving in faith the payment for his sins. The scripture says, "He who believes and is baptized will be saved; but he who does not believe will be condemned." It does not say He who is not baptized will be condemned, right? Baptism is not for God; it is for us. It is a point of contact for our faith. If the devil comes along ten years later and challenges you on whether you are a Christian or not, you can say, "Oh yes, I am! I was born again and then baptized on such and such date." You might not remember the exact date or time when your feelings changed toward God and you made that important decision for Him because sometimes it is a gradual realization, but you will probably remember your baptism day.

Most churches have a time and place for water baptisms, and many times they use a special water tank or tub there at the church, but any pool or lake or river will do. John the Baptist used a river. The idea is for you to show that you have been raised from death to life. Someone dunks you, or at least your head, under the water (that's the death part) and lifts you back out (that's the raising to life part). Some churches baptize folks by sprinkling them with water, but that sort of misses the whole point of showing the outward sign of being buried in death and raised to life, doesn't it? In Mark 7:13, Jesus said, "Thus you nullify the word of God by your tradition that you have handed down. And you do many things like that." Sprinkling water on someone to baptize them is an example of a well-meaning tradition that nullifies the Word of God concerning the identifying of ourselves with Jesus's death, burial, and resurrection. It is not the presence of water that is important; it is the action of burial and resurrection. The Greek word *baptizo,* translated "baptism" in the Bible, means "to immerse." You *baptizo* your doughnut in your coffee. I was baptized (sprinkled) as a baby, but then years later, after I had been born again, believing God for the forgiveness of my sin, I was baptized again, immersed in water so that it meant something to me. I'm not saying you have to do this, but it's what God led me to do. Let everybody follow the Spirit for himself.

Matthew 3:13 gives this account. "Then Jesus went from Galilee to the Jordan River to be baptized by John. But John tried to talk Him out of it. 'I am the one who needs to be baptized by You,' he said, 'so why are You coming to me?' But Jesus said, 'It should be done, for we must carry out all that God requires.' So John agreed to baptize Him." If Jesus was baptized and you know who He was, it must have been important, so I'm in. How about you?

Holy communion

The other tradition set up by Jesus for the Church is to take Holy Communion, or just Communion, on a regular basis. The tradition of Communion is based on the last supper that Jesus shared with His disciples before He went to the cross. The story is found in both the gospels of Matthew and Mark, and Paul records Jesus's words at the Last Supper in 1 Corinthians 11. Jesus told them to continue to do what He did as a tradition in remembrance of Him. The act of taking Communion involves the eating of a small piece of bread and drinking a sip of wine. Many people substitute things like crackers for the bread and juice for the wine. That's perfectly fine. Just like with baptism, the act of the tradition is secondary to the meaning behind it. There is an element of bread, which means something, and an element of wine, which means something. Let's see what it means.

The Lord Jesus on the same night in which He was betrayed, took bread; And when He had given thanks, He broke it and said, "Take eat; this is My body which is broken for you; do this in remembrance of Me."

In the same manner, He also took the cup after supper, saying, "This cup is the new covenant in My blood. This do, as often as you drink it, in remembrance of Me."

For as often as you eat this bread and drink this cup You proclaim the Lord's death till He comes. (1 Corinthians 11)

When you take Communion, these words of the Lord are usually recited in some form to remind us of the two important things that Jesus did for us: He came to forgive our sins, paying for them with His own blood, and He came to heal our bodies, exchanging His body for ours.

Let's take a look at the cup first. When Jesus said the wine was His blood, you can look at it two ways—either He meant it was literally His blood and He wanted you to drink it, or He meant it was symbolic of His blood, and by drinking it you symbolically become a partaker of His suffering and death. Since baptism is a *symbol* of His death and resurrection and God does not expect you to actually drown, I tend toward believing the second way about the wine and this tradition. Drinking the cup reminds us that Jesus shed His own super valuable and powerful God-blood in order to save our lives and bring us into His Kingdom. He said, "As often as you do this…" We need to do this *often*, not once or twice a year. Some believers take Communion every day. It is not important where you take Communion. Ministers take Communion elements to people in the hospital and people in their homes all the time. Actually, there is no need to have a minister bless the elements first. Jesus has already blessed them (Mark 14:22).

Now let's look at the bread. Jesus said, "The bread of God is He who comes down from heaven and gives life to the world," referring to the manna that God provided in the Old Testament. He also said, "I am the bread of life" (John 6:33, 35). The bread represents the sustenance of *life*, not only the going-to-heaven life but this life now. The bread represents the body of Jesus, who is *life* personified. Imagine what His human body was like for a moment. He was the last Adam, a perfect man. Think about that. He was like Adam before the fall. No curse, no sickness, no weakness, perfect skin, no marks, no freckles, moles, or pimples. His eyes were perfect, ears perfect, hair perfect. His muscles were strong and toned. He was so beautiful, and full of energy. Every cell, every tissue pulsated with the life of God. This was His body, and this is what He crushed and broke voluntarily for you and for me.

Why the broken bread? Why not just the wine representing His blood shed for us? Because salvation is a two-pronged blessing. We are cleansed of sin, and our bodies are healed. During Jesus's ministry, He preached the gospel and then healed everyone who came to Him to prove it was true. The word used for salvation—what Jesus accomplished for us—in the Bible is *sozo*. According to Strong's Concordance of Greek words, this word means "to save, deliver, or protect, *to heal, preserve*, save, do well, *be (make) whole*." Included in the meaning of salvation is physical healing for our bodies. Thayer's Greek Lexicon says *sozo* means "to save a suffering one (from perishing), i.e., one suffering from disease, to make well, heal, restore to health."

First Peter 2:24 tells us, "And He Himself bore our sins in His body on the cross, so that we might die to sin and live to righteousness; for by His wounds you were healed."

There is no doubt. Jesus came to heal us as well as give us His righteousness. He healed our spirits by transforming our sin nature back to God's nature, and He healed our souls (mentally and emotionally), and He healed our physical bodies as well. It was a thorough job and well done, although we don't always see the results on the outside immediately. More on that later.

When you take Communion, the bread is broken in two. Sometimes a bigger loaf is broken off into pieces and passed around. If you have a cracker, you break it. The concept is that *Jesus's body was broken so that ours could be healed!* Ours could be put back together! Just as Jesus takes your ugly sins by shedding His perfect blood and gives you His beautiful holiness, new blood, new God DNA, He also takes your diseased and imperfect body and gives you His perfect body, which was broken for you. It is an exchange. When you take Communion, you can receive healing for every part of your body. But it's not automatic. It is received by faith—faith in what the Word says, not in what you see. Many miracles of healing have happened during the taking of Communion. So take it often. You don't need a pastor or someone else to bless the elements first. That is a man-made tradition. You just need the Word of God. Say what Jesus said and do what Jesus did. If you are sick, take Communion like you would take medicine, two or three times a day. Jesus created this tradition as a way for you and me to be healed. Let's use it!

Discussion Questions

1. Have you been baptized? How was it done?

2. Have you ever taken Communion at home?

3. How would you know what to say if you took Communion at home?

LESSON 8

BAPTISM IN THE HOLY SPIRIT (PART 1)

Now that you are born again and baptized in water, what comes next? Something wonderful! Something powerful! A precious gift from God, the dove, the baptism in fire!

When you become a believer, the Holy Spirit, the presence of God, comes to live with you, and in you, and you are saved forever. You become a citizen of the Kingdom of Heaven, the Kingdom of Light. Then get ready for this... the Lord Jesus Christ *baptizes* you in His Holy Spirit, immersing you in His love and equipping you with the power and boldness to become witnesses and to minister to people in His name. It's absolutely amazing! We are turbo-charged! I tend to believe that one of the reasons for God giving us the act of water baptism is to show us what is happening when we are baptized in the Holy Spirit, the gift promised to us and our children (Acts 2:38–39). Definitely cool! When you become a believer, you get Jesus. When you are baptized in the Holy Spirit, you get more of Jesus, His power for ministry.

Jesus talked a lot about the Holy Spirit. He said, "It is to your advantage that I go away; for if I do not go away, the Helper will not come to you; but if I depart, I will send Him to you... When He, the Spirit of truth has come, He will guide you into all truth...He will glorify Me" (John 16:13–14).

Some people do not believe that there is a second experience for Christians. They believe that the Holy Spirit comes once, and that's all there is to it. However, the scriptures do not support that view.

In John 20:20–22, Jesus appears to His disciples after the resurrection, showing them the nail prints in His hands and sword mark in His side. "So Jesus said to them again, 'Peace to you! As the Father has sent Me, I also send you.' And when He had said this, He breathed on them, and said to them, 'Receive the Holy Spirit.'" This was the beginning of the release of the Holy Spirit to the Church, lovingly given to us by Jesus personally. This was when the disciples were *born again*. Up until the time of the resurrection, being born again was not possible because the price of sin had not yet been paid and the Holy Spirit would not have been able to live in anybody.

But if that's all there is to it, as some people believe, then why the separate experience on the Day of Pentecost?

The Book of Acts tells us that before Jesus ascended to heaven (after He had breathed on them to receive the Holy Spirit), He commanded His disciples not to leave Jerusalem but to wait for the Promise of the Father, which He had told them about before. "For John truly baptized with water, but you shall be baptized with the Holy Spirit not many days from now… You shall receive power when the Holy Spirit has come upon you; and you shall be witnesses to Me in Jerusalem, and in all Judea and Samaria, and to the end of the earth" (Acts 1:4–5, 8). His disciples were already believers. They were already born again because Jesus had breathed on them to receive the Holy Spirit inside them. They had been baptized by John in water. Jesus was not talking about the baptism into the kingdom; He was talking about something else, a separate experience where the Holy Spirit would come *upon* them and would empower them to be witnesses, to show what God could do in their midst.

Peter said, "And we declare to you glad tidings—that promise which was made to the fathers, God has fulfilled this for us their children, in that He has raised up Jesus" (Acts 13:32–33). While the resurrection of Jesus is definitely a fulfillment of God's prophecy and a promise, Jesus mentions another promise, or perhaps a deeper level of the promise, calling it the promise of the Father (Acts 1:4). After Jesus had been raised from the dead, He told His disciples to wait for the promise of the Father. This promise was the power of the Holy Spirit that would rest on all believers, just as the dove rested on Jesus when He was baptized.

In the past, the Holy Spirit would come upon a select person for a short time to accomplish a certain task, such as Samson becoming super strong to defeat the Philistines or Elijah prophesying to the king or Elisha raising the dead son of the Shunammite woman. God's plan was to eventually give all His children the power of the Holy Spirit, but He couldn't empower them until they had been washed in the blood of Jesus and been regenerated into pure spiritual vessels. He said, "Nor do they put new wine into old wineskins, or else the wineskins burst, the wine is spilled, and the wineskins are ruined. But they put new wine into new wineskins, and both are preserved" (Matthew 9:17). Only after the people's spirits had been made new, only then could the Holy Spirit take up residence in a big way in each of our beings. When Jesus was born as a baby, He was already the Son of God, and He never sinned like Adam, so He didn't need to be "born again." But He didn't do any miracles until the Holy Spirit, in the form of a dove, came and rested upon Him. It wasn't until He was baptized in the Holy Spirit on the day of His water baptism by John, as evidenced by the dove from heaven coming down and landing on Him, that Jesus began His ministry. So it is with us.

John the Baptist had predicted, "I indeed baptize you with water, but One mightier than I is coming, whose sandal strap I am not worthy to loose. He will baptize you with the Holy Spirit and fire" (Luke 3:16). Other believers, pastors, friends can baptize you in water. Jesus Himself now is the baptizer in the Holy Spirit.

And just like Jesus and the Father had promised, when the Day of Pentecost had come, the disciples were all gathered together in an upper room. (Pentecost was a feast day of the Jews that celebrated the giving of the Ten Commandments to Moses on Mount Sinai. Jews from all different nations made a pilgrimage to Jerusalem at that time.) "Suddenly, there came a sound from heaven, as of a rushing mighty wind, and it filled the whole house where they were sitting. Then there appeared to them divided tongues, as of fire, and one sat upon each of them (like the dove came and sat on Jesus). And they were all filled with the Holy Spirit and began to speak with other tongues, as the Spirit gave them utterance" (Acts 2:1–4). It caused a big commotion because people from all different regions had come to Jerusalem for the feast, and they each heard the disciples speaking in their own varied native languages instead of Hebrew or Aramaic. Suddenly, after the Holy Spirit came and sat on him, Peter—a commercial fisherman, a regular guy—became a super bold preacher! He had been a believer before, but now he was turbo charged! He preached so well that three thousand people became believers that day. This is what the baptism in the Holy Spirit is for. It gives you boldness (*fire*) to be a witness, gives you a heavenly language, and brings supernatural ability for certain situations, depending on how God wants to do things. The end result is that people come to know Jesus. *The Holy Spirit always glorifies Jesus.*

Peter said on that Day of Pentecost when all the people wondered what was happening, "Repent, and let every one of you be baptized in the name of Jesus Christ for the remission of sins; and you shall receive the gift of the Holy Spirit. For the promise is to you and to your children, and to all who are afar off, as many as the Lord our God will call" (Acts 2:38–39).

This baptism in the fire of the Holy Spirit (or Holy Ghost in some translations) is available to every believer, but it is not automatic. Just like everything else with God, it is activated *by faith*. Remember, Jesus had told the disciples it was coming and to wait for it. They had heard about it. Many Christians don't know about it because, unfortunately, it isn't preached as often as it used to be. And you can't have faith for something that you don't know exists. Here is what happened to a group of new Christians in Ephesus that were in the same boat.

> And it happened, while Apollos was at Corinth, that Paul, having passed through the upper regions, came to Ephesus. And finding some disciples he said to them, "Did you receive the Holy Spirit when you believed?" So they said to him, "We have not so much as heard whether there is a Holy Spirit." And he said to them, "Into what then were you baptized?" "Into John's baptism." Then Paul said, "John indeed baptized with a baptism of repentance, saying to

the people that they should believe on Him who would come after him, that is, on Christ Jesus." When they heard this, they were baptized (in water) in the name of the Lord Jesus. And when Paul had laid his hands on them, the Holy Spirit came upon them, and they spoke with tongues and prophesied. Now the men were about twelve in all. (Acts 19:1–7).

These disciples (believers) had not *heard* about baptism in the name of Jesus. So when they *heard*, they were baptized in His name (even though they had already been baptized into something else). Neither had they *heard* about the baptism in the Holy Spirit. They had not been with the other disciples in the upper room on the Day of Pentecost. But as soon as Paul told them and laid hands on them, they also received the baptism of the Holy Spirit, as evidenced by their speaking in tongues and prophesying. This gift of the Holy Spirit is for *every believer*, not just special ones.

In another instance, Philip had gone down to Samaria and preached the gospel, doing miracles.

When they believed Philip as he preached the things concerning the Kingdom of God and the name of Jesus Christ, both men and women were baptized… Now when the apostles that were at Jerusalem heard that Samaria had received the word of God, they sent Peter and John to them, who, when they had come down, prayed for them that they might receive the Holy Spirit. For as yet He had fallen upon none of them. They had only been baptized in the name of the Lord Jesus. Then they laid hands on them, and

they received the Holy Spirit. And when Simon
saw that through the laying on of the apostles'
hands the Holy Spirit was given, he offered them
money... (Acts 8:12–18)

In Acts 10:44–47, Peter was sent to teach Cornelius, a
Gentile, and all his friends and relatives who had come to
hear about Jesus. As they were *hearing* the words, the gift
of the Holy Spirit was also poured out on them. Peter and
the Jewish believers that had come with him knew what was
happening because they *heard* them speak with tongues and
magnify God. They hadn't even been water-baptized yet! The
Holy Spirit is not so much into rituals and religious things
as we have been led to believe. He is all about life! He can't
wait to bless us!

You may have been a Christian for a while and never
heard about the baptism in the Holy Spirit because they
don't teach about it in the church that you attend, or your
parents didn't know about it. That's okay. Those Ephesians
didn't know about it until Paul came and told them. Or
you might have *heard* that it is not for today. Or maybe
you *heard* that the baptism in the Holy Spirit is the same
as becoming a Christian. The Bible says that "faith comes
by hearing and hearing by the Word of God." So your faith
for something depends on what you have *heard about it*,
right? And some people assume that because *they* have not
experienced this supernatural power of God in their lives, it
must not be available for anyone else. But we receive things
on an individual basis from God *by faith*. The Holy Spirit
included those experiences in the Book of Acts so that we
would know:

- It is possible to miss something due to not having heard about it. That's why it becomes important where you go to church and who you are listening to.

- Man's tradition is not always the same as God's plan. Some churches actually have a tradition *not* to believe in the baptism of the Holy Spirit. Peter broke tradition by teaching Gentiles about Jesus. It's okay to break tradition to follow God's plan.

- It is possible for people to have different experiences. Some people are baptized in water first, some are baptized in the Holy Spirit first, but all are believers first.

- If you desire to get close to God, He will reveal more of Himself to you. Eventually, Paul or Peter or somebody will come along and tell you what you need to know, or you might learn it in a Bible study, or God might just tell you. He likes variety.

Is it possible to believe one spiritual concept and not another? Sure it is! We know it is possible to believe in a historical Jesus without believing He paid for your sins. It is possible to believe Jesus paid for your sins but that He didn't heal your body. It is possible to believe He healed you of one thing but not of another. It is possible to believe that Jesus saved you and healed you but that He is not coming back, etc. So yes, it is possible for a Christian to believe in all those things about Jesus without believing he can receive the gift of the baptism in the Holy Spirit. But that's not you, right? Now that you've heard, you can receive. Go for it! Believe

God for the baptism in the Holy Spirit. Pray that Jesus will baptize you, and He will.

Sometimes, like with the Ephesians and Paul and the Samaritans, someone that has already been baptized in the Holy Spirit can lay hands on another believer, and that person will receive what the other has experienced. And sometimes, like with Peter and the centurion's family, it doesn't require another to lay hands on you. My advice, whatever it takes, get it done. You want this. Jesus said you need this, so don't brush it aside like it isn't important. Remember what He told His disciples. Basically, "Wait in Jerusalem until the Holy Spirit comes." Jesus felt it was crucial.

You: So what you are saying is that there are two separate events where Jesus gives the Holy Spirit?

Me: Yes, that is what I am saying. The first one is when you become a believer and are born again. The Holy Spirit comes to live *inside* you. The second is when you are *baptized* in the Holy Spirit. This is when He comes *upon* you for boldness and power to witness.

Let's look at this another way.

In John 4:13–14, Jesus refers to salvation as a well of water. He was sitting near the well in Samaria when a woman came to draw water. Jesus told her, "Whoever drinks of this water will thirst again, but whoever drinks of the water that I shall give him will never thirst, But the water that I shall give him will become in him a fountain of water springing up into everlasting life." The Greek word here means fountain, spring, or well, a source of water. When the Holy Spirit comes to live inside us, when we are born again, we have personal access to His wisdom, His peace, His love, His character, His comfort, His healing touch, the life of God, the source, a well of living water. That is pretty powerful by itself. The born-again believer has power over sin and the power to walk in newness of life. "Therefore we are buried with him by baptism into death: that like as Christ was raised up from the dead by the glory of the Father, even so we also should walk in newness of life" (Romans 6:4).

But then, in John 7:37–39, Jesus is referring to the water in another way. "He who believes in Me, as the Scripture has said, out of his heart will flow rivers of living water.' But this He spoke concerning the Spirit, whom those believing in Him would receive, for the Holy Spirit was not yet given, because Jesus was not yet glorified." The Greek word for rivers here means running water, river, stream, flood, flowing out with a current. When we are baptized in the Holy Spirit, He flows out of us to affect others. Ministry should come from this flow. There is a current, so jump in and you can flow with God. You are not on your own.

Do you see the difference? There's *inside* you and then there's *upon* you. Well and rivers.

God is doing all kinds of supernatural things all the time. Some of us don't see them because we don't expect to see them. Faith is having the expectation that God will do something amazing. If you are not seeing the supernatural workings of the Holy Spirit in your life or some area of your life, perhaps you are not expecting to see them. Jesus said in Mark 16, "And these signs shall follow them that believe: In My name they shall cast out demons; they will speak with new tongues; they will take up serpents; and if they drink anything deadly, it will by no means hurt them; they will lay hands on the sick and they will recover." If you don't expect it to happen, it won't. You always get what you believe.

Discussion Questions

1. What are the two baptisms we are told we need to have?

2. Have you been baptized in water? When?

3. Have you, or do you know anyone who has been baptized in the Holy Spirit?

Okay, you are saying to yourself, *I'm in! I want everything the Lord has for me. But whoa, Nellie! Back it up, back it up… what in the world is this tongues thing all about and what is prophesying? Clearly this needs to be explained.*

More of a Good Thing

The Holy Spirit is the ultimate gift of the presence of God Himself living in you, which happens when you are born again. There is nothing of greater value or importance than that the Spirit of the great God Jehovah, Creator of the universe, would come to live inside us, His tiny creations! I may seem to be redundant, but so many people are confused by this that it bears repeating. With the baptism of the Holy Spirit, you just get *more* of His power, a bigger dose, so to speak, specifically for ministering to others. Remember, in Acts 1:8, Jesus told His disciples, "But you shall receive power when the Holy Spirit has come upon you; and you shall be witnesses to Me in Jerusalem, and in all Judea, and Samaria, and to the end of the earth." The word *power* is the Greek word *dunamis*, which means force, miraculous power, and ability. It is where our word *dynamite* comes from. *He, the person of the Holy Spirit, is what is most important.* When He comes upon a believer, when you are baptized in the Holy

Spirit, He brings all of His supernatural abilities with Him. They are supernatural.

God's plan is redemptive. He is in the construction and restoration business. Think of the Holy Spirit like a repairman opening the back of his utility truck filled with specialized tools, also referred to as gifts. We are His apprentices working alongside Him, and we use these power tools as they are needed—for fixing, repairing, restoring all the things God likes to do.

The nine gifts (tools) of the Spirit mentioned in 1 Corinthians 12 are these:

- *Gift of knowledge*—supernaturally knowing a fact or facts about something or someone

- *Gift of wisdom*—supernaturally knowing what to do

- *Discerning of spirits*—supernaturally seeing into the spirit realm, identifying angels or demons

- *Gifts of healing*—supernatural miraculous healing, not normal or medical healing

- *Gift of faith*—supernatural faith for some situation, not regular faith

- *Gift of working of miracles*—supernatural manifestations of God's power in a natural situation, like multiplying food or calming a storm

- *Gift of prophecy*—supernatural utterance of exhortation or direction

- *Gift of diversity of tongues*—supernatural utterance of a known language but not known to the speaker

- *Interpretation of tongues*—supernatural interpretation of the gift of tongues

These gifts are operated by the Church *as the Holy Spirit wills*, or as He feels like it. Included in the category of diversity of tongues is a special heavenly language that is operated *as the believer wills*. It is also referred to as tongues, so it can be confusing if you don't know the difference.

A Gift of Tongues for You

"These signs shall follow those that believe: In my name they shall cast out demons; they will speak with new tongues…" (Mark 16:17). When we are baptized in the fire of the Holy Spirit, the first thing that changes is that we have a new boldness to step out and share the good news. This is the main difference, and every gift or tool following is dependent on that boldness for its administration. One of these tools is the ability to speak a new heavenly language known only to God. When you speak in this language, you are praying a *perfect prayer*. You can't mess it up with unbelief because you don't know what you are saying, and the devil can't understand it either, so he stays clueless to the plan of God. Good thinking, Holy Spirit!

Words and speech are important to God. Remember, His own Word is called His Son. He has a relationship with His Word. Animals do not have the ability or intelligence, amazing as they are, to speak words. Humans are a higher life-form than animals, even though some people would have us believe we are evolved from them. We are created in God's own image. Words are what God uses to create everything, not thoughts. In Genesis, the scripture says "And God said, let there be light…" Go back and read it for yourself. He spoke everything into existence; He didn't just think it. In the old cowboy movies, the heroes would say, "My word is my bond." That meant a man's word was as good as his own self, a binding contract. It meant he would surely do what he promised. Back even just a few years ago, it was considered bad form to deceive someone or to break a promise. Not so much anymore, unfortunately. But God hasn't changed with the culture like we have. He remains steadfast and true through thick and thin. His Word is His bond. He cannot lie. His Word is the same as Him. We can learn a lot by observing what God does.

Your words, God's words, are important and binding. The devil came along, like he does, and tricked Adam and Eve by twisting and manipulating God's words. Habitual sin over time further corrupted our speech and language. But now, God, who restores all things, is restoring holiness to our speech by giving us this new language that cannot be corrupted, even by our own thoughts. In Genesis chapter 11, we read the story of the Tower of Babel, when God confused the only known language at that time, supernaturally turning it into many different ones. Because they couldn't understand each other, they eventually separated and never finished the tower. Funny how the word *babble* means speaking words that are not understandable. The people spoke, but different words came out. Well, now He has changed things again. He gave all the believers one language, *unifying them*, and it sounds to the world like babbling. Doesn't God have a sense of humor!

Have you ever intended to say something and then a different word came out by mistake, or have you ever said something and then wondered where that came from? Just in the same way, when we speak in our heavenly language, it is our own mouth and tongue speaking, but the words are coming from our spirits, not our minds, so we don't make the mental connection to what it means. God doesn't make you talk differently or make you open your mouth. You step out boldly and speak whatever comes to your mouth to say. You are releasing your spirit to pray. Your spirit is born again and wants to pray according to the mind of Christ, to which we are now connected. "For who hath known the mind (thoughts) of the Lord, that he may instruct him? But we have the mind of Christ" (1 Corinthians 2:16).

When we pray in our new language or "pray in the spirit," we can start and stop whenever we want to. We are totally in control. Praying in the spirit is *our* spirit that is praying. It is our own spirit that is communicating with God's Spirit. "For if I pray in an [unknown] tongue, my spirit [by the Holy Spirit within me] prays, but my mind is unproductive..." (1 Corinthians 14:14 AMP). In other words, our minds (physical brains) don't understand what we are saying, but our spirits sure do!

When you pray in the spirit or pray in tongues, your spirit will fill your mouth with the words, but your mouth will have to say them. Your will, your decision. I know, it feels weird at first, but you'll get used to it. The thing is, you won't understand what you are saying. Your mind will object at first, calling it nonsense, but remember, the whole point is that your mind is *not* involved. You are praying for impossible things. First Corinthians 14:2 calls them mysteries. "For he who speaks in a tongue does not speak to men but to God, for no one understands him, however in the spirit he speaks mysteries." If your mind was involved, you would start analyzing what was being said, and your doubt and unbelief would kick in, and that would mess up the whole thing. God doesn't want that. *You* don't want that.

Some people are able to release beautiful, flowing sentences immediately after they are baptized in the Holy Spirit, but many people start with a syllable or one word, then two, then three, then a whole phrase. It's like priming a pump. The more you speak, the easier it becomes. Listening to a room full of believers all praying in tongues or singing in the spirit is so beautiful! It all sounds like the same language, which it is. God must get a kick out of watching us learn, like we enjoy our children's first words.

Praying in Tongues Makes You Stronger

This language is used for praying when we don't know what or how to pray, when we or someone we know is in a dangerous situation and the situation is urgent, or when we are praising God and thanking Him for stuff or just everyday praying. Jude 1:20 tells us that speaking in our heavenly language edifies us. The Bible definition of *edify* means to build up, construct, confirm, to make stronger, embolden. "But you, beloved, building yourselves up on your most holy faith, praying in the Holy Spirit…" Paul agreed. "He who speaks in a tongue edifies himself…I thank my God I speak with tongues more than you all" (1 Corinthians 14:4, 18). So if you are intending to go to help or minister to someone, pray in the Spirit first to build yourself up.

The prophet Isaiah in the Old Testament prophesied (told before it happened) about this heavenly language. "For with stammering lips and another tongue He will speak to this people, to whom He said, 'This is the rest with which you may cause the weary to rest,' and this is the refreshing" (Isaiah 28:11–12). In the Old Testament, other tongues referred to other nations, especially nations that fought against the Jews and many times conquered them. But this prophecy foretold the coming of the Church, a new group of people speaking in a heavenly language, those tongues speaking *for* them, not against them. Praying in the spirit is refreshing to us, like the scripture says. It is restful because it builds us up, like a dose of vitamins. It is like a little visit to heaven, one that revitalizes us. This type of speaking in tongues is speaking in a heavenly language and is available for every believer who is baptized in the Holy Spirit. There is another type of speaking in tongues, and that is a gift for the assembly of the Church. That one needs an interpreter. We will come to that.

Praying in Tongues Is Not Emotional

Many people have been taught that praying in the spirit means they are praying inwardly, silently, in their hearts or what they think of as their spirits. Their silent feelings and yearnings toward God may be intense. Paul talks about groanings in the spirit (Romans 8:26). This is certainly a type of intercessory prayer and is valuable for certain situations, but it is not the same thing as "praying in the spirit" because Paul says we should feel refreshed as we pray in the spirit and that we are edified. Intercessory prayer is led by the Holy Spirit, and one of its characteristics is a heaviness or heavy burden that is felt by the believer to pray for someone or some situation. In contrast, when you pray in the spirit, you feel stronger, more vitalized. It is not the same as intercessory prayer or an emotional connection with God, although you can pray in the spirit when you are interceding, and you should feel a connection with God whenever or however you pray. It is not the same as what some call "ecstatic prayer." Praying in the spirit is not necessarily emotional at all. It is not like an out-of-body experience. Your spirit is the real you and lives in your body. You don't need to go anywhere.

Praying in the spirit is not praying silently to yourself; it is praying out loud, speaking to God, using your voice. It is not an "in your heart" kind of thing. Words and speech, saying something, is important to God. We are created in His image, and He speaks.

> For if I pray in a tongue, my spirit prays, but my understanding is unfruitful. What is the conclusion then? I will pray with the spirit, and I will also pray with the understanding. I will sing with the spirit, and I will also sing with the understanding. Otherwise, if you bless with the spirit, how will he who occupies the place of the uninformed say "Amen" at your giving of thanks, since he does not understand what you say? For you indeed give thanks well, but the other is not edified. (1 Corinthians 14: 14–17)

In this passage, discussing praying in the spirit, Paul is referring to something that someone can hear, not a silent prayer in the heart. If you interpret this scripture to mean praying in the spirit is silently praying in your heart, then you would also have to interpret singing in the spirit as being silent, from the heart. And if you "bless with the spirit," along those same lines, Paul's words would contradict, as he defines it as "what you say," not what you think in your heart.

Paul said, "What is the conclusion then? I will pray with the spirit, and I will also pray with the understanding. I will sing with the spirit, and I will also sing with the understanding... I thank my God I speak with tongues more than you all..." (1 Corinthians 14:15, 18). He is showing us that it's not that we never pray in our own language, we still do that, but we have added to our arsenal a way to pray that the devil can't understand and that we can't mess up. And Paul thanked God that he spoke with tongues more than anyone. That's because he wanted to. It's up to you. Paul said, "I wish you all spoke with tongues," so it is a good thing. Let's do it!

Paul talks about speaking in tongues a lot, especially in 1 Corinthians 14. This particular letter that Paul wrote was a response to a letter that the Corinthians had written to him, asking questions about things he had taught them earlier. We don't have a copy of the letter with the questions, but we have Paul's answers with references to questions. One of the things Paul wanted to clear up was the idea that speaking in tongues was a sign of spirituality, a sign to believers that they were really cool. In the Corinthian church, it was like the people were showing off, praying in the spirit, prophesying, talking over each other and not listening.

Paul said that if an unbeliever were to walk in, he would think everyone was crazy! Paul was saying that this isn't what the gifts are for. They are for helping and building up the Church.

Gift of Tongues for the Assembly

Praying in the spirit, a heavenly language, speaking to God, is for the believer. There are times in an assembly that you can use it, like during certain times of prayer or worship, when the other people are not listening to you in particular and everyone is communicating with God individually. But there is another type of speaking in tongues, a supernatural gift for the Church assembly, and this is what people saw and heard on the Day of Pentecost. This is supernaturally speaking a *known* language that you haven't learned, one that is an earthly language, like French or Chinese, not a heavenly language. (This is how all those travelers in Jerusalem each heard their own languages being spoken in Acts 2.) You still have to open your mouth yourself. Then God fills it with words that someone who knows that language could understand. The gift of *interpretation of tongues* goes along with this kind of gift of tongues, and someone else, or even the same person, will interpret to the rest of the congregation what was said. It is all supernatural. The interpreter doesn't know the language by his own natural ability. As an example, suppose you were ministering the gift of tongues in a Sunday service. You were speaking some kind of language, but you are unfamiliar with it. Maybe it was Swahili. Then I receive a prompting by the Holy Spirit to interpret what you said. By faith, after you are done, I begin to speak out words from the Holy Spirit. It's by faith because I don't know how to speak Swahili either! The point of this gift is to show a supernatural sign to unbelievers (1 Corinthians 14:22, Acts 2).

I was in a church service one time, and someone spoke out a message in another language. It was "Greek to me," as they say. I didn't understand a word of it. The congregation waited, but no one offered an interpretation, so some of the people thought that the one who had spoken out in tongues had made a mistake. However, after the service, a woman came forward and said she had heard the words in her own language of Croatian. She said the language had been spoken perfectly, and it was praising God. The person that spoke them had never learned the Croatian language.

It was a supernatural manifestation of the presence of God. The interpretation was most likely given to someone else in the congregation, but they were not sure and were hesitant to speak it out. Do you see how God will give us the words, but it is up to us whether we use our mouths, our tongues to say them?

We are all learning. People will make mistakes, and that's okay. We would rather have an occasional mistake than never have a manifestation of the presence of God in our church. I have lots of good memories of my children's first words. My daughter used to say "perkle" for purple, and my son called a cupcake a "pupcake." Did I get upset and not allow them to talk anymore? No, ability comes with experience. Where else could someone go to exercise the gift of tongues and interpretation? You can't practice it at home with no congregation, so the experiences will have to come in the church. I chuckle every time I think of those early mistakes my children made. They are heartwarming. God feels the same way about us. Let's allow people some learning curve.

There have been times when missionaries have super-naturally been given the gift of tongues to speak to the natives they are ministering to. This use of tongues, the knowledge of what to say, happens as *God* wills. The other use of tongues happens as *we* will.

As the Spirit Wills

When you are in a church assembly, the gift of tongues can be manifested to the congregation as the Spirit wills.

"As the Spirit wills" means that if He wants to, the Lord will impress on a person in some way, maybe a thought or a special feeling of some sort, that He wishes to speak to the congregation. That person, at an appropriate time, understanding the prompting to be God and not himself, begins to speak out whatever the next words are that come into his head. The words can continue to flow out without the person's thoughts being further engaged. When the Holy Spirit is finished, there are no more words left to say, and the person stops speaking. The Holy Spirit doesn't force someone to speak anything. He works in partnership with us. If He urges someone to speak, that person will always have a choice to follow the prompting or not. If the person does not choose to speak, the Holy Spirit will then find someone else to move through. If there is no one who is willing or understands what God wants to do, He will not speak. In many churches, God remains silent, but hopefully, we are all learning. We need to hear what our Father wants to say!

Discussion Questions

1. Do you remember any words you said incorrectly as a child?

2. In your own words, what is the difference between "as the Spirit wills" and "as the believer wills"?

LESSON 9

BAPTISM IN THE HOLY SPIRIT (PART 2)

To review, the gift of tongues is a supernatural gift for the Church assembly and is usually accompanied by the gift of interpretation, which obviously is the translation of whatever the speaker of the language was saying. A believer operating in the gift of tongues may speak out in the service at an appropriate time and then either translate it himself or someone else will speak out, operating in the gift of the interpretation of tongues, and translate the message. These two gifts work together and are part of the whole package, that "repair truck of tools" that the Holy Spirit has given to the Church. The gift of interpretation of tongues, like the gift of tongues, is for someone who does not normally know the language being spoken. This is not a heavenly language. It is a language known in the world, like Norwegian or Hindi or Filipino, just not by the person speaking it in the assembly. It requires boldness to operate in these gifts. They are spoken words, not thoughts. The message spoken is from the Holy Spirit and will exhibit His personality. It will glorify Jesus, never the speaker. The message will be words of instruction or exhortation (encouragement), something to help us. It is usually short and sweet but could be longer. It's up to Him.

In the assembly, as you listen to someone speaking words from God, you are drawn closer to Him. He is there, talking to you! How amazing! It may be a confirmation of something God has said to you individually, or it may not apply to you at all but rather to someone standing next to you. The overall purpose of this supernatural utterance is to show that God is there. It is a sign to point to the presence of God in the service. Unbelievers become believers when witnessing such an event, and of course, it's amazing for us believers too! We never get tired of the supernatural manifestation of Jesus!

The manifestation of the gift of tongues in the assembly is *God speaking to the Church*. Praying in the spirit is different. It is *you speaking to God*. Sometimes, people mistake the one type of speaking in tongues for the other or think they are the same thing. They wonder why someone who is praying in the spirit doesn't have an interpreter. But praying in a heavenly language doesn't need an interpreter because you are speaking to God, and He doesn't need one. And if you would like to know what you have prayed for in the spirit, Paul told us in 1 Corinthians 14:13 to ask God for the interpretation. Although both types of utterance can be referred to as speaking in tongues, it is probably helpful to call the heavenly language "praying in the spirit" in order to avoid confusion.

Evidence

One other thing that I want to mention about speaking in tongues is that in the Bible, whenever the event of the baptism of the Holy Spirit was mentioned, the others around could tell that those people had been baptized in the Spirit and that something supernatural was happening because of evidence. That evidence was that the newly baptized believers were speaking in tongues and glorifying God. So in some groups of believers, when they are praying for a person to be baptized in the Holy Spirit, they get so excited and want to see the evidence that they end up trying to force the person to speak instead of letting God, in His gentle way, show that person how to receive. Some people have said that they've had a bad experience with other believers trying to force them to speak in tongues, and that made them think the whole baptism in the Spirit event was not from God because of all the pressure and focus on the tongues part. I don't blame them! God will never force His kids to do anything. He's a gentleman and He is kind. Some people who have received the baptism in the Holy Spirit at a church meeting begin to receive the tongues part as they are on their way home. Some people receive later on that night. Everyone that asks receives eventually. Ministry is not bullying, so be careful. Jesus is the baptizer, not people, even well-meaning Christian people. Tongues are a blessing to the believer, a sign of the baptism of the Holy Spirit, not of your level of spirituality.

Is it possible to be saved without the baptism in the Holy Spirit? Of course, absolutely, no question about it! You receive the Holy Spirit as soon as you are born again. Baptism in the Holy Spirit is just receiving power for ministry, the same power that Jesus had when He ministered to people. Is it possible to receive the baptism in the Holy Spirit without speaking in tongues? Ah, this is the more controversial issue.

Five Examples

Scripture gives five references in the Book of Acts to people being baptized in the Holy Spirit.

- Acts 2:4
- Acts 8:17–18
- Acts 9:17

- Acts 10: 44–46

- Acts 19:6

Three references show specifically that speaking in tongues was the evidence that the witnesses of the event heard. In addition, there are two references in which it was inferred that the people spoke in tongues. One was Acts 8:14–18, where a man, Simon, "saw that through the laying on of hands the Holy Spirit was given." What evidence did he see? Was it like on the Day of Pentecost? Many people believe Simon saw and heard those folks speaking in tongues. And in Acts 9:17, the other reference, Saul, who later became Paul, was "filled with the Holy Spirit." We know he spoke in tongues because later on, he told us he did. This makes it pretty much unanimous that speaking in tongues is evidence of being baptized in the Holy Spirit. In 1 Corinthians 14:5, Paul says, "I wish you all spoke with tongues." Some people interpret this to mean that not all believers baptized in the Holy Spirit could "pray in the spirit." But Paul was not saying, "I wish you all *could* speak in tongues." He was saying, "I wish you all *did*." Big difference. The praying in the spirit gift of tongues is subject to the will of the believer. The believer speaks if he wants to, and Paul was saying he should make it a habit. God is not preventing anyone from praying in the spirit, and He doesn't make anyone do it against their will. It is a fulfillment of the promise to the believer and evidence that he has been baptized in the Holy Spirit.

But could you be baptized in the Spirit, showing other signs, like new boldness to witness, prophecy, or other gifts without the tongues part? That seems possible, but with five scriptural examples connecting the baptism with tongues, you can see why so many folks tend to stick to the theory that the *best* evidence of the baptism is the ability to pray in the spirit. Tongues are not the greatest of the gifts, but they tend to be the most common. I would say that if someone thinks they have been baptized in the Holy Spirit and they are demonstrating other signs but have not yet spoken in tongues, they have probably just not released the ability they already have. It takes a bit of faith. My advice would be to have someone they trust to lay hands on them to help them release their faith, and their heavenly language will most likely begin to flow. Tongues or praying in the spirit, Paul said, is available for every believer, so Jesus must feel that they are important. We should too.

In 1 Corinthians 12:28–30, Paul talks about people that God has appointed in the Church. "And God has appointed these in the church; first apostles, second prophets, third teachers, after that miracles, then gifts of healings, helps, administrations, varieties of tongues. Are all apostles? Are all prophets? Are all teachers? Are all workers of miracles? Do all have gifts of healings? Do all speak with tongues? Do all interpret?" The answer to all of his questions is no. Not everyone is an apostle. Not everyone is a prophet, etc. What Paul is speaking about here is the operation of these gifts in the Church organization, the *public* assembly, not in *private* life. The church congregation needs administration, help, and all these things. Some people take the verse *"Do all speak with tongues?"* out of context and use it to confirm that tongues or praying in the spirit is not for them individually. But Paul was talking here about speaking in the *assembly*. He is describing "varieties of tongues," the kind that requires interpretation. Later in 1 Corinthians 14:18–19, he says, "I thank my God I speak with tongues more than you all; yet in the church I would rather speak five words with my understanding, that I may teach others also, than ten thousand words in a tongue."

That just makes sense. Your heavenly language is not a public gift. It is a private communication between you and God.

Boldness to Witness

I have been with many believers who have not yet received the baptism in the Holy Spirit. How do I know they haven't received it? Because there is no evidence of it. They do not have new boldness; they are timid. They are not dramatically hungry for the Word, they do not have a strong desire to witness or minister to people, they do not prophesy or acknowledge miracles happening around them every day, and they do not sense the spiritual realm. (Oh, by the way, they don't speak in tongues either.) In fact, there is *no fire* in their walk with Jesus. Not that everyone has to experience all of those things, but one or two of them should pop up occasionally. Jesus said, "You shall receive power when the Holy Spirit has come upon you, and you shall be witnesses to me in Jerusalem, and in all Judea, and Samaria, and to the end of the earth" (Acts 1:8). Christians with no power are generally ineffective and not that excited or "fired up" about spiritual things. It is not necessarily their fault. Probably no one at their church ever talks about the baptism in the Holy Spirit, or if they do, it's in a negative way. Remember, Romans 10:17 says, "Faith comes by hearing, and hearing by the word of God." That's why it is so important where you go to church. If you don't hear about it, you will never have faith for it.

The evidence of *salvation* should be seen on the outside by the changes in a person's character and lifestyle. Character changes start from the inside. The evidence of a person's born-again experience on the inside is a change in their character on the outside as they begin to grow to become more like

Jesus. For some people, the born-again experience seems to be gradual. The born-again experience is for unbelievers that change into believers. Some folks, especially those raised in the church, don't even remember the day they made that eternal decision, but these folks believe what Jesus has done for them, and they know they are saved. Their hearts have been cleansed from sin, and they are heaven-bound. Their lives are gradually changed from glory to glory as they learn and grow in the Word. This is all wonderful. The thief on the cross next to Jesus was saved, but as the experience of salvation or being born again is for unbelievers, so the baptism in the Holy Spirit is for those who are already believers. The baptism in the Holy Spirit is a change in the boldness of the believer. A new fire comes upon us, flames of spiritual fire crackle and spark and swirl within us, and we become witnesses of who Jesus is to us and what He has done for us. We almost can't help it. We become ministry-minded "fishers of men," as Jesus said, and other people's spiritual conditions take on a new importance in our lives.

How you get the baptism varies a little by individual experience. Jesus is the baptizer, and He can accomplish the task all by Himself, but sometimes He uses us to lay our hands on people as a point of contact for them to receive. As far as the evidence is concerned, the baptism in the Holy Spirit is not so much about your character becoming more like Jesus as it is about the boldness to express that character in ministering to others. Don't be afraid of it. It's just Jesus. And He's not scary.

Discussion Questions

1. Can you be born-again without the baptism of the Holy Spirit?

2. Why did Jesus command His disciples to wait for the baptism of the Holy Spirit before going out to witness (Acts 1:4–8)?

Prophecy

It says in the scripture that believers that were baptized in the Holy Spirit spoke in tongues and *prophesied*. What's this prophecy thing all about? Prophecy in the New Testament is the equivalent of speaking in tongues and interpreting the message. It is speaking the words of God in the moment but in *your own language*. These "utterance" gifts are usually speaking out loud the words of God at the moment in the church assembly, and both these gifts are the Holy Spirit speaking with His personality. Paul called prophecy a greater gift than tongues because it is speaking words that can be understood, and that is more helpful to those who are listening.

Paul said, "He who speaks in a tongue edifies himself, but he who prophesies edifies the church" (1 Corinthians 14:4). Then he goes on to say, "He who prophesies is greater than he who speaks with tongues, unless indeed he interprets, that the church may receive edification." So if you speak in tongues in the assembly and interpret the language, it is equal to prophesying. The idea is, we all want to understand, so we will be strengthened and helped by what Jesus is saying. Why doesn't God just always speak to us in our own language? Good question. When there is a manifestation of tongues in the assembly, people perk up. It is different and unique. God usually seems to have multiple reasons for why He does something. He is the original multitasker. My own opinion is that He likes to mix things up a little, keep things exciting. Isn't it interesting how many different ways God uses language? He is all about words.

In the Old Testament, the Holy Spirit came upon certain men chosen by God to speak to the people on His behalf. Basically, prophecy is God speaking through a man. It is the man's voice you understand, not a booming what-we-think-he-should-sound-like voice. And the thoughts and words are not the man's ideas, they are God's own words. Wow, how cool is that! Sometimes God would speak through a prophet and would tell about things to come in the future, and sometimes it would be just about how God felt about a situation. Futuristic stuff is usually what people think of when they think of prophecy, but God also spoke to us through prophets to show us how He was feeling, and not only that, but why there would be judgment or blessing. This is one of the reasons to read the books of the prophets in the Old Testament. It gives us a bigger picture of God's story. Here are some examples:

- Isaiah 43:1 shows us God's affection for His people. "But now, thus says the Lord, who created you, O Jacob, and He who formed you, O Israel; Fear not, for I have redeemed you; I have called you by your name; You are Mine."

- In Deuteronomy 5:29, God is expressing his desire for His people. "Oh, that they had such a heart in them that they would fear Me and always keep all My commandments that it might be well with them and with their children forever!"

- Ezekiel 6:9 shows us God's sadness over Israel's unfaithfulness to Him and worshiping other gods. "Then those of you who escape (judgment by war) will remember Me among the nations where they are carried captive, because I was crushed by their adulterous heart which has departed from Me…"

- Isaiah 42:1 shows us God's love for Jesus. "Behold! My Servant whom I uphold, My Elect One in whom My soul delights!"

Besides revealing the heart of God, these prophets foretold all kinds of future events. Other religions also had prophets. God called them false prophets. The devil is a counterfeiter, a copycat with no new ideas of his own. Anyone can "prophesy" or claim to prophesy, but if it doesn't come true, that person is not a true prophet. True prophets in the Old Testament predicted Jesus would come, and He did. There are over three hundred fulfilled prophecies about Jesus. Here are a few of them:

- He would be born of a virgin (Isaiah 7:14).

- He would be born in Bethlehem (Micah 5:2).

- He would be heir to the throne of King David (Isaiah 9:7).

- He would spend some time in Egypt (Hosea 11:1).

- A messenger would prepare the way for him (Isaiah 40:3–5).

- Little children would praise him (Psalm 8:2).

- He would be rejected by his own people (Isaiah 53:3).

- He would be betrayed (Zechariah 11:12–13).
- The price of his betrayal would be used to buy a potter's field (Zechariah 11:12–13).
- He would be spat upon and struck (Isaiah 50:6).
- He would be crucified with criminals (Isaiah 53:12).
- He would be given vinegar to drink (Psalm 69:21).
- He would be forsaken by God (Psalm 22:1).
- His hands and feet would be pierced (Psalm 22:16).
- Soldiers would gamble for his garments (Psalm 22:18).
- Soldiers would pierce his side (Zechariah 12:10).
- He would be buried with the rich (Isaiah 53:9).
- He would be resurrected from the dead (Psalm 16:10, 49:15).
- He would ascend into heaven (Psalm 24:7–10).

The mathematical odds of even one of those coming to pass are ridiculously impossible.

1 person fulfilling 8 prophecies: 1 in 100,000,000,000,000,000 1 person fulfilling 48 prophecies: 1 chance in 10 to the 157th power 1 person fulfilling 300+ prophecies: Only Jesus!

It is the magnificent detail of these prophecies that mark the Bible as the inspired Word of God. Only God could foreknow and accomplish all that was written about the Christ. This historical accuracy and reliability sets the Bible apart from any other book or record.

The New Testament was written after the death of Jesus Christ. Archeologists have found thousands of manuscripts of the New Testament. Some of these pieces of manuscript are dated less than 100 years after the original letters were written. In terms of historical reliability, the Bible is superior to any other ancient writings. (CBN.com)

In the New Testament Church age, the gift of prophecy is not so much telling the future, although it can be, but it is more expressing the heart of God. It is often used to confirm information that has been brought to us in some other form first, like an idea, an impression, a dream, a situation, or concerning a direction that we should go. For instance, if a church group has been considering a new building program, the Holy Spirit might speak through a prophecy telling the church to go forward with their plans or to wait or to go in a different direction. A prophecy might come forth in the church to dispel fear or to declare a time of rejoicing. The words of the person speaking will almost always be encouraging and caring because the Holy Spirit loves us, and His intention is to build up, not tear down. First Corinthians 14:3 says, "But he who prophesies speaks edification, and exhortation, and comfort to men." The NLT says it this way: "But one who prophesies strengthens others, encourages them, and comforts them." Because the words are not always futuristic, New Testament prophecy cannot usually be judged like Old Testament prophecy, which is if the thing predicted comes to pass. Instead, it is judged by the Spirit of Jesus and the confirmation in a believer's heart. "For the testimony of Jesus is the spirit of prophecy" (Revelation

19:10). If the prophetic words lift up and glorify Jesus, if the words are helpful, comforting, encouraging, then you can probably receive them as coming from the Lord. If the words are negative, demeaning, oppressive, and do not glorify Jesus, then it's not the Holy Spirit speaking. Does that make sense? But there are some exceptions. The Holy Spirit can and does bring words of correction as well as comfort, and believers should be able to tell by the confirmation in their hearts if the words are from God. In general, we try to keep in mind that believers are operating at all different levels of maturity. We don't get mad at someone who prophesies something funky; we just try to encourage them so that they will do better next time. This same attitude applies to every believer operating in any of the gifts of the Spirit. We are all learning.

Of course, as I said, there is also such a thing as deliberate false prophecy, and God even warned against it. He told us how to know the difference. If it comes to pass, it's real.

> But the prophet who prophesies peace will be recognized as one truly sent by the Lord only if his prediction comes true. (Jeremiah 28:9)

> When a prophet speaks in the name of the Lord, if the thing does not happen or come to pass, that is the thing which the Lord has not spoken; the prophet has spoken it presumptuously; you shall not be afraid of him. (Deuteronomy 18:22)

God was not happy about so-called prophets that continually spoke their own words but called them God's. In the Church today, where prophecy is less about future events, be wary of people who just like to hear themselves talk and seem to need the spotlight.

For the believer giving a prophecy, the Lord will sometimes give you an idea, a thought, a phrase to share with the group. As you say the first thought or words, the next thing will come, and you just keep sharing God's thoughts and words as they come. A person giving a prophecy should be conscious of the heart of Jesus, a love for the people, and a desire for them to connect to the One Who loves them. It is a gift for ministry. From personal experience, sometimes when I give a prophecy, my body seems to get a kind of adrenaline rush. It's not really adrenaline, but rather, it's the feeling of the Spirit of God like a river current. But I have also given a prophetic message or "words from the Lord" when I felt nothing like that. Feelings are not dependable. Prophecy is usually a public gift, but it might operate occasionally in a more private way. A believer may have "a word from the Lord" for another believer from time to time. This could be a word of knowledge or word of wisdom or a prophecy. All the utterance gifts work toward the same goal—communicating God's thoughts. The thing about personal prophecy, just like in the public assembly, is that if the word is truly from the Lord, you will sense a confirmation in your spirit that it is true. It will likely be a confirmation about something the Lord has already been speaking to you about. For instance, if you have felt like God is leading you to make a decision about something, another believer who doesn't know what you are dealing with may confirm the direction of the decision by a word from the Lord (prophecy). When this gets out of hand is when a "personal prophet" goes overboard and tries to tell you how to run every little thing about your life. Believers don't need a personal prophet, thank you. We have the Holy

Spirit that lives inside us. Personal prophecy is a once-in-a-while thing, a ministry of Jesus for a special occasion.

Many years ago, I had been struggling with an overwhelming schedule and feelings of insufficiency to accomplish it all, leading to severe headaches to where I felt like my mind was splitting in two. I wondered if that is what people that develop schizophrenia felt like. I had never felt so oppressed. This went on for several weeks. One day, I received a phone call from a Christian friend who told me that she had been praying for me and that the Lord told her to tell me that the giant's head had been cut off. That's all she said, but it was enough. That prophetic word from the Lord was a lifeline to me. I received it as having come from the Lord, and from that time on, the headaches left, and I was able to make decisions about how to simplify my situation. I have never felt that horrible oppression again. Thank you, Jesus!

Five Ministry Gifts to the Church

One more thing, a person who prophesies once in a while is not necessarily a "prophet." Any believer can prophesy if the Holy Spirit moves him, but the office of prophet is a special focus for ministry. There are other qualifications involved. The Holy Spirit of Jesus sets the offices of apostle, prophet, evangelist, pastor, and teacher in order in the Church. Ephesians 4:11–13 says, "And He Himself gave some to be apostles, some prophets, some evangelists, and some pastors and teachers, for the equipping of the saints for the work of ministry, for the edifying of the body of Christ, till we all come to the unity of the faith, and of the knowledge of the Son of God, to a perfect man, to the measure of the stature of the fullness of Christ." These are sometimes called the fivefold ministry gifts. These gifts are people, not just abilities, and are given to the Church to help believers grow and be successful. You probably recognize most of these minister functions.

- *Apostle*—Basically, he is a minister who is led by the Holy Spirit to gather groups of believers, to start a church or churches, and to oversee their growth. An apostle can be an overseer of many or few churches. An apostle needs lots of gifts working alongside him or her, like preaching ability, administration ability, and many other things. They are the ones who get things going. Apostles are not pastors and do not always stay with the churches they plant.

- *Prophet*—he is someone who declares the Word of the Lord to the Church. This person tends to see things as more black and white than most people. They call it like it is. They may have spiritual dreams and visions where God shows them things for the rest of us. The intent and heart of God is important for them to understand. Prophets help us see the bigger picture.

- *Evangelist*—He is someone who feels a strong desire to preach, especially about salvation. Helping people become believers is what evangelists are all about. They don't want anyone to miss it. Evangelists are not necessarily teachers or pastors. They help birth the baby believers, and then the pastors and teachers help grow them up.

- *Pastor*—He is someone who feels responsibility for the sheep (local church members). A pastor is a caring, nurturing, shepherd who cares for the little ones as well as the older ones in the flock. A pastor may not necessarily be a good preacher, but he or she loves the sheep. Pastors know their flock, their names, their family members, and probably go to little Billy's soccer game. They are there for the family when someone in the flock dies, they marry people, and they do counseling.

- *Teacher*—He is someone who studies the Word of God and breaks it down into smaller bite-size pieces for the rest of us so we can understand what is going on. A teacher is not necessarily a charismatic evangelist or preacher. Teaching is a separate gift.

Some believers operate in more than one of these gifts, and some move from one to another depending on the season of their lives. It is possible for a minister to operate in a preaching gift and switch to a teaching gift in the same message. We are grateful to God for providing these amazing helpers for the Church. He has thought of everything!

The Parable of the Sower

Listen! Behold, a sower went out to sow. And it happened, as he sowed, that some seed fell by the wayside; and the birds of the air came and devoured it. Some fell on stony ground, where it did not have much earth; and immediately it sprang up because it had no depth of earth. But when the sun was up it was scorched, and because it had no root it withered away. And some seed fell among the thorns; and the thorns grew up and choked it, and it yielded no crop. But other seed fell on good ground and yielded a crop that sprang up, increased and produced:

some thirtyfold, some sixty, and some a hundred. (Mark 4:3–8)

In this parable, Jesus is talking about the seed of the Word of God, and the ground that it falls on is our hearts.

We all receive revelation from the Lord through that Word and are at different levels of increase, depending on the condition of our hearts. This is where we can see the five-fold ministry gifts come into play and why they have been given to the Church. Specifically, these three are:

- Evangelist—The seed sown by the wayside was picked off easily by the birds. An evangelist comes to throw out more seed for these people and to chase the birds away. An evangelist has thick skin and keeps on preaching, talking about Jesus, even if it looks like no one is listening. He is throwing seed on the surface, not necessarily teaching deep doctrinal concepts. An evangelist is interested in getting the seed into the ground, away from the birds, where it will begin to grow.

- Teacher—The seed sown on stony ground will not make it unless someone breaks up that ground and gets rid of the stones and adds fertilizer. This is what the teacher does, making the scriptures easier to be understood, building a foundation or a root system that can withstand the scorching sun. Teachers reach people at all stages in their spiritual growth. They can teach basic doctrine or deep spiritual truths. Their interest is in growing root systems.

- Pastor—The seed choked by weeds and thorns is where the pastor comes in. The weeds are the cares and circumstances of our everyday lives. Sometimes we need someone to walk through the times of pain with us, slashing down the weeds, removing the thorns, clearing the area to let the light in so we can see clearly again. Pastors minister to the people around them, to stay mainly in one place, and to help people clear the thorns from their lives so that they will continue to grow and produce fruit.

These offices are available to all believers, both men and women, who have the faith and diligence to pursue them. We sometimes think it is only a special few who are gifted, but God is no respecter of persons. First Timothy 3:1 tells us that if anyone desires the position or office of a bishop, "he desires a good thing." The word *bishop* means overseer, an elder, someone in a position of leadership. We are to desire to attain these offices, and we don't have to wait for a special calling.

Discussion Questions

1. Have you ever heard someone say something that just made all the difference in your thinking?

2. When might a word of prophecy be important to the church assembly?

3. Which ministry gift (apostle, prophet, evangelist, pastor, teacher) do you identify with the most? Why?

Introduction to Know Your Enemy

I think the thing that stands out the most to me about dealing with the devil, as I have read and listened to experienced and knowledgeable teachers, is the lack of fear they displayed. That has impressed me more than anything they have said. Jesus confirmed this approach multiple times, saying, "Fear not! Don't be afraid! Just believe!"

Interestingly, in many religious settings, people are afraid to even discuss the devil, fearing his unwanted attention and retribution, but not so with the Christians that seem to know what they're talking about. Unfortunately, the enemy does not just go away if we hide our heads under the covers. He plays with us, like a cat pouncing on whatever is moving under the blanket.

Fear *attracts* the enemy. That is the opposite of what we want to do, right? The best way to defend ourselves is not to play his game. Faith is the opposite of fear, and we are believers.

Flip the covers off your head, get up, and take the cat out! Boy, will he ever be surprised!

You are the boss because Jesus has left you in charge.

Smith Wigglesworth, a noted Bible teacher, once told a story of how he was awakened in the middle of the night and saw Satan in person sitting on the edge of his bed. His response was, "Oh, it's only you." Then he rolled over and went back to sleep.

This is the kind of thing that impresses me. This is how Jesus responded to the devil. He exposed him and cast those demons out right and left. Then he sent his disciples, first the twelve and then seventy others (or seventy-two, depending on the translation), to do the same thing, and they came back with a glowing report that even the demons were subject to them in the name of Jesus (Luke 9:1–2, 10:1). But I can't remember any Sunday message or Bible study covering much on this topic. The philosophy has seemed to be that the less said about the devil, the better. And that just plays right into his grubby little hands. You've probably read somewhere that the enemy's biggest ploy is encouraging people to believe he doesn't exist. Clearly that has been a successful move on his part.

The truth is, if Jesus spent so much time showing us how to deal with the devil, then it must be important. Do we really think that the devil has gone away? In Mark 16, right before He ascended into heaven, Jesus charged his disciples to continue to cast out demons and put Satan in his place. Are we completely walking in the light of the Gospel if we neglect this side of things? Personally, I don't think so. Just like healing is for the believer, deliverance from oppression is as well. Jesus is not going to do this for us. He gave *us* the authority. It's our job.

The Bible tells us we are not ignorant of the devil's devices. Think about it. We know he is a liar. We know he is a thief and a murderer. Why are we allowing him to take our territory without a fight? He has weaseled his way into our culture, our education, the arts, the political arena, the media, even the churches, and yet there is little outcry. We turn our resistance on to those in our own ranks, while the real culprit and his cronies remain hidden, shielded by our unbelief. And those who are his children interpret our folly as weakness. Their mockery of the Church is becoming increasingly intense. Ironically, when someone attempts to expose the devil, to tell the truth about his involvement, the response, even from the Church, is not supportive. We don't want to talk about it. Does this seem practical? In fact, it is counterproductive.

If the enemy's biggest strategy is convincing people that he doesn't exist, the second biggest is that he doesn't matter. Yes, he matters. He is the single most destructive entity we know. He doesn't just come to bother us; he comes to steal, kill, and destroy according to Jesus in John 10:10. Our lives and the lives of those we care about are in danger. If we say nothing and do nothing to protect ourselves, we are foolish.

> Finally, be strong in the Lord and in His mighty power. Put on the full armor of God, so that you can take your stand against the devil's schemes. For our struggle is not against flesh and blood, but against the rulers, against the authorities, against the powers of this dark world and against the spiritual forces of evil in the heavenly realms. Therefore, put on the full armor of God, so that when the day of evil comes, you may be able to stand your ground, and after you have done everything, to stand. Stand firm then, with the belt of truth buckled around your waist, with the breastplate of righteousness in place, and with your feet fitted with the readiness that comes from the gospel of peace. In addition to all this, take up the shield of faith, with which you can extinguish all the flaming arrows of the evil one. Take the helmet of salvation and the sword of the Spirit, which is the word of God. And pray in the Spirit on all occasions with all kinds of prayers and requests. With this in mind, be alert and

always keep on praying for all the Lord's people.
(Ephesians 6:10–18)

It's time for the Church to rise up and take a stand against the real enemy, not in fear but in faith and in the grace of the Son of God, King Jesus, who lives forever.

> The thief does not come except to steal and to kill and to destroy. I have come that they may have life and that they may have it more abundantly. (John 10:10)
> Greater is He that is in you than he that is in the world. (1 John 4:4)

That's the good news!

LESSON 10

KNOW YOUR ENEMY (PART 1)

First Peter 5:8-9 tells us, "Be sober, be vigilant; because your adversary the devil walks about like a roaring lion, seeking whom he may devour. Resist him, steadfast in the faith, knowing that the same sufferings are experienced by your brotherhood in the world." The devil is the "elephant in the room." Many people tend to stay away from this subject, kind of like it's some big secret (ssshh!), but I think it's better to have it all out in the open.

The Bible says we have an adversary. Adversary means one's opponent in a conflict, contest, or dispute. To the devil, this world is a chessboard. It is a life-and-death game between him and God. He is playing for his life and cannot afford to lose. If he should win, which he has to believe he has a chance, he would win big. God would be defeated. Jackpot! Then Satan would sit on the throne of heaven. How he thinks that is even a possibility shows how delusional he is—delusional but dangerous. Because humans have been made in God's image, because God has taken a personal interest in us, and because God loves us, we have become the main focus of attack in this game. *We* now have an adversary that is looking for ways to oppose us on a daily basis. Ever since the time of Adam, he has been annoying people all over the world, not just us. Heads up, we are in a battle zone, and even if you don't realize it or feel like fighting with him, he is trying to take you down anyway. You can't say, "I don't want to play this game." I mean, you can say it, but it won't do you any good. He doesn't care, it's not about you. It's all about him and God. Even if you are not a Christian, you are his enemy just by being human. God loves you, so the devil hates you. He is so predictable. We are surrounded by the devil's kingdom of darkness. Mosquitos come out when it gets dark. They bite. They can carry dangerous disease. Some people get allergic reactions and complications to a mosquito bite. But are there times you can go outside and there are no mosquitoes? Yes. Can you wear protective clothing? Yes. Can you spray yourself with insect repellent? Yes. Do you stop living your life because there are mosquitos? No. You protect yourselves and swat them. The devil and his crew are like buzzing mosquitos. Sometimes their attack on us is simply annoying, and sometimes it is overwhelming. But be of good cheer, we need not be helpless victims subject to the whims of the enemy. Jesus has overcome the world. He has defeated the devil legally. "You are all children of the light and children of the day. We do not belong to the night or to the darkness" (1 Thessalonians 5:5). And we have insect repellent. His name is Jesus.

Profiling the Devil

"The FBI method of profiling is a system created by the Federal Bureau of Investigation (FBI) used to detect and classify the major personality and behavioral characteristics of an individual based upon analysis of the crime or crimes the person committed" (Wikipedia.org).

Think of these next two lessons as a profile, an analysis of the personality and behavioral characteristics of our enemy based on the Word of God with a little personal experience thrown in. This is the same tactic the devil uses on us. He studies us and profiles us to find out what we are likely to do or say in a certain situation. Then he uses that information against us. He always copies someone else's ideas. This time, we are going to use his own tactic to learn about him. Satan has a few different names in the Bible. He is called Lucifer, Satan (accuser), the devil, the destroyer, the Assyrian, the king of Tyre or Tyrus, Leviathan, that old dragon, the god of this world, the prince of the air, and some other things. I call him trouble. You know that he tried to overthrow God, the great high King, and his attempt failed. Satan was created beautiful and had a powerful position in heaven. Ezekiel 28:12 describes him as the "seal of perfection, full of wisdom and perfect in beauty."

The name Lucifer appears only once in the Bible (Isaiah 14:12). It is a Latin translation of the Hebrew word *heylal* and means "brightness, morning star." Some Bible translations just use the term "daystar" or "bright one." The word *heylal* comes from the word *halal*, which means "clear" or "shine." It also has the meaning of "boasting" or "to make a show" (the devil is a show-off) and is actually where we get the word *hallelujah*. Lucifer was made to praise the Lord. He was a musician with musical instruments in his own body that played music when he walked. Some say he was probably the worship leader in heaven, although in heaven you probably don't need one. He was covered in precious jewels and might have even sparkled! He must have been something amazing at one time. From the meaning of his name, we can surmise that God created Lucifer as something special to behold, a literal shining example of the Creator's ability. The angels might have even thought he was the best thing God had ever made…until He made man. Man was created in God's own image. Now there was competition. Perhaps that is where the trouble erupted. Perhaps that is when the name of Lucifer became Satan, the accuser—the jealous accuser.

In Ezekiel 28, the Bible prophesies over the leader of the kingdom of Tyre, calling him the prince of Tyre. A few verses later, the tone shifts, and the Lord begins prophesying to someone else, called the *king* of Tyre. This was the demon spirit ruling over that region and the entity behind the destructive actions shown by the prince. The word *Tyre* means a sharp stone or a knife. It comes from a root word meaning "adversary." It becomes clear as you read through the passage that this particular evil spirit was in the Garden of Eden. Now we know who it is talking about—Satan himself.

> Son of Man, take up a lamentation for the king of Tyre, and say to him, "Thus says the LORD God: You were the seal of perfection, full of wisdom and perfect in beauty. You were in Eden, the garden of God; Every precious stone was your covering:
>
> The sardius, topaz, and diamond, beryl, onyx, and jasper, sapphire, turquoise and emerald with gold. The workmanship of your timbrels and pipes (musical instruments) was prepared for you on the day you were created. You were the anointed cherub who covers; I established you; You were on the holy mountain of God; You walked back and forth in the midst of the fiery stones. You were perfect in your ways from the day you were created, Till iniquity was found in you. By the abundance of your trading you became filled with violence within, and you sinned. Therefore, I cast you as a profane thing

out of the mountain of God; And I destroyed you, O covering cherub, from the midst of the fiery stones. Your heart was lifted up because of your beauty; You corrupted your wisdom for the sake of your splendor; I cast you to the ground, I laid you before kings, that they might gaze at you. You defiled your sanctuaries by the multitude of your iniquities, By the iniquity of your trading; Therefore, I brought fire from your midst; It devoured you, And I turned you to ashes upon the earth In the sight of all who saw you. All who knew you among the peoples are astonished at you; You have become a horror and shall be no more forever." (Ezekiel 28:12–19)

Through the clues in Ezekiel, we can tell a few basic things about him.

- *He was anointed.* He had some kind of limited access to the creative power of the Holy Spirit of God; anointing means "consecrated with oil." Priests were anointed in the Old Testament. Kings were anointed. Oil is a type of the Holy Spirit.

- *He was the cherub who covers.* He was a guardian angel who had administrative authority to protect. The ark of the covenant in the Old Testament was covered by two guardian cherubim.

- *He was on the holy mountain of God and walked in the midst of the fiery stones.* He had privilege that other angels did not share.

- *Iniquity (wickedness) was found in him.* He turned his eyes away from beholding God and onto himself.

Jesus said in Matthew 6:22-23, "The lamp of the body is the eye, If therefore your eye is good, your whole body will be full of light. But if your eye is bad, your whole body will be full of darkness. If therefore the light that is in you is darkness, how great is that darkness!" Evil imaginations and ideas come from the devil.

- *He was an abundant trader (dealer).* He is a salesman, a con artist, a liar, a deceiver, and a cheat.

- *He became filled with violence.* He is an assassin, a murderer, a thug.

- *He sinned.* God cast him out as a profane thing.

- *His heart was lifted up because of his beauty.* He is puffed up and full of pride.

- *He corrupted his own wisdom for the sake of his splendor.* He is not as smart as he thinks he is. He makes mistakes.

- *God cast him to the ground.* He came down to the earth.

- *God laid him before kings that they might gaze on him.* We are learning from watching him.

- *He defiled his own sanctuaries with a multitude of iniquities, especially unfair trade.* Jesus said a kingdom divided against itself will not stand. The devil's kingdom will fall.

- *All who knew him are astonished at his end.* He has become a horror story. Astonished means "to stun, grow numb, stupefy, make amazed, astonish."

- *God brought fire from his core.* This is the creation of hell. It will devour him, and he shall be no more forever. Beauty turned to ashes.

Jesus calls the devil a thief and the father of murder and the father of lies. He is the parent, the progenitor of wickedness.

The Anointed Cherub

Ezekiel 28 tells us that Lucifer was originally the anointed cherub that covers.

A cherub (cherubim for more than one) is a special angel—in particular, one that spreads his wings over the throne of God. Carved cherubim made to God's specifications covered the ark of the covenant, the presence of God, in the tabernacle and later the temple in Israel. The word *cherub* means to bless. Sometimes we see an artist's rendering of cute little babylike angels shooting arrows around Valentine's Day. Cherubim are pretty much the opposite of that picture. They are big and strong and hold a place of honor and importance in heaven. The fact that the devil was a cherub tells us he was super close to God. He was there to bless God, to bless the throne, to bless the Kingdom. But he wasn't just a cherub; he was the "anointed" cherub. The word *anoint* means to rub or paint on something. In the Bible, a priest sometimes anointed a person with oil, touching them with the special oil, as a symbol of God's touch, His blessing, the Holy Spirit's assistance to accomplish a special task. Kings and priests were always anointed as part of the ritual of installation. Lucifer had been anointed. He had been anointed to bless and to cover. The Hebrew word there for *cover* in the Bible means "to entwine as a screen, to fence in, to protect, to defend.

His job was to protect the throne, to defend God's position. Instead, what did he do? He tried to tear it down.

Not just for ritual, the anointing is also a connection to the power of God. The Holy Spirit's power is often referred to as the anointing in the New Testament Church. People are healed through the anointing, the blind can see, the deaf can hear, the lame can walk. Miracles have happened, prophecies were spoken, wars were won, all because of the anointing of the Holy Spirit. It is the symbol of the powerhouse of God. Lucifer had been anointed (given the creative power of God) for a particular purpose. As he moved, musical instruments played from his body. Other angels probably admired him and his position, which appealed to his pride. He felt the anointing, the power of God on him for service. He liked that feeling. He liked it a lot! Under the anointing, when God's power and strength combines with yours, you feel like you can do anything, be anything. The potential is more than enough to accomplish whatever the task, as nothing is impossible with God!

The word *anoint* also has the meaning of expansion, such as the outstretched wings of a cherub over the throne of God. It is possible that "anointed" in this case refers not only to this cherub's expansion of wings but also to the expansion of his imagination. This is where Lucifer stepped over the line. He imagined what it would be like to be God. He imagined what it would be like to sit on the throne himself with God out of the picture. Lucifer imagined it, and then he meditated on it, dreamed about it, and projected his faith for it. But with God out of the picture, all the love and light and righteousness go out of the picture too. All you are left with is the absence of those things, the negative consequence or opposite. When you take away all light, darkness is left.

When you take away all good, a black hole, evil is left. Lucifer imagined a godless throne, with himself taking God's place. He imagined mutiny, and evil and darkness, by default, followed, filling his being. And he became Satan, the devil, the father of evil.

> How you are fallen from heaven, O Lucifer, son of the morning! How you are cut down to the ground, You who weakened the nations!
>
> For you have said in your heart: 'I will ascend into heaven, I will exalt my throne above the stars of God;
>
> I will also sit on the mount of the congregation On the farthest sides of the north;
>
> I will ascend above the heights of the clouds, I will be like the Most High.
>
> Yet you shall be brought down to hell, To the lowest depths of the Pit. (Isaiah 14:12–15 KJV)

The Destroyer

I've heard it said that people worship what they fear. It's possible that God, in His mercy, postponed much revelation about Satan's influence in the world until Jesus came and helped us see how to defeat the devil. He didn't want people fearing the devil so much that they would worship him. That's what Satan desires, of course. He wants to be worshiped like God. There are some glimpses into the influence of the devil in the Old Testament—in Ezekiel, Isaiah, and Job—but usually he is portrayed as just the destroyer, or something to that effect. For instance, in Exodus 12:23, the story of the

Passover, when the Israelites were delivered from the bondage of slavery in Egypt, the scripture reads: "For the Lord will pass through to strike the Egyptians; And when He sees the blood on the lintel and on the two doorposts, the Lord will pass over the door and not allow the destroyer to come into your houses to destroy you." Who was the destroyer? Satan. He comes to steal, kill, and destroy.

Why would God allow Satan to destroy anything? Because Adam allowed it. Remember, Adam's sin had brought judgment and death on the whole world. The devil was then legally allowed to steal, kill, and destroy on the earth. Adam had given the keys to the devil. The earth had become his own dominion, and he filled it with evidence of his own evil imagination. God said the wages of sin is death. The devil is not doing anything illegal by killing and destroying; only God set boundaries for him and prevented him from acting in many cases. The earth itself still belongs to God. You might think of it like He leased it to Adam, and Adam subleased it to Satan. When the lease is up, the tenant has to move. Jesus told parables about a landlord leasing his fields out. In those parables, He said the landowner would come back one day. The true owner of the earth, Jesus, is coming back shortly to takeover, and the devil will be out.

In the New Testament, Jesus (God in the flesh) exposed the devil as a loser and defeated him in his own territory. The debt of sin has been paid by Jesus Himself, and for born-again Christians who have accepted Jesus's payment for their sins and signed the contract by their faith, the devil no longer has the right to steal, kill, and destroy *their* lives. Not that he doesn't try. The world is still his domain, but it is temporary because Jesus is coming back to set up His own amazing Kingdom, and He will fix all the things the devil has broken. In the meantime, believers are operating under a different contract from the other people in the world. They live in the world but are not *of* the world, and as citizens of a different Kingdom, they are not legally subject to the devil's evil whims. Of course, if the believers don't know what the Bible says about that, they will end up living just like the other people of the world do.

God is light and the devil is dark, but they are not equal in power, oh no! Darkness is swallowed up in light, death is swallowed up in life. When a light turns on, the darkness is dispelled. God will always win, and the devil will always lose.

The devil from the very beginning has been a con man, the cartoon characterization of the sleazy car salesman and slick lawyer. He is the inventor of the disinformation department and the original propaganda expert. He has sold us on the lies that he is just as powerful as God, that he can do whatever he wants, that he holds all the cards. None of those things are true. He foolishly tried to overthrow God and lost. That part's true. Jesus said, "I saw Satan fall like lightning from heaven" (Luke 10:18).

Why Did the Devil Think He Could Win?

Why would the devil chance it? Why would he take the risk of trying to fight God? The reason, I believe, is that Satan thought he had found a weakness in God. Yes, God is super powerful, righteous, holy, and just, but he is also wonderfully merciful and kind. He is love. That was where the devil thought God's weakness was. He might have even thought that God's love for him would overlook his treachery. He planned his coup in heaven, and when that failed, he tried again on the earth. He might have thought that because of

God's mercy he would never have to face any consequences. After all, he was God's special angel. And when there seemed to be limited retribution after his mutiny, when he was allowed to remain at large, he was sure his assessment of God's weakness had been right. Sure, certain privileges had been revoked, but he was still active and able to speak his lies. So he began to make another plan, focusing his attack this time on the earth and mankind— God's special project. If he couldn't rule heaven, he could certainly rule the earth! The devil gambled again that God's character trait of mercy would win out over his character trait of justice. Psalm 89:14 tells us that righteousness and justice are the foundation of God's throne. If Satan could somehow trick God or put Him in such a position that He would have to choose mercy over justice just once, he could destroy the foundation of heaven, the right of God to sit on the throne. However, the devil was so wrong! There is another scripture that says, "And in mercy (or love) shall the throne be established" (Isaiah 16:5). He wasn't paying attention. Love is not weak; it is the strongest thing there is. *Love never fails.*

Satan vs. Jesus

God allowed the devil to think he had sabotaged His plan with Adam, but God already knew what would happen and He let it play out. (Jesus is called the Lamb slain from the foundation of the world—Revelation 13:8). God's plan is long term. He allowed the devil to remain as god of this world, but when the time was right (God is so patient), Jesus came, and everything changed.

Satan knew a savior was coming. It had been prophesied from the time of Adam. God said to the serpent after he had tricked Adam and Eve into eating the forbidden fruit,

"Because you have done this, You are cursed more than all cattle, and more than every beast of the field; on your belly you shall go, and you shall eat dust all the days of your life. And I will put enmity between you and the woman, and between your seed and her Seed; He shall bruise your head, and you shall bruise His heel" (Genesis 3:14–15). God was prophesying that a child would be born who would bruise the serpent's head or the devil's power and authority in the world. Some translations use the word *crush* instead of *bruise*. God was saying right from the beginning that the devil was on a short leash. His days are numbered.

When Adam and Eve had their first two children, Cain and Abel, the devil thought one of them must be the special child. It looked to him like Cain was messing up and that God was favoring Abel, so it must be Abel who was the savior! So Satan whispered lying thoughts into Cain's ear, stirring up jealousy. Eventually, Cain was so jealous that all the devil had to do was point him in the right direction, give him a little push, and Cain slew Abel, his own brother. Cain was exhibiting his "father's" nature—the devil's murdering violent nature. The inheritance of sin was already manifesting. *That's that*, the devil probably thought, all full of himself.

Only it wasn't over. There continued to be prophecies of a coming Savior, a King that would reign forever. The devil was in a continual frenzy to identify the one who was foretold. He stirred up people to murder prophet after prophet, trying to obliterate the threat to his dynasty. After the wise men came to Jerusalem to find out from King Herod where the baby Jesus would be born, King Herod sent them to Bethlehem and had every male child slain from birth to two years old (Matthew 2:16). Was that butchery really King Herod's idea? No, that was Satan's input. He is the one who put that evil thought in the king's mind, stirred him to jealousy just like he did with Cain. The devil operates in the same pattern every time. But God knew what he was up to and sent Joseph a dream, warning him to take Mary and Jesus into Egypt until after Herod was dead. For several years, the devil didn't know where the Savior was. He probably assumed he had been killed with the other children. Do you see that Satan does not know everything? He is clever and usually pays attention, but he is not like God. He makes all kinds of mistakes. Remember, he corrupted his wisdom because all he can think about is how beautiful he is. And actually, he's not that good-looking anymore. You've seen pictures of demons. They are not handsome, they are monsters. Sin corrupts beauty. The Bible says Satan can transform himself into an angel of light temporarily, but he used to look like that all the time. He's definitely gone downhill.

God did not reveal who Jesus was until the right time. Timing with God is everything. Jesus grew up just like a natural boy. He did not do any miracles until the time of His ministry as an adult. We know that because the Gospel of John records the turning of the water into wine at the wedding in Cana as being the first miracle that Jesus did. All through the years, the devil kept searching for the Savior, riling up the religious elite to kill the prophets and anyone whom he thought might be the one sent from God to "crush his head." But he never knew for sure if he had killed the right one. Then one day, when Jesus was baptized by John the Baptist at the age of thirty, the heavens opened up, the Holy Spirit alighted on Jesus in the form of a dove, and God the Father said these words out loud. "This is my beloved Son, in whom I am well pleased" (Matthew 3:16–17). Whom do you suppose He was announcing this to? Jesus already knew who He was, and John the Baptist had been looking for a dove as the sign (John 1:32–33), which he saw, so it wasn't him. It was to Satan that God was talking to. He was saying, "Here he is, this is the Savior, the one who will step on you and crush your head with his heel!"

Did Satan hear God's voice giving him a hint? Yes! And he immediately went to work on Jesus, but he couldn't budge Him. The Bible gives us a picture of the devil's frontal attack. You can find this account in Matthew 4 and Luke 4. Jesus fasted for forty days, praying in the wilderness before He started his ministry. First Peter 5:8 tells us, "Be sober, be vigilant; because your adversary the devil walks about like a roaring lion, seeking whom he may devour." Imagine the devil pacing back and forth like a lion in a cage, trying to find a weakness in Jesus. All he had as a weapon against this man was *words*. (That's all he has against us too.)

Jesus was hungry after fasting for forty days and nights. (You would be too.) The devil saw a potential weakness in the human flesh body of Jesus and tried to exploit it by tempting Him to turn the stones into bread. Wasn't that reminiscent of the temptation he had used with Eve back in the garden? I guess the devil thinks that all us humans want to do is eat. Jesus basically answered, "I'm not *that* hungry." No, really, what He said was, *"It is written, man does not live by bread alone, but by every word of God."* Jesus fought back with *words*—not just any words but *scripture*. The devil realized Jesus was stronger in that area that he had guessed, so he tried a different way. He tempted Him to throw himself off a high precipice to see angels come and save him, to prove He was the Son of God. This attack was against a human's desire for pride and fame. Jesus didn't "fall" for it. Instead, He said, "I don't have to prove anything to you," or in His own words,

"It is written, you shall not tempt the Lord your God." He kept throwing the Word at him.

Then the devil, extremely frustrated and beginning to understand that this Jesus might be a real threat to his continued kingdom of darkness, tried the biggest temptation he could think of for a human being: riches and power! He went all out, got out the big guns, the trump card, the one that always works for weak human beings (Luke 4:5– 8). "Then the devil, taking Him up on a high mountain, showed Him all the kingdoms of the world in a moment of time. And the devil said to Him, 'All this authority I will give You, and their glory; for this has been delivered to me [by Adam], and I give it to whomever I wish. Therefore, if You will worship before me, all will be Yours.'" Basically, he was saying, "I am in charge of everything here, but I'll let you share the kingdoms of the world with me," something like, "You can be the king on Tuesdays." But what did Jesus say to that? "And Jesus answered and said, 'Get behind Me Satan! For it is written, "You shall worship the Lord your God and Him only shall you serve.""'" Satan's strategy didn't work. "Then the devil left Him, and angels came and ministered to Him" (Matthew 4:11).

Frustrated, Satan left Him for a more opportune time (Luke 4:13). He doesn't like to quit. Throughout Jesus's three-year ministry, the devil kept popping up, whether it was through demons that were oppressing people or a storm threatening to capsize His boat or the Pharisees who opposed Him, scheming and trying to trap Him in his speech. Jesus cast out the demons, calmed the storm, and exposed the Pharisees' sneaky attacks as being from their father, the devil. Everywhere Jesus went, He uncovered Satan's lies and showed everybody that the devil has been the problem all along.

One day, Jesus walked into the temple and got really upset at the commerce He saw going on there. Sleazy salesmen all over the place! It was a trader's market, not a temple of worship. Dealers were taking advantage of the people coming to worship, selling blemished animals for sacrifice that were supposed to be unblemished and pure. Money changers that traded coins for "official" temple money were cheating the people, giving them less than a fair exchange. Everywhere He looked, Jesus saw evidence of the devil's influence, the trader, the con man, the cheater. John 2:14– 16 tells us,

> In the temple He found those who were selling oxen and sheep and pigeons, and the money-changers sitting there. And making a whip of cords, He drove them all out of the temple, with the sheep and oxen. And He poured out the coins of the moneychangers and overturned their tables. And He told those who sold the pigeons, "Take these things away; do not make My Father's house a house of trade."
>
> And He said to them, "It is written, My house shall be called a house of prayer, but you have made it a den of thieves." (Matthew 21:13)

Satan knew he would have to do something drastic about Jesus. He would have to kill Him, but not being able to harm Jesus himself, he had to get others to do it for him, so he stirred up the scribes and Pharisees to get the job done.

The Resurrection

After Jesus was crucified, the devil thought he had finally won. He had bruised the Savior's heel! The Savior was defeated! *My theory was right*, he thought and patted himself on the back. Jesus, with all His focus on love, even loving one's enemies, made Him, who had the potential to be so powerful, weak, weak, weak. He went down so easily to the grave like every other man before Him. True, it was a little touch-and-go while Jesus was on the cross. Would God display mercy over justice and save His Son's life? Would He nullify the agreement between Adam and the devil, going back on His word? The one that states that all men must die? No, God kept the justice thing going, and Jesus died. Okay, so God didn't fall for that trick. That part of his plan didn't work, he thought, but look on the bright side. At least the prophecy in Genesis about the Savior crushing him was null and void. What a relief! The devil must have been giddy with delight. He had actually fooled God! No more Savior! The earth was all his to rule forever! Look out mankind! Things for them were about to get a lot worse.

However, what the devil had not taken into account was that Jesus's death was voluntary. He was a sinless man, and so the curse of sin—that sin DNA—was not in Him. Death is only legal for us because it is the wages of sin (Romans 6:23). Jesus the Man, by Himself, should not ever have died. He should have lived forever. So the death that Jesus submitted to was voluntary. He endured death on behalf of all mankind as payment for *our* sins, not His own. Keep in mind, Satan makes mistakes all the time. This was a big one. If he had known what Jesus was doing…but he didn't. The sacrifice that Jesus made on our behalf was successful, all the sins of the world were paid for, and He rose from the dead as living proof of the receipt of payment. What a merciful God! He paid for all of our sins by Himself! So God's mercy side was satisfied, and God's righteousness and justice were satisfied as well. The sins of the world had been paid for with the blood of a perfect Man, and the righteous requirement of the law had been legally met. Case closed; court adjourned. God is seriously so clever!

After He died, Jesus went down to hell, took the keys of the earthly kingdom back from the devil and his gang, and paraded him around as a defeated enemy, showing all the demons that Jesus is Lord and Satan is a loser (Colossians 2:15). Then Jesus rose from the dead, sealing the deal and proving to the world that "it is finished!" (John 19:30). That's why the resurrection is so important to us as Christians! Without the resurrection, we would have no *proof*, no assurance of eternal life. But because of the resurrection of Jesus, we know we will all be resurrected one day too. "For as in Adam all die, even so in Christ shall all be made alive" (1 Corinthians 15: 22).

There is now a *new* covenant. God's new covenant with man is that if anyone believes in Jesus, he will be "born again" out of the kingdom of darkness and back into the Kingdom of Light. So get this! Adam, before his fall, was created a human being, a little lower than the angels. After Jesus's resurrection, when someone is born again, he becomes a new creation, made a little higher than the angels, and a joint heir with Christ. Better covenant, better promises! (Hebrews 8:6). *We are better off now than before the devil interfered!* Jesus said believers will reign with Him (Revelation 5:10). Who will sit on a throne? Not the devil. *We* will, in the place right next to our Savior Jesus. Satan didn't see *that* coming!

Discussion Questions

1. Why is it a good idea to know our enemy?
2. How did Jesus counter the devil's attacks?
3. Why could Easter be considered the most important Christian celebration?

LESSON 11

**KNOWING YOUR ENEMY (PART 2)
WHY IS THE DEVIL STILL HANGING AROUND?**

I know of two reasons why the devil is allowed to hang around. I'm sure there are probably more, since God is the original multitasker. The first reason goes back to Ezekiel 28:17. God has laid him out before us so we could gaze on him. Of course, there will be literal gazing at the end, but for now, we're doing figurative gazing. And the angels want to look too. They want to see what is going on with the devil and what is going on with the Church.

> Concerning this salvation, the prophets, who spoke of the grace that was to come to you, searched intently and with the greatest care, trying to find out the time and circumstances to which the Spirit of Christ in them was pointing when He predicted the sufferings of the Messiah and the glories that would follow. It was revealed to them that they were not serving themselves but you, when they spoke of the things that have now been told you by those who have preached the gospel to you by the Holy Spirit sent from heaven. Even angels long to look into these things. (1 Peter 1:10–12)

The scripture says angels *long* to look into these things. They know what the scriptures say, but they have not experienced the forgiveness and mercy and love of God like we have. They want to see how we are going to react, what God is going to do, and what the devil is going to do. They are watching us like a reality TV show. That's the first reason the devil is still here. God is using him to show what a bad king will do as opposed to what a good king will do for his people (1 Samuel 8:4–22).

The second reason I believe the devil is still allowed to hang around is that he makes life tough for us. You know it! But it's through those tough times that our faith grows and is exercised or sharpened. God is using the devil and his agenda to help us grow up spiritually. When we are born again, we are like newborn babes. All we can do is eat and cry and make messes. We are hungry for the milk of the Word of God. That's normal! As we grow and mature, we learn to lean on God for everything. This goes against the independent spirit of the world, but we are not of the world. We begin to realize we need the Word, His promises in the Bible, like food and water, in order to prosper in this life. We learn about our Father and learn about ourselves as we go through these trials. With every time of trouble our faith stretches, and with every trial we mature a little more if we lean on God. We pray, and He answers. We get into trouble, and He delivers us. We need God!

Mature Christians understand and have lived this out. "My brethren, count it all joy when you fall into various trials, knowing that the testing of your faith produces patience. But let patience have its perfect work, that you may be perfect and complete, lacking nothing" (James 1:2–4). Look out! Here come the obstacles!

When things are going well, we tend to forget about God. When we're confronted with an obstacle, we suddenly remember to pray. God knows how we are. The Bible says we should pray without ceasing, but many of us don't—that is, until the devil kicks up some dust, and we have to call on God for help. As we begin to grow up spiritually, we start to remember to pray even when there are no obstacles. That's what God likes! He wants us to be communicating all the time. Jesus prayed all the time and talked to the Father through the communication of prayer. He said He only did what He saw the Father do. The Father talked to Jesus too: "For all things I have heard from my Father I have made known to you" (John 15:15).

Prayer is simply communicating with God. It is often making requests but not always. Sometimes it is just telling Him how much we appreciate Him and thanking Him for what He has done for us. (Don't forget to thank Him when He answers your prayer!) Sometimes it is asking Him what He would like us to do next. Sometimes it is just listening to Him talk to us. He likes all kinds of prayer; in fact, He just likes us! Prayer changes things for us. Prayer can make a way around an obstacle. Sometimes it smashes right through it!

"Rejoice always, pray without ceasing, in everything give thanks; for this is the will of God in Christ Jesus for you" (1 Thessalonians 5:16–18).

If you can't think of something to talk to God about, then just thank Him for all those wonderful blessings in your life. The more you acknowledge what God has done, the more you will see all the other little things He is doing in and around you. He is alive and active in your life, whether you see it or not. Don't you think it is way more fun if we are paying attention and can see what He's doing? God's plan is long term. We are thinking here and now, but He is thinking eternity.

> All praise to God, the Father of our Lord Jesus Christ. It is by his great mercy that we have been born again, because God raised Jesus Christ from the dead. Now we live with great expectation, and we have a priceless inheritance—an inheritance that is kept in heaven for you, pure and undefiled, beyond the reach of change and decay. And through your faith, God is protecting you by his power until you receive this salvation, which is ready to be revealed on the last day for all to see. So be truly glad. There is wonderful joy ahead, even though you must endure many trials for a little while. These trials will show that your faith is genuine. It is being tested as fire tests and purifies gold—though your faith is far more precious than mere gold. So when your faith remains strong through many trials, it will bring you much praise and glory and honor on the day when Jesus Christ is revealed to the whole world. (1 Peter 1: 3–7 NLT)

Our end reward is a sure thing. We already have a priceless inheritance reserved for us in heaven. It's safe. *You* are safe. So we don't go through trials in order to get to heaven but so that we can grow our faith and grow our character, which, after we are born again, becomes the character of our Father God instead of the character of the devil. It's a process of growing that takes time. This is God's purpose for keeping us here on the earth. We are learning.

The end "reward" for the devil is also a sure thing. He is *not* safe. Isaiah 14:24–27 tells us,

> The Lord of hosts has sworn, saying, "Surely as I have thought, so it shall come to pass, and as I have purposed, so it shall stand: That I will break the Assyrian (Satan) in My land (Israel), and on the mountains tread him underfoot. Then his yoke shall be removed from them, and his burden removed from their shoulders. This is the purpose that is purposed against the whole earth, and this is the hand that is stretched out over all the nations, For the Lord of hosts has purposed, and who will annul it? His hand is stretched out and who will turn it back?"

God is using the devil to help train us, but when his value as a training tool is over, there will no longer be a reason or purpose for the devil to be here, causing all this mess. His time will be up.

So the Devil Is Still Here, But What Can He Actually Do?

This Bible study is not meant to cause fear but to expose all the crazy things the devil has got going on, so we will be aware and not fall for his tricks. The devil has been around for a long time and has a whole network operation. He's got his fingers into everything. Once you start unraveling the thread of his involvement, it's like a government conspiracy movie. His influence seems to be everywhere, but let's draw some parameters. First of all, the devil himself is not like God. He can only be in one place at a time, whereas God is literally everywhere. (That's called omnipresence.) The devil does not know everything like God does (omniscience). The devil does not have all the power like God (omnipotence), so Satan is limited. He does have a network of demons, though, that serve him, and so he can organize and spread out doing more damage than he could do alone. But just like a cellphone network, demons are not everywhere, and even though there are a bunch of them, they are limited in number. So along with the information to come, keep in mind that these are things he is able to do but is not necessarily doing them everywhere to every single person 24-7. This network is vast, but it is not invincible. They, like him, make lots of mistakes. Ezekiel 28 tells us that Satan's pride corrupted his wisdom and that he defiled his own sanctuaries with all his shenanigans. The word translated here as "defiled" comes from the Hebrew *chalal*, which means to bore (a hole into), to wound, to dissolve, or to profane. He has made his own sanctuaries, his palace, his innermost sacred places, his kingdom, demons included, weaker by his actions. We should not be afraid of them. They should instead be very afraid of us.

Demons all know that Jesus won the victory over them, and their final punishment draws nearer every day. The Bible says that Satan drew one-third of the angels to his side (Revelation 12:4). Those became the demons. Even though we don't know how many thousands or millions that represents, we know that leaves two-thirds of the angels that remain and still serve God. There are way more on our side than his side.

Second Corinthians 2:11 talks about his devices, "Lest Satan should get an advantage of us: for we are not ignorant of his devices." The word *device* is defined as a thing made or adapted for a particular purpose, especially a piece of mechanical or electronic equipment; a plan, method, or trick with a particular aim. What is the aim? To steal, kill, and destroy the people God loves and the planet He created for them. The Bible definition tells us a bit more. The word *devices* comes from the Greek *noema*, meaning perception (i.e., purpose or the intellect, disposition, mind, thought). It comes from the root word *noieo*, meaning to exercise the mind (observe), i.e., to comprehend, heed, consider, perceive, think, understand. In other words, Satan's devices are primarily mind-related. He uses thoughts, memories, feelings, perceptions, ideas, imaginations, etc. This is where our struggle and ultimate victory for truth is fought. God's Word is the truth. The devil is lying. Remember, don't let these things about the devil's abilities scare you. He has already been defeated at the cross, and his power over you, if you are born again, is only what you *allow* him to have.

Be a Gulliver

If you have never read *Gulliver's Travels*, it is about a man who sails to a strange land where all the people are very tiny, and so he looks like a giant. He is shipwrecked and washes up on the beach, and while he lies there unconscious, the little people try to tie him down with their strongest cords because they are afraid of him. They tie down his hair and his clothes and anything they can so he won't be able to move. He seems to be totally immobilized, paralyzed, and then he wakes up. He is a giant. The little dinky cords they wrapped him in break immediately as soon as he begins to sit up. This is a picture of the Church, tied up by Satan and his team. It looks like he has thought of everything and has all this power, but in reality, Jesus has given *us* the authority and power over him. We just need to wake up. As soon as we sit up, those bondages will break from around us, and we will be free. So read this with the idea that you will *never* let him have dominion in your life. You belong to Jesus, and He is your King. He will protect you and teach you how to counter every attack from the loser devil and his crew. Those who do not know Jesus (the Word of God) may not fare as well. Now let's be more specific.

The main strategy of the devil is deception. He is a con artist and a trickster. He sets up traps and snares to trick us into making decisions that are bad for us and will lead us away from God's protection and blessings. Matthew 16:23 says, "And having turned, He (Jesus) said to Peter, 'Get behind Me, Satan! You are a stumbling block to Me. For your thoughts are not of the things of God, but the things of men.'"

The word used here for stumbling block, or offense, in some translations, means a snare, a trap. The devil tried to snare Jesus by getting Him to think protectively about Himself. But that wasn't God's purpose, and Jesus exposed the lie. The devil tries to trick us, snare us, trap us, stop us, so that we cannot fulfill our destinies, the call of God on our lives. When we fall for his deception, we may end up going around and around in circles, stuck in an emotional turmoil, trapped in unforgiveness, chronically ill, never making progress until it is too late and our lives on earth are over. If we don't know that this is a possibility, we will assume that life has just been hard and unfair for us. Some people blame God for the obstacles in their lives, and that hinders their relationship with the Father that loves them. It is imperative that we expose the intent and devices of our enemy because our best defense is knowing what's really going on.

Satan's most successful deception is that he does not exist. His second is that he doesn't matter.

The devil is a pathological liar. Of course, he is! Deception is his game. He lies all day long. He accuses, he slanders, he twists and spins the truth, and if you believe him, he will convince you that black is white and up is down. He will try to sell you swamp land and the Brooklyn Bridge. Conversely, lying is a big deal to God. He hates it. Jesus said, "I am the way, the truth, and the life…" (John 10:10). Not only is lying the opposite of what God likes, but it is the opposite of who He *is*. The devil tries to get you to lie constantly. If you get in a habit of lying as a way out of trouble or just for the fun of it, you are setting yourself up for demonic activity. There is such a thing as a lying spirit. If a lying spirit sets up camp in your mind, you will find yourself lying when you didn't even "need to." The real trouble begins when you want to tell the truth, and no one believes you. Like the boy who cried wolf, once you get a reputation for being a liar, it is very hard to change people's minds in your favor. Don't do it! Lies are traps. Also good to remember is that if the devil is spreading a lie, then the opposite of the lie must be true. If the lie is that you are sick, the truth is that you are well. If the lie is that someone doesn't like you, the truth is that they really like you. Try to get in the habit of turning those negative thoughts around to make them into victory statements. You'll be glad you did!

The devil has a loud roar. He doesn't just whisper his lying and intimidating thoughts quietly, although that can be how it starts out at first. If you appear not to be paying attention to him, he screams louder and louder in your head until you use the name of Jesus against him. He can be relentless if he thinks there is a chance you might capitulate.

His goal is to wear you down so you will finally agree with him, whether it is in the area of fear, sickness, depression, unforgiveness, immorality, or whatever button he chooses to push to get you to react in his favor. The scripture says, "Be sober, be vigilant, because your adversary the devil walks about like a roaring lion, seeking whom he may devour" (1 Peter 5:8). Lions that are growing old and weak use their last defense, the loud roar, to try to strike fear in approaching predators. *Who is the devil's predator? You are!* A born-again, Spirit-filled believer is the dreaded enemy of the devil because in the name of Jesus, we can cast him out. The devil hopes he can scare you and make you afraid of him so you won't notice that he is, in reality, a loudmouth with no teeth, no authority. Jesus has *all* the authority. He told his disciples, and we are included, "Behold, I give you authority to trample on serpents and scorpions, and over all the power of the enemy, and nothing shall by any means hurt you" (Luke 10:19). That statement made Jesus happy. "In that hour, Jesus rejoiced in the Spirit and said, I thank You, Father, Lord of heaven and earth, that You have hidden these things from the wise and prudent and revealed them to babes. Even so, Father, for so it seemed good in Your sight" (Luke 10:21). Jesus rejoices at the thought of us taking down the devil. Tee-hee! Talk about a plot twist! So don't wait until the devil has talked and talked your ear off. Tell him to go away in the name of Jesus right in the beginning of his sales pitch. Hang up the phone!

The devil profiles people. Satan and his crew cannot read minds, but they have been around long enough to figure out what you might be thinking. They know human beings, they study them. They know you and study you. They are looking for a weakness that they can exploit and use against you. That's why the Bible tells us to live moral, peaceful, selfless lives, walking in the character of our Father God, who cannot be exploited by the devil. It's for our own good. He knows that in our flesh (our mortal bodies and minds), we are selfish, greedy, vain, and insecure. These are weaknesses that can be used against us to ruin our relationships and cause us to fail in our endeavors. And then when we are depressed, full of fear, and hopeless, the devil thinks we will turn against God. Many times his plan works, so he keeps trying it, but once we are born again, we are able to counter those fleshly desires with a new desire to be like God, who is unselfish, patient, humble, loving, and secure. Plan foiled!

The devil uses our emotions against us. We all have human emotions. We were created in the image of God, and He has emotions. Joy, peaceful feelings, love, affection, excitement, hope, expectation, secure feelings are all good emotions that God has blessed us with. The devil is not going to encourage those because it's not to his advantage. On the other hand, negative emotions like anger can be manipulated and magnified to an extent that they cause real damage to our lives. Jealousy, envy, fear, panic, greed, hatred, rage, insecurity, strife, violence, depression, hopelessness, confusion, lust, and many more are all susceptible to magnification by the devil. There are spirits that personify these ugly emotions and when you allow yourself to accept those things in your life, the devil considers it an open door to come in and harass you.

By **accepting something in your life**, I mean accepting it as belonging to you, being a part of your own identity, the real you. Emotions alone are not actually a part of us. We exhibit them. We use them, if you will. You could be feeling peaceful one minute, and then something happens to surprise you and you could be in panic mode the next. Emotions come and go according to our responses to daily situations.

You are not excited or hopeful or envious every minute, but if you let yourself be talked into assuming negative emotions as being part of your personal identity, saying to yourself, "Well, that's who I am, I'm shy, I'm angry, I'm jealous, I'm depressed," then the demons will be "high-fiving" in delight and will encourage that thinking.

Once an evil spirit has settled comfortably in your mind, it can become a stronghold of *irrational* thinking and irrational behavior. *Key words to locating a demonic presence: irrational, unusual, out of balance, weird, and crazy.* You do and say things you would never do or say because you have been blinded to the truth, and so you no longer listen to it. All you hear is the coaxing of the evil spirit. Your emotion, whichever one has been targeted, becomes super charged, so to speak, and seems way out of balance to the situation. Have you ever noticed someone who is subject to bursts of irrational temper? Irrational fear and panic attacks? Blind jealousy? Bitter hatred for minor reasons? It is quite possible that these people have "help" from the dark side. Those demons need to be bound in the spirit and escorted out.

If left alone, these evil spirits invite others to join them. It is no longer the person himself that has to give permission for those demons to enter (Luke 11:24–26). That is how an opening to a demon of jealousy can escalate into oppression by demons of hatred, violence, and murder, etc. And that is how someone can become eventually possessed (completely taken over). However dire and dangerous as that sounds, though, our Savior, Jesus the King, showed us how to cast them out!

The devil steals from us. Jesus called him a thief. He and his thugs can cause theft or loss in your life in any number of ways. When you lose things through theft or through accident, natural disaster, all the so-called "acts of God" written on insurance policies, this is most likely the devil stealing from you. Or "acts of the devil" can be more subtle. Things can just leak out of your life, and there seems to be no reason for it. Your money doesn't go as far as it used to, your relationships seem to be headed in the wrong direction, your health isn't as robust as it used to be, etc. He steals your stuff, your health, your joy, your progress, and your time. But when time is lost, things take too long; months or years of ineffectiveness go by, and you feel like you will never have that time back to succeed in some area of your life, I want you to know that *God can restore* the effects of that time stolen from you by the devil. Relationships can be interfered with and lost, stock markets can crash, finances can be stolen, peace and joy can be stolen, but God is the *restorer* of all things. The trick is to identify who is behind the theft, cast him out, and lock your spiritual doors and windows so it won't happen again.

Then pray and ask the Lord to restore everything that has been lost. He will.

If you have lost a loved one, know that God understands your loss and weeps with you. Isaiah 53:4 says, "Surely, He has borne our griefs and carried our sorrows…" Although your loved one has passed, God can send new relationships into your life, not to replace the other but to help fill the aching hole that loss can make in your life. In fact, He would like to fill it with Himself if you will let Him. When you are filled with the Spirit of God, He brings along love and joy and the peace that passes all understanding. You are able to live and love again. That is restoration. I have some personal experience with this process myself. God is faithful always and is true to His name, the Comforter. And as believers, we know that we will see our loved ones again, never to be parted for all of eternity. What an amazing promise! The world does not and cannot promise anything like that.

The devil is a murderer. This seems to be a hard concept for people to understand. They attribute to God the power to give life, which is true, and they attribute to God the ability to take it, but there is another who can take it and frequently does. We all have an appointed time to die (Ecclesiastes 3:2), but it is God's idea that we live a long life. "You shall walk in all the way that the Lord your God has commanded you, that you may live, and that it may go well with you, and that you may live long in the land that you shall possess" (Deuteronomy 5:33). But we live in a fallen world, one where sin is rampant, and the payment for sin is death. Romans 6:23 puts it this way: "The wages of sin is death." Satan, as god of this world, has set himself up as judge and executioner over sinners, and he has no mercy. Why do many people die young? Why do fatal accidents occur? If you don't realize that there is an enemy causing these things, you may think that God is causing them. But Jesus was very clear about that. He said, it is the devil that comes to steal, *kill,* and destroy (John 10:10). Jesus came to *give life* and that more abundantly. God, when speaking to Satan in Job 2:6, says, "Behold, he (Job) is in your hand, but spare his life." In other words, the normal pattern would be for Satan to take Job's life. God was restraining him in this instance, but Jesus gave us the authority over Satan now, so now *we* need to do the restraining.

The devil is a legalist. He doesn't care what the circumstances or reasons are and why you do or say what you do or say. If you at any time for any reason side with him, even temporarily, he will count that as a victory and an open invitation from you to come into your life and make a big mess. It reminds me of the game "You *said…*" we played as children.

Mom says, "Don't run in kitchen." You run in the living room.

Mom says, "I told you not to run."

We say, "You didn't say we couldn't run in the living room. You *said* the kitchen!"

Mom says, "You know what I meant."

But the devil plays that game, and he doesn't care what you *mean*. He only cares what you *say*.

For instance, if you say things like, "I'm getting sick…," "I'm going to get fired…," "I'm so stupid…," "Nothing goes right for me…," "Cancer runs in my family…," etc., you are, in the devil's opinion, giving him the green light to actually make those things come to pass in your life, even if you don't really mean what you are saying. *Don't agree with him or his agenda—ever!* Everything you say can and will be held against you in his perverted court of law. But as I said before, he makes mistakes, he's not everywhere, and he can't hear everything. If I slip up and say something dumb, I try to immediately cancel it out by saying what the Word says. As an example, if I forget myself, being led by emotions at the time, I say, "I'm so stupid!" My spirit objects immediately with, "No, you're not!" So out loud, to myself but audibly, I say, "Oops, no, I'm *not* stupid". First Corinthians 2:16 tells us we have the mind of Christ, and He is super smart! I don't want the devil messing with my brain. Our words can condemn us, and our words can vindicate us. Jesus said in

Matthew 12:37, "For by your words you will be justified, and by your words you will be condemned." We don't want to give the devil any "legal" reason to come in and mess up our lives.

What about Job?

People love to quote Job 1:21 at funerals. "And he said: 'Naked I came from my mother's womb, And naked shall I return there. The Lord gave, and the Lord has taken away; Blessed be the name of the Lord.'" But God doesn't take away life prematurely. Let that sink in. Some well-meaning folks claim things like God "needed another angel in heaven," so He took someone's brand-new baby. That certainly does not make any sense. Why not just keep it there then? God is sensible. In Isaiah 1:18, God says, "Come now, and let us reason together..." God is reasonable. Taking innocent young life is not reasonable or sensible. It is not God's way. God is all about life. In fact, He's all about abundant life (John 10:10). Ephesians 6:2–3 tells us, "'Honor your father and mother,' which is the first commandment with promise: that it may be well with you and *you may live long on the earth.*"

Using Job's quote is not an accurate picture of the will of God. For one thing, this wasn't God saying it, it was Job. Lots of people say things in the Bible that are not truths. The truth is, right before Job's words, God has a conversation with—guess who? Satan. The devil says, "Have you not made a hedge around him (Job), around all his household, and around all that he has on every side? You have blessed the work of his hands, and his possessions have increased in the land. [That sounds like God.] But now stretch forth Your hand and touch all that he has, and he will surely curse

You to Your face!" Not a nice guy, that Satan. Anyway, God replies, "Behold all that he has in your power; only do not lay a hand on his person." Job's donkeys, oxen, sheep, camels, servants, and seven sons and three daughters were all killed that day. Who killed them all? The murdering-thief devil, that's who. The devil was sure Job would fall apart and turn against God, but surprisingly, he didn't.

You may be wondering why God would even allow the devil to get away with this. I know I did. But there was a reason. There was already a crack in the hedge around Job's life. The devil was able to gain access to Job through his *fear*. Job was worried that his children were sinning.

Job 1:4–5 says,

> And his sons would go and feast in their houses, each on his appointed day, and would send and invite their three sisters to eat and drink with them, So it was, when the days of feasting had run their course, that Job would send and sanctify them, and he would rise early in the morning and offer burnt offerings according to the number of them all. For Job said, "It may be that my sons have sinned and cursed God in their hearts." This Job did regularly.

Maybe they were or maybe they weren't sinning and acting crazy, we don't know, but Job was afraid they were. (He knew them better than we do.) The thing is, Job was not just a little worried, but he was filled with fear. He knew he was a blessed man and that everything he had was a gift from God. He was afraid his children were sinning, and he was afraid that the blessings of God would stop either because of that or maybe just because God had changed His mind, giving and then taking away. He said, "For the thing which I greatly feared is come upon me, and that which I was afraid of is come unto me" (Job 3:25). "Greatly feared" is our clue to Job's problem. The Hebrew word *greatly* here means "vehemently." Lots of fear.

As a side note about God allowing Satan to attack Job, what God said was, "He is in your hands." If we interpret that to mean, "Here, I'm giving him into your hands," we think God has literally helped the devil to destroy Job. But if we interpret that to mean, "He is already in your hands due to him being filled with fear," we get a different perspective. We know God is all about life and not about death. He does not have a split personality.

The devil uses fear to intimidate and paralyze his victims. Like a serpent that spits out poison to paralyze its victims, one of the devil's biggest tactics is to scare you with the possibility of destruction. It is not the real thing, you understand, just the fear of it. That alone can change even a strong someone into a quivering pile of mush. But if you realize that fear is a weapon being used against you and that you and the fear are two separate things, you can speak to the fear and command it to leave in the name of Jesus. It will obey you.

Fear attracts the devil. Fear is the opposite of faith and works like an open door for demons to come in and bring destruction in your life. So get a grip and don't be afraid. "Trust in the Lord with all your heart and lean not on your own understanding. In all your ways acknowledge Him, And He shall direct your paths" (Proverbs 3:5–6). Turn your fear into faith, which attracts *God!*

Jesus said, "Don't be afraid," or "Fear not," many times, including once when a man had asked Him to come and heal his daughter. As Jesus was going with him, a messenger came up and told the man his daughter was already dead, but Jesus's reaction was to say, "Don't be afraid, only believe, and she will be made well" (Luke 8:50). He healed her and brought her back to life. That is what faith versus fear can do. Counter the fear thoughts with the Word of God and with faith, and you will beat the devil every time. There are all kinds of testimonies (stories) about people who have conquered cancer and other scary diseases by their faith in the Word of God.

Fear cancels out faith, stops God, and allows the devil to work in your life.

Faith cancels out fear, stops the devil, and allows God to work in your life.

If there is a flu epidemic coming around, don't fall for it right away. Don't say, "I know I'll get the flu this year. I get it every year. It'll probably turn into pneumonia like it did last time. Maybe it will kill me this time." Saying things like that are fear-based and the opposite of what God wants us to say. We should say something more like, "Thank God, He is protecting me, and I won't get the flu this year!" A statement like that stops the devil in his tracks. He doesn't know how to work with that. It confuses him because most people go with the negative flow. Most of the time, we see good results, miraculous results by speaking the Word. We are in training. We are still learning. We don't throw everything out at one minor defeat. Jesus didn't quit, and neither do we. We are in this war for the long haul. So what if the enemy wins a battle occasionally? We won the war!

We know by the Bible account of Job that the devil is able to kill and destroy. In Job's story, there was another conversation with God. Satan whined, "'Skin for skin! Yes, all that a man has he will give for his life. But stretch out Your hand now and touch his (Job's) bone and his flesh, and he will surely curse You to Your face!' And the Lord said to Satan, 'Behold, he is in your hand, but spare his life. So Satan went out from the presence of the Lord and struck Job with painful boils from the sole of his foot to the crown of his head'" (Job 1:4–7). This leads us to the next thing the devil can do.

The devil uses sickness and disease. Satan has surrounded himself with a hoard of demons that imitate symptoms of sicknesses and all kinds of diseases, just like they imitate our emotions. These demonic powers can manipulate your feelings and your body to the extent that you let them. Sickness and disease are a part of the curse of this world, but demons can also mimic symptoms that, left alone, will be just as annoying and deadly as the real thing. These are fake symptoms, but they have the ability to turn real if the person accepts them as real. If it looks like you have some sort of sickness and you feel the pain of it, you will probably believe that you really have it. But that is not necessarily so. Jesus showed us that. The accounts of Jesus healing in the Gospels are often linked with casting out demons. Some people that came to Him were obviously demon-possessed in their minds as demonstrated by demonic convulsions, seizures, and weird evidence, but some demon-afflicted people had symptoms of sicknesses. No problem for Jesus. He healed the blind, the lame, the mentally ill, fevers, leprosy, fake demon symptoms, and everything else.

> When evening had come, they brought to Him many who were demon possessed. And He cast out the spirits with a word, and healed all who were sick, that it might be fulfilled which was spoken by Isaiah the prophet, saying: "He Himself took our infirmities and bore our sicknesses." (Matthew 8:16–17)

Do you see how the scriptures connect the two problems? When the demons were cast out, then the symptoms were eliminated.

> As they went out, behold, they brought to Him a man, mute and demon possessed. And when the demon was cast out, the mute spoke.
> (Matthew 9:32–33)

> Then one of the crowd answered and said, Teacher, I brought to you my son who has a mute spirit. And whenever it seizes him, it throws him down; he foams at the mouth, gnashes his teeth, and becomes rigid… When Jesus saw that the people came running together, He rebuked the unclean spirit, saying to it; "Deaf and dumb spirit, I command you, come out of him and enter him no more!" (Mark 9: 17–18, 25)

In these scripture account, the spirit is named with the symptom it caused. We know there is a mute spirit and a deaf and dumb spirit. These are symptoms of a physical nature, not just spiritual.

And behold, there was a woman who had a spirit
of infirmity eighteen years, and was bent over and
could in no way raise herself up. But when Jesus
saw her, He called her to Him and said to her,
"Woman, you are loosed from your infirmity."
And He laid His hands on her, and immediately
she was made straight, and glorified God.
(Luke 13:11–12)

We know by this that there is an evil spirit of infirmity.
The definition of the Greek word for infirmity here is:
feebleness of body or mind, malady, frailty, disease, infirmity,
sickness, weakness. So evil spirits exist that can mimic disease,
sickness, weakness, etc.

The account in Luke goes on to explain,

But the ruler of the synagogue answered with
indignation, because Jesus had healed on the
Sabbath; and he said to the crowd, "There are
six days on which men ought to work; therefore
come and be healed on them, and not on the
Sabbath day." The Lord then answered and said,
"Hypocrite! Does not each one of you on the
Sabbath loose his ox or donkey from the stall,
and lead it away to water it? So ought not this
woman, being a daughter of Abraham, whom
Satan has bound—think of it—for eighteen
years, be loosed from this bond on the Sabbath?"

Here is another account of healing.

Now He (Jesus) arose from the synagogue
and entered Simon's house. But Simon's wife's

mother was sick with a high fever, and they made request of Him concerning her. So He stood over her and rebuked the fever, and it left her. And immediately she arose and served them.
(Luke 4:39)

Jesus rebuked the fever. We don't as a rule rebuke things that can't help themselves. So what was Jesus admonishing? The evil spirit behind it, the spirit masquerading as a fever symptom in the woman's body.

Okay, so are all symptoms of sickness and disease caused by demons? No, of course not. There are not enough demons on the earth to pull that off. We live in a fallen, cursed world where things are not going as God planned them originally. Disease germs exist, viruses exist, accidents occur, and bad things sometimes happen. But what we are saying here is that there is also an influence from the demonic realm that likes to mimic these things to use against us. They get a kick out of faking you out. What you don't know can hurt you, but if his game is exposed, the devil won't be as successful. He likes to work in the dark, and we are turning the lights on. We are exposing the devil's antics following in Jesus's footsteps. "How God anointed Jesus of Nazareth with the Holy Ghost and with power: who went about doing good, and healing all that were oppressed of the devil; for God was with him" (Acts 10:38).

It is God's will that you be whole and well. The Greek word for "salvation" in the Bible includes healing. "By His stripes (whip lacerations on His body), you have been healed" (1 Peter 2:24). For those of us who have never heard that before, it might seem too good to be true. Look around, isn't everybody fighting sickness or pain of some sort, especially as they get older? If God wanted everyone healed, why are they still getting sick? This is a good question to ask. The Bible supports God's will is to heal, not give sickness and disease. Adam was not sick. Heaven is not filled with diseased people. When it is up to God, people are whole and well. But if it is up to the devil…that's another story. The way you fight this demonic strategy is the same way you fight the others—through faith, not fear.

Does God Use Sickness to Teach Us Things?

Some of us are skeptical about the devil and attribute to God everything that happens, good or bad. After all, He is God, they think, so He must be in charge. (If you were God, wouldn't you want to be in charge?) Well, the truth is, He is in charge in general, but He gave authority to man in the garden to rule the planet and has never taken it back. Man gave it to the devil. So here we are. People have tried to come up with a reason for why bad things happen on the earth aside from the devil—we don't like to talk about him. If bad things have to happen, why do they happen to good people just minding their own business? They reason that because God's ways are higher than our ways, bad things like accidents or sickness must somehow really be *good* things in His eyes. You may have heard it said that God uses sickness to teach us things, or maybe someone you know thought God put them in the hospital to slow them down, give them time to think about their lives and prioritize or something to that effect. Maybe there has been something good that came out of a bad situation, but that's because God has intervened and used the opportunity to our advantage. *He brings good out of bad situations*. He doesn't cause them.

People usually want to give God the benefit of the doubt. They want to think He is good, so when trying to figure out why sickness exists (apart from the devil), they reason that sickness could be a good thing (in some convoluted way), that maybe you might learn something from it. But just imagine teaching your own children that way. Think of what you are saying. Would you put cancer on your child to teach him how good you are? Would you put dementia on an older person? Would you put blindness on a teenager, cripple a mom with three kids? Obviously, no. Those things are terrible. And we know that God is good always. He is all love. God loves to restore, not destroy. Instead of putting sickness on us, taking lives prematurely, He laid His own life down for us, taking our sins and sickness on the cross. Jesus came to show us God's heart and His will. He never put sickness on anyone but healed everyone that came to Him. We would expect that if God uses all that sickness and calamity to bless us, Jesus would have shown that side at least once during His earthly ministry. But no, He only healed, He helped, He restored, He raised people from the dead. He is the resurrection, not the death.

Death vs. Sleep

First Corinthians 15:26 says, "The last enemy that will be destroyed is death." The Bible calls death an enemy! In fact, death is thrown into the lake of fire in Revelation 20:14, along with his pal, the devil. God is not into death. He is all light. John says in Him there is no darkness whatsoever. Are we better than God? Do we love our children more than He loves His? No, a thousand times no! God is way more kind, more thoughtful, more helpful, more loving than we are. But if that's all true, and it is, why are sickness and disease so rampant? We know God is not and cannot be the author of ugly and devastatingly painful disease. But we *do* know someone who is a killer and a thief. We know someone who is a terrorist and will torture, twist, and maim with glee. He is a thug that wouldn't hesitate to take a life before its time. That guy is the devil.

Someone might say, "Well, we all have to die in order to go to heaven, so that's why we have sickness." My answer to that is, many folks in the Bible did not die of any sickness. Enoch did not get sick in order to die (Genesis 5:24). Elijah did not get sick in order to die (2 Kings 2:11). Stephen fell asleep in the middle of being stoned (Acts 7:60), David "died of a good old age" (1 Chronicles 29:28). Moses died at 120 years old on the mountain with God, not of sickness. The scripture says, "His eyes were not dim, nor his natural vigor diminished" (Deuteronomy 34:7). It is not necessary for us to be sick in order to die. Jesus showed us how to live, and He showed us how to die. He released His spirit. "And Jesus cried out again with a loud voice, and yielded up His spirit" (Matthew 27:50). "So when Jesus had received the sour wine, He said, 'It is finished!' And bowing His head, He gave up His spirit" (John 19:30).

When your allotted time is up, you don't have to come down with some crazy sickness or disease in your body to help you out of this world. God will receive your spirit. He will help you, and it will seem like you are merely falling asleep. That's what Jesus called dying, falling asleep.

"After He had said this, He went on to tell them, 'Our friend Lazarus has fallen asleep; but I am going there to wake him up,' His disciples replied, 'Lord, if he sleeps, he will get better.' Jesus had been speaking of his death, but His disciples thought He meant natural sleep" (John 11:11–13).

Here are a few more scriptures about that:

> Then falling on his knees, he (Stephen) cried out with a loud voice, "Lord, do not hold this sin against them!" Having said this, he fell asleep. (Acts 7:60)

> And Solomon slept with his fathers and was buried in the city of his father David. (1 Kings 11:43)

> After that He appeared to more than five hundred brethren at one time, most of whom remain until now, but some have fallen asleep. (1 Corinthians 15:6)

We tend to interpret scripture in the light of what we already think is true. Instead, we should interpret what we know to be true by the light of the scriptures. Instead of assuming "falling asleep" to mean some foul sickness had to occur in this person's body, let's assume these people really just fell asleep. Doctors call it "natural causes," for lack of a better term. When your body dies, your heart will stop, and probably your lungs will fill up with fluid. Cardiac arrest and pneumonia are the common *go-to* explanations of death when there is no other obvious cause. If we are able to die of natural causes (basically falling asleep and not waking up), then sickness is revealed to be our enemy, not a necessary part of the circle of life. Why do we so easily accept that as you get older, you will lose your health? Could it be that the devil has played one of his tricks on us, and the reality is that we can live long and strong? Deuteronomy 34:7 tells us about Moses, "Moses was a hundred and twenty years old when he died, yet his eyes were not weak, nor his strength gone." Hmmm. Don't we really know inside that sickness is bad? That's why we go to the doctor and take medicine in order to get better.

If we really thought it was God's will to make us sick, why would we keep trying to get rid of it?

The transition from this life to the next is like walking through a door. We are simply changed from one body to another. "Behold, I tell you a mystery: We shall not all sleep, but we shall all be changed—in a moment, in the twinkling of an eye…for this corruptible must put on incorruption, and this mortal must put on immortality…then shall be brought to pass the saying that is written: 'Death is swallowed up in victory'" (1 Corinthians 15:51–54).

Demon Possession

Now back to the weirdo devil. Even though demons can possess people (and they like to show off with all that foaming and growling and such), every fake sickness symptom is *not* evidence of demon possession. Possession is a major takeover of someone's spirit, a deeper level than his or her mind and body. That doesn't happen overnight. Most of the time, demons are just harassing people, oppressing them in their minds and bodies. *Born-again believers can be temporarily oppressed by a demon but never possessed.* The Holy Spirit has taken up residence in our spirits, and there is no room for a demon to move in. So if you are fighting some sort of oppression, like a sickness or depression that doesn't want to go away, don't imagine you are possessed by a demon and panic and get hysterical, but do pray and ask God to help you learn how to cast it out. God will not do it for you.

That's your job. You have the authority on earth. You can use the name of Jesus just like His disciples in the Bible did. They had great results, and so will you!

The Devil's Strategy

At the risk of redundancy, let us restate the obvious. There is no secret here. The devil wants to *steal, kill, and destroy.* Jesus said, "The thief does not come except to steal and to kill and to destroy" (John 10:10). Some people have been fooled into thinking the devil will help them in some way. He lies to them and tells them he will give them power, maybe riches, or fame. He offered the same to Jesus, but Jesus turned him down. Some people have made what they think are deals with the devil. They agree to worship him if he makes them successful in this life. Come to find out, the devil is a liar and a cheat, and he doesn't keep agreements or stick to the deals he has made. He has no code of honor. He uses people for his own ends and throws them away when he is done. He has no respect for people or human life. Who do you think is behind the push to encourage abortion? The truth is, the only things the thief, or the devil, will do for you is steal, kill, and destroy. He does not come except to do those things. He will steal your joy, your peace, your stuff, and your life if you let him. He will interfere with your health, your job, your social life, your children, your marriage, your plans, and your future *if you let him.* He will attempt to bring destruction in whatever way he can. He is like the mean kid who stomps on everyone's carefully built sandcastles. He is like the kid who uses a magnifying glass to burn ants in the sun (if you ever did this, the idea didn't come from you). Then there's his serious side. He can carefully scheme and build a complicated plot to destroy, but he can also get distracted. He doesn't see everything. He has lost the big war, and gradually this fact is driving him more crazy than he already is. He is like the villain in a movie that realizes his evil plot is falling apart, and he gets increasingly anxious, which leads to him being sloppy and eventually exposed through his own mistakes.

The way the devil's strategy operates is like this. He clouds our minds with false thoughts, anti-God thoughts, fearful thoughts, insecurity, anger, hatred, unforgiveness, greed, and lusts of all kinds. He gets us all upset about stuff for no reason. He will send conflicting thoughts just to cause confusion. We conclude it's *us* thinking all that! It sounds like us in our minds. We think we are the ones who are crazy, but it's not us—it's him. On the other hand, God is *not* the author of confusion. He is the author of peace. "For God is not the author of confusion but of peace, as in all the churches of the saints" (1 Corinthians 14:33).

Demons like to start quarrels, stir up strife, encourage people to hold grudges, fill our minds with thoughts of insecurity, lie to us that our loved ones don't love us back, strangers don't like us, friends are traitors, people can't be trusted, a white lie is okay, sexual immorality and perversity are okay (it's not hurting anybody) and that it's okay to steal if no one catches you. They constantly accuse other people (in our minds) of whatever they think we don't like. They twist morality issues, parade thoughts of unfairness, loneliness, boredom, anything and everything that goes against the laws and heart of God. The devil is the personification of lawlessness, and he attempts to lure us and sway us into his way of thinking. *What we think will greatly influence what we say*, and what we say will influence how we act. The battle begins in the mind, in the thoughts which we assume to be secret and private, but demons can whisper thoughts in your head. If you spend time reading and listening to the Word of God or God's thoughts, you will know right away when a demonic thought tries to weasel its way into your mind. You respond, "No, I don't think that way," and toss that thought out. It's not that hard.

If he can't get us to move in an ungodly direction in our thought life, then he might throw physical obstacles in our way. Demons can influence obstacles to move and influence animals. Satan possessed a serpent's body in the Garden of Eden. When Jesus cast out demons one time, they requested to go into a herd of pigs. We know they went into the pigs because the pigs all ran in fear down the steep bank into the sea (Matthew 8:28–34). Demonic activity can cause crops to fail, natural disasters that destroy (Jesus rebuked the winds and the storm that had been set up to stop Him from crossing to the other side of the lake), and accidents to happen. He can also cause things to go right when it is to his advantage. He can turn himself into an angel of light and make something look good that is really not, tempting us to go down the wrong path.

The Occult

Think of what you have heard about paranormal activity, seances, ghosts, witchcraft, and spells. Those things are all influenced by demons, so we Christians don't participate in them. New age pyramids, psychics, mind control, crystals, incense, potions, telepathy, Ouija boards, any type of thing, activity, or practice that puts another entity, Mother Nature, angels, or man himself at the center of power instead of God is commonly referred to as the occult, which operates in the realm of darkness, and we are not of that kingdom. White magic or white witchcraft is no different than black. That is a deception. The same demons are behind it.

Halloween

Should we participate in Halloween? Think about what Halloween represents. It glamorizes the occult, demons, death, skeletons, fear, murder, perversion, witchcraft, etc., all in the name of fun. Couldn't we think of something else that would be fun instead? Halloween is a high holy day to the Satanic worship community. And every year Halloween seems to take on a more significant presence in our culture. This is not an accident. It is part of the devil's agenda to make evil and darkness seem like fun and harmless. Don't be fooled. It may start out to seem like fun, but it's not harmless. Years ago, I remember an ad campaign to warn children not to get into cars with strangers. The picture was of a man offering candy as an incentive to climb in. "Want some candy, little girl?" Is this what is going on here?

Demons are also involved in fake UFO activity and any kind of fake alien encounters. Bigfoot, Loch Ness monster sightings, abominable snowman, you name it, the devil is behind it. What do you think will be the narrative after Christians disappear in the rapture? Aliens took them? Most likely. People are already intrigued by that storyline and ready to accept it. Ironically, the reality is that in all of our scientific quest for life on other planets, there has never been any evidence that life exists anywhere other than the Earth. On the other hand, our earth, which God made for us to live on, is teeming with life. From microscopic life in a drop of pond water to huge elephants in Africa to the bazillions of birds in the trees and skies to the countless fish in the sea, there is pretty much life everywhere on planet Earth. Even the most remote parts of the world, Antarctica, the bottom of the ocean, the equator, the Sahara desert, everywhere there is some kind of life-form. Compare that with any other planet ever discovered. They have nothing, no life anywhere. At best, there could have maybe, possibly at one time, existed the chemicals necessary for a living being, but there is no real evidence of life now. The planet Earth is the place where God planted His garden and placed His Adam. The planet Earth is where Adam was given dominion as a training for rulership. God asked Adam to name all the animals and enjoy his dominion on the earth. Perhaps God will continue creating where He left off once Jesus returns. Perhaps He will create new planets and He will let us name the new creatures on them. We know we will rule and reign with Jesus, but the scriptures do not specify where. We know that time and space will no longer be issues for us in our immortal bodies, so interplanetary travel will not only be possible but also probable, given mankind's curiosity about outer space.

Worship of Saints and Angels

Some people have been taught that God is so holy (which He is) and so busy (which He can easily handle) that we shouldn't bother Him about every little thing. They are taught that the saints that have gone before us will watch out for us and take care of all our little problems if we ask them instead. They have been taught that these saints will intercede for us, try to convince God to do things for us. My grandma used to tell us to pray to St. Anthony if you lost something. Some people think of angels this way as well. We know that angels are around and are helping us, but nowhere in the Bible does it ever say to pray to angels or pray to saints. In fact, in the Book of Revelation, John has this experience with an angel.

Now I, John, saw and heard these things. And when I heard and saw, I fell down to worship before the feet of the angel who showed me these things. Then he said to me, "See that you do not do that. For I am your fellow servant, and of your brethren the prophets, and of those that keep the words of this book. Worship God."
(Revelation 22:8–9)

The only person we pray to is God. We don't need any other mediator but Jesus. He said the Father loves us and desires to give us what we pray for when we ask Him. We don't need anyone to convince Him. Anything else that we set up in between us and God is an idol, and idolatry is expressly forbidden.

Worship of Mary

Many people have also been taught to pray to Mary, the mother of Jesus. Many people attribute special characteristics to Mary that are not scriptural and lead to idolatry. Some people pray to Mary, hoping she will talk Jesus into helping them because she is His mother and has some sort of authority over Him. That is ridiculous! Jesus is the one (the Word of God) that originally created Mary. She was the human vessel chosen to carry His human body as a baby and to care for Him until He reached adulthood. That's all. It was a tremendous privilege, but let's not read into her role something that is not there. She is not in the same position as God. She was not born sinless, nor did she ascend to heaven like Jesus. These are false teachings. Mary is like us, a born-again Christian. She was there in the upper room on the Day of Pentecost with the other disciples and was baptized in the

Holy Spirit just like the other disciples. She even had other children, which some people have not been taught. Matthew 12:47–49 tells us, "Someone told Him, 'Look, Your mother and brothers are standing outside, wanting to speak to You.' But Jesus replied, 'Who is My mother, and who are My brothers?' Pointing to His disciples, He said, 'Here are My mother and My brothers…'" Jesus honored His mother, but He clearly separated His earthly connection with her from His ministry. In Luke 11:27–28, a woman from the crowd calls out to Jesus, "Blessed is the womb that bore You and the breasts that nursed You!" But He said, "More than that, blessed are those who hear the word of God and keep it!" He elevated all believers to a higher level or position than that of the position of His earthly mother. When He hung on the cross, John 19:26–27 tells us, "When Jesus therefore saw His mother, and the disciple whom Jesus loved (John) standing by, He said to His mother, 'Woman, behold your son!' Then He said to the disciple, 'Behold your mother!' And from that hour that disciple took her into his own home." This shows Jesus again honoring Mary but clearly separating His earthly connection with her from His ministry. Absolutely nowhere in the scriptures are we taught to pray to Mary or worship her as if she was part of the Trinity. That is idolatry. She did not die for us, Jesus did. She did not shed her own blood to remove our sins, Jesus did that. Interestingly, Mary is called by her worshipers the queen of heaven, as if she somehow mysteriously became the mother of us all. The "queen of heaven," referred to in Jeremiah 7:18, 44:15–18, is a demonic influence that down through the years has been called by many names, such as Astarte, Ashtoreh, Doumu (Chinese goddess), Isis, Demeter, and Inanna. Is this what we are really worshiping when we think we are worshiping

Mary? Let's not put Mary into the same category as the demons. She is one of us.

Wrap Up

So to wrap this up, the devil uses devices against people. These devices are usually related to lying thoughts fed into the mind, but they can be physical too. Demons or evil spirits can oppress individuals by their proximity or presence, just as the presence of God sets them free. As we said before, demons masquerade as symptoms of illness, fear, doubt and unbelief, mental instability, anger, strife, addictions, lying, and sexual perversion, to name a few. *The devil is a bully*. Remember, when Jesus was on the earth, he was constantly casting out demons that were causing illness symptoms like fevers, blindness, deafness, and insanity. Does that mean all illness is caused by the devil? No, as I said before, not necessarily. We live in a fallen world where viruses and disease have been allowed to roam. But that said, if you get sick, remember that there is a possibility it is just a demonic smoke screen and not even real. Go to the doctor, take medication, but also pray for healing, take Communion, and tell that sickness to go in the name of Jesus! You may be surprised at how fast you get better. If you are dealing with something else that seems oddly wrong or inappropriate, irrational, tell that thing or feeling to go in the name of Jesus as well. We have the legal right to use the name of Jesus, and as Christians, we have the authority to cast out demons in His name. Even a baby Christian has this authority. Be a Gulliver! Stir up your faith and get rid of those invaders! Tell them no! Jesus is the boss, not them! And by the delegated authority we have been given in Jesus's name here on the earth, *we* are the boss and still not them!

Living Without Oppression

I heard it said once that the devil cannot get very far with a grateful man. That's why the Bible says to give thanks continually. If you are wise, you will let the Holy Spirit guide you, and when you read something in the Bible like, "Be slow to anger," take the advice and control that temper of yours! Forgive people that step on your toes, even the ones who have really messed up your life. God said it is a better way to operate. God has forgiven you so you can afford to forgive someone else. Do it for God, and He will help you. Remember, God is not trying to ruin your life by putting lots of conditions on His love for you. He already loves you. These other guidelines are to help us *live free from oppression.*

The thing is, when you sidestep the will of God, when you sin, you open the door to the devil and his crew. It's as if you are saying, "Here I am, a little defenseless sheep, all alone. Come and get me, wolf!" That is so unnecessary, my friends. If you realize you have stepped over into darkness or strayed down a dark road just a little too far, just repent and run back home again. The blood of Jesus cleanses us continually. Our Savior is there to save us continually day or night. Jesus is not worried about the devil. He kicked his backside. He gave us the authority to walk in that same confidence, knowing that we are called by His name. When you tell a demon to go in the name of Jesus, it has to go! God is backing you up with all the power of His throne.

Remember, demons cannot read your mind, but they can whisper thoughts into it. We think our thoughts are all originating with us, but not so, according to the scriptures. What do you do if a thought comes into your mind that is contrary to what you normally would have thought? Judge it by the Word of God. Does the thought agree with God, or does it agree more with the devil's agenda? Does it bring peace or confusion? Is it kind or mean-spirited? Does it go in a dark direction or a light direction? Does it lead you to God or away from Him? You get it. That's what Christians need to do all day long. We can get good at it if we practice. I have had the craziest thoughts down through the years. I remember driving along and having the thought enter my head that I should drive off the road into a tree just to see what it would feel like. Crazy, right? I knew enough about the devil's devices to cast that thought aside. Just because you have a thought doesn't mean you have to agree with it or act on it. Be wise!

How to Fight Depression

Depression is often a spiritual thing. It is an attack of oppression, thoughts that suppress the joy in your life by telling you all is hopeless and that your future is bleak. Depression starts by thoughts, lies from the enemy. There is a demonic influence behind self-pity. The way to combat depression is by replacing dark thoughts with light thoughts from God, thoughts of good, thoughts of peace, and thoughts of victory. "The Word says…" is like someone throwing you a rope when you have fallen into a deep pit. Listening to praise and worship music also dispels demonic oppression. When David played his harp for King Saul in 1 Samuel 16:23 the evil spirit that was bothering him departed. Demons can't stay around praise music, so if you don't have any handy, make up a praise song and sing from your heart like it says in Ephesians 5:19, "Speaking to one another with psalms, hymns, and songs from the Spirit. Sing and make music from your heart to the Lord."

Praying in the spirit edifies us and gets rid of oppression. Get together with other Christians and talk about how good Jesus is. Remember the prayers He has answered in the past and how He has blessed you so often. Do something nice for someone else. Get your mind off you and on to someone or something else. These are tools for you to use when depression tries to intimidate you and paralyze you. The Bible says that the joy of the Lord is your strength. You can laugh your way out of depression. Isn't that funny, I mean, amazing? The devil hates to be laughed at! He is full of pride. Think of a funny joke, watch a funny show, or just laugh at the devil. The Bible says, "A merry heart does good like a medicine" (Proverbs 17:22). There is something very healing about having a good belly laugh. LOL!

> For the weapons of our warfare [against evil] are not carnal [worldly] but mighty in God for pulling down strongholds [long held beliefs], casting down arguments [and imaginations] and every high thing that exalts itself against the knowledge of God, bringing every thought into captivity to the obedience of Christ...
> (2 Corinthians 10:4–5)

The responsibility is ours to *think right*.

Who Are You Agreeing With?

The devil's agenda is to steal your joy, make your life miserable, turn you against God, and, if that doesn't work, take you out. We know the devil can put thoughts in our heads. He can't read our minds, so how does he know if his tactic worked? How does he know if he tricked us? He can't read our minds, but he knows what we're thinking by what we *say out loud* and by what our actions tell him. If his trick worked, he will use it again and again. Say, for instance, he puts a thought in your head that your boss thinks you are not doing a good job. If you don't say anything in agreement with that thought or you say something opposite to that thought, the devil will conclude that the trick didn't work. He will try something else, but if you listen to the lie and respond by telling a coworker or your spouse, "No matter what I do, my boss doesn't think I'm doing a good job," you have just agreed with the devil, and he knows he has you right where he wants you. He will keep up the lies and the pressure. Eventually those thoughts will escalate into feelings of discouragement and hopelessness. Then you don't work as hard because in your mind it won't make any difference. The devil sees his tactic is working and continues to hammer similar thoughts into your mind. Before you know it, things have spiraled, and you are fired. And it was all based on a lie.

If he can do that to you, he can do that to others around you too. He can influence the way they think about you. The quickest way to diffuse a lie from the devil is to communicate the truth. Talk to your boss, talk to your friends, your family, saying kind and loving words. Don't let the lies the devil has told about you take root in someone's heart, and likewise, don't let the lies he has told you about others grow unchallenged. Believe the best about people, especially people that love you. "Love bears all things, believes all things, hopes all things, endures all things" (1 Corinthians 13:7). Remember who the real enemy is! The devil lies about everything. These are some examples. You could probably come up with fifty more in five minutes.

- Your wife or husband doesn't understand you.

- Your neighbor is spying on you.

- Everyone else gets a good night's sleep but you.

- You can eat four pieces of cake, it won't matter.

- You are so fat no one could love you.

- What about you? What about your feelings?

- Why don't you try those drugs just once to see what it feels like.

- Everybody's doing it (one of his favorites).

- That's impossible.

- God doesn't care about you—He let that bad thing happen.

- Nobody's watching.

- Everything bad always happens to you.

- With your rotten luck…

- It figures things would go wrong for you.

The devil's strategy doesn't stop at one thought or one attack. One thought leads to another and another. Thoughts can become overwhelming and oppressive. The picture here is more like a group of wild dogs attacking a deer. One dog nips at its heels, and then another nips at its side until it falls, and then the whole pack of dogs comes and tears it to pieces. The agenda is to take us down, not just annoy us. And then next will be our families and our friends. He will turn a good marriage into a divorce or a financially prosperous business into a bankruptcy. It is not pretty. You can't just let the devil have his way once, hoping he will then leave you alone.

But God has thought of everything. He loves you and is training you for the future to reign as a king. So even though this is battle training, and it can get intense, Jesus has already won the victory, and we are just playing it out. And don't forget, the Church is a team effort. Find another Christian and pray together. The Bible says that one can chase a thousand, and two can put ten thousand to flight (Deuteronomy 32:30). And Matthew 18:19 says, "Again, truly I tell you that if two of you on earth agree about anything they ask for, it will be done for them by My Father in heaven."

Little g god of This World

A good thing to also keep in mind is that the devil, though he is defeated in the long run, is still operating as "god" of this world. He is especially involved in things matching his own interests, the system of commerce, the political system, the music culture, idolatry of all kinds, religions, and the education system. He is also interested in keeping people from becoming born again, learning the truth, having a relationship with God, or having relationships with anybody. He's "livin'" the dream, but it's a delusion and coming to an end. The closer it gets to the return of Jesus, our true King, the more the devil tries to grasp power. He is now at the point of making a play for global domination, something he's never been able to pull off before. Up until now, he's been trying to be devious and subtle, but it's now or never for him, and he knows it. The devil likes to operate in the dark, but we are children of the day, and our job is to shine the light of the truth right in the middle of his lie. That is how you bust it wide open. Light destroys dark.

Lambs among Wolves

Keeping us alone and away from the herd is a tactic the wolf uses. Luke 10:3 says, "Behold, I send you out as lambs among wolves," and Matthew 7:15 also says, "Beware of false prophets, who come to you in sheep's clothing, but inwardly they are ravenous wolves." In other words, be alert! There are things going on that look normal (sheep's clothing) but aren't on your side. We need the Word of God to reveal the dangers and the Holy Spirit to guide us. Thankfully, Jesus is the Good Shepherd! He will send someone to come and find you if you lose your way and get stuck in a bush or fall down a ravine. But if you stay with the herd, you are less likely to have all those problems. Hebrews 10:25 says, "Not giving up meeting together, as some are in the habit of doing, but encouraging one another—and all the more as you see the Day approaching." If you don't have a church, go find one. Look for a church that teaches from the Bible and has a victorious and faith-filled message. Stick together!

Knowing your enemy is the best way to avoid the pitfalls of life. You will still have trials, but you have weapons! That is our next lesson.

Discussion Questions

1. Why does God allow the devil to bother us?
2. How often should we pray? Why?
3. The mind is the battleground for a Christian. How do we fight off evil thoughts?

LESSON 12

KNOW YOUR WEAPONS—OR FIGHTING BACK

We know that God allows Satan and his crew to be here for our training purposes. Jesus made it clear that we are to *resist the devil.* In fact, James 4:7 says, "Submit yourselves, then, to God. Resist the devil, and he will flee from you." We are going through resistance training. In the natural, resistance training is a form of exercise that improves muscular strength and endurance. Resistance training is simply a form of training in which you're working against some type of force that "resists" your movement, forcing you to work those muscles and get stronger. This is what the devil does for us. As we resist him, and by that, I mean we don't just accept his encroaching advance into our territory and our lives; we are exercising spiritual muscles and gaining strength and endurance. How do we resist? We tell him no!

Here are a couple of other scriptures that confirm our statements.

> For everyone who lives on milk [basic, elemental teachings of the faith] is still an infant, inexperienced in the message of righteousness. But solid food is for the mature, who by constant use have trained their senses to distinguish good from evil. (Hebrews 5:13–14 BSB)

> Stay alert! Watch out for your great enemy, the devil. He prowls around like a roaring lion,

looking for someone to devour. Stand firm against him, and be strong in your faith. Remember that your family of believers all over the world is going through the same kind of suffering you are. (1 Peter 5:8–9 NLT)

The purpose for trials is to test and purify, like gold in a furnace. Gold ore taken out of the ground must be purified before its real value can be determined. Gold is melted and mixed with chemicals to extract the impurities out of it. The melting point of gold is 1,948 degrees Fahrenheit, and regular fire heat can't melt it. So if you are feeling like you have been going through an especially intense season of life where everything seems to be going wrong, perhaps the furnace has been heated up to close to 2,000 degrees in order to purify you and make you come out shining like gold! "In all this you greatly rejoice, though now for a little while you may have had to suffer grief in all kinds of trials. These have come so that the proven genuineness of your faith—of greater worth than gold, which perishes even though refined by fire—may result in praise, glory, and honor when Jesus Christ is revealed" (1 Peter 1:6–7). The scriptures describe us often as gold or silver. We are precious to Him. "But He knows the way that I take; when He has tried me, I shall come out as gold" (Job 23:10).

Interestingly, real, pure gold, when exposed to the flame, will get brighter after a while as it gets hotter but will not darken. Imitation gold, like fool's gold (actually pyrite, an iron sulfide) and objects made of brass, iron, or copper alloys, will darken or change color when exposed to a fire's heat. God is after purity in our lives, pure motives, pure actions, pure speech, pure love, pure understanding, and pure worship. He wants us to shine!

As we resist the devil, we grow stronger in our faith toward God and burn brighter, just like resistance training in the natural helps firm our muscles and makes us look good. What are we resisting? The devil's agenda: anti-truth, anti-good, anti-moral, anti-law, and just anti-God. When you realize those things are at the bottom of what's happening, you know by experience that is *not* the way to go. Resist! Don't go along with it. Turn around! Say no!

Our Strategy

Our initial response to some random attack of the enemy should be to walk away, ignore him. Don't play with him. In his games, he wins, you lose. If his attack is using thoughts, cast them away and fill your mind with opposite thoughts, preferably scripture. You've heard of the "glass is half empty" guy. That is what the lies of the enemy tend to be. They tend to be negative and depressing, offering you what is the worst that could happen. If those types of thoughts come to you, decide that you will be the "glass is half full" guy. Turn your thoughts toward what is the *best* that could happen. With a God on your side who loves you, the best-case scenario is where you should place your faith. Scripture says: "Nothing is impossible with God," "No weapon formed against you will prosper," "I wish above all things that you may prosper and be in health even as your soul prospers," "A thousand shall fall at my side, ten thousand at my right hand, but it shall not come near me," "No plague shall come near my dwelling," "God works all things together for good for them that are called according to His purpose."

Exposing Lies and Fear

The enemy's most common weapons are lies and fear. Our strategy is focused on exposing the lies and quelling the fear. Remember, the devil is a liar. Therefore, the opposite of what he is whispering or screaming at you must be the truth. FEAR = False Evidence Appearing Real.

One time, I was driving along, and I felt a pain in my chest. I didn't respond immediately, but the thought entered my head that I was beginning to have a heart attack. I tried to ignore the thought, but for one second, I entertained the idea that yes, I must be having a heart attack, and from then on, I couldn't shake it off. I began to imagine myself either crashing the car or ending up in the emergency room at the hospital. I saw my funeral and my family trying to deal with a loss. The thoughts became ridiculously loud in my mind. I was past the point of ignoring them. I went back and forth thinking it might be the devil, but fear was all around me, and it seemed like it was real. I prayed, asking the Lord for wisdom. The lying thoughts bombarded me. So in a desperate attempt to stop the madness, and I believe God was answering my prayer, I turned the car around and drove to a walk-in emergency clinic. They checked my heart and did tests, and as a result, the doctor told me, "Whatever it was, it was *not* your heart." I was, of course, very relieved, but more than that, I had learned again that the devil is a liar and that the presence of fear does not necessarily mean anything is wrong. The truth was, I was fine. Fear can be a response to real danger, but *fear can also be a false response*, and there is *no* imminent danger.

Second Timothy 1:7 says that "God has not given us a spirit of fear, but of power, love and a sound mind." One morning, I woke up to thoughts of fear all around me. Everything I had been praying for seemed hopeless. I knew it was fear, but I was like a deer in the headlights. It was paralyzing. Suddenly, the Holy Spirit spoke to me, saying, "Where did that fear come from?" I thought for a second, well, it didn't come from God. I knew 2 Timothy 1:7, so I began to quote that scripture out loud. I said it a few times, and after a few minutes, the fear began to subside. I was able to shake it off because I measured it against the Word of God. God always tells the truth. If we believe that scripture, we can say fear doesn't come from God, and that means it has no power over us.

Capture Those Enemy Thoughts

> For the weapons of our warfare [against evil] are not carnal [worldly] but mighty in God for pulling down strongholds [long held beliefs], casting down arguments [and imaginations] and every high thing that exalts itself against the knowledge of God, bringing every thought into captivity to the obedience of Christ...
> (2 Corinthians 10:4–5)

The idea here is that *thoughts can be our enemy*—not every thought, just the ones that lie to us.

The Word of God tells us how to fight them. Pull down beliefs, even long-held beliefs that do not match with the truth of the Word of God. Cast down arguments that side against the Word of God. Other translations use the word *imaginations*. We are to cast down any kind of ideas that form against the truth. Those thoughts are our enemy, and there is no place for them in our minds. We have the mind of Christ, 1 Corinthians 2:16 tells us. Jesus is not imagining all sorts of weird things that counter the truth, right? We are to bring every thought into *captivity*. That means we capture the enemy's thoughts and put them in "thought jail." We don't spend time thinking about them, rolling them around in our minds for fun.

If the attack is not just thoughts, if a demon has riled up someone to argue verbally with you, refuse to enter the fight. Walk away. If you are switching TV channels or YouTube videos and something inappropriate comes your way, don't fall for it. Pictures produce thoughts. That's the whole point of pictures. Temptation seeps in through our eyes and ears. Walk away or, in this case, keep switching to something else. You get it. The enemy has not changed and uses the same tactics he used in the Garden of Eden with Adam and Eve. Demons are prowling around looking for an opening, searching for a way to get into your life and mess it up. They try things, like a burglar tries a locked door. But if you are on the alert, the Holy Spirit will expose those tactics, and you will be able to sidestep the trap. And…in the event that you may need something a little stronger in your stand against the enemy, the Lord has got you covered. This is where the weapons of our warfare come in handy. We have a whole arsenal at our disposal! Let's take a look at those. We'll start with the offensive weapons.

Offensive Weapon #1 The Mighty Name of Jesus

Jesus defeated him and, therefore, Satan has legally lost the war. However, as long as he remains on the scene, it is up to us, the Church, to enforce the victory. We are the sheriff's deputies. He said in Matthew 28, "All authority has been given to Me, therefore (you) go…" Jesus has given us the use of His name, like a sheriff's badge, and we have every right to use it, to set ourselves free and help set others free too. It is an offensive weapon. It's like saying, "Stop in the name of the law!" Jesus sent out seventy of His disciples to preach the gospel and heal the sick. They returned with joy, saying, "Lord, even the demons are subject to us in Your name!" (Luke 10:17).

In the Book of Acts, the early Church was threatened by religious leaders and ordered not to use the name of Jesus because it was causing miraculous healings and making them look bad.

> And when they had set them in the midst, they asked, "By what power or by what name have you done this?" Then Peter, filled with the Holy Spirit, said to them, "Rulers of the people and elders of Israel… let it be known to you all to all the people of Israel, that by the name of Jesus Christ of Nazareth, whom you crucified, whom God raised from the dead, by Him this man stands here before you whole… Nor is there salvation in any other, for there is no other name under heaven given among men by which we must be saved." (Acts 4:7–12)

> The council confirmed among themselves, saying, "What shall we do to these men? For indeed that a notable miracle has been done through them is evident to all who dwell in Jerusalem and we cannot deny it. But so that it spreads no further among the people, let us severely threaten them, that from now on they speak to no man in this name." So they called them and commanded

them not to speak at all nor teach in the name of Jesus. But Peter and John answered and said to them, "Whether it is right in the sight of God to listen to you more than to God, you judge. For we cannot but speak the things we have seen and heard." (Acts 4:15–20)

It was the religious leaders that threatened the disciples not to use the name of Jesus, but who was behind that intimidation, and who was it that gave them the idea that the biggest problem was the use of that name? You guessed it, the devil.

The Devil Must Bow to the Name of Jesus

Therefore God also has highly exalted Him (Jesus) and given Him the name which is above every name, that at the name of Jesus every knee should bow, of those in heaven, and of those on earth, and of those under the earth, and that every tongue should confess that Jesus Christ is Lord, to the glory of God the Father. (Philippians 2:9–11)

Whenever you or those around you are in trouble, use the name of Jesus to stop the devil in his tracks! It is Jesus that is Lord, not the devil. And we have been empowered to enforce that!

Offensive Weapon #2
The Power of the Blood of Jesus

The blood of Jesus is also a weapon, both defensive and offensive. The blood of Jesus was so powerful that it freed the whole world from sin. Like a nuclear blast, the debt of everyone ever born and ever to be born was forgiven, the slate wiped clean. In the Old Testament, the Israelites were held captive as slaves by the Egyptians. God raised up Moses to deliver the people from the Pharaoh and to bring them to a land God had promised to give them. Pharaoh, a symbol of the devil, who holds people captive and enslaved in his kingdom of darkness, refused to let the people go. As a result, God sent ten different plagues to the country of Egypt. The last one was a curse on the first-born of every Egyptian family, including the house of Pharaoh. The firstborn in every family died when the destroyer came through the land. The Israelites were safe from the plague because God (through Moses) had told them how to block it! He told each family to sacrifice a lamb and smear the blood over their doorposts and hide inside the house. So that's what they did. When the destroyer saw the blood, he had to "pass over" their houses, leaving the firstborn untouched. The Jews continue to celebrate the Feast of the Passover to this day. This true story is filled with symbolism, or as they call it in Bible study, typology.

Pharaoh = Type of Satan, holding people captive, making them slaves in his kingdom

Israelites = Type of the Church

Blood of the lamb = Type of the Blood of Jesus, the Lamb of God

Destroyer = Type of the devil again, looking for a way in to cause death and destruction

The same blocking technique works today. You still need the blood of a lamb, only we don't have to personally sacrifice that lamb (thank goodness!) because it has already been done.

God did the hard part for us. John 1:29 says, "The next day John saw Jesus coming toward him, and said, 'Behold! The Lamb of God who takes away the sin of the world!'" Our lamb is Jesus.

"All who dwell on the earth will worship him, whose names have not been written in the Book of Life of the Lamb slain from the foundation of the world" (Revelation 13:8).

When you "apply" the blood of Jesus by faith to your house or to your situation, the destroyer must pass over you and not harm you. "Applying the blood" just means acknowledging your faith in its power to heal you and deliver you. "For the life of the flesh is in the blood, and I have given it to you upon the altar to make atonement for your souls; for it is the blood that makes atonement for the soul" (Leviticus 17:11– NKJV). Another Bible version reads: "For the life of a creature is in the blood, and I have given it to you to make atonement for yourselves on the altar; it is the blood that makes atonement for one's life" (NIV). The payment for sin from the beginning has always been death or shedding of blood, representing death. When the destroyer sees that blood has already been given or a death has already occurred in payment for the sin, he must pass over you and move on.

How Does the Blood of Jesus Protect Us against the Devil?

The blood of Jesus has removed our sin, which is the culprit, and why the devil has had any legal right to oppress us in the past. But now, as believers, with no sin laid to our charge and our robe of righteousness shining in his face, the devil has zero ground with which to proceed against us. Our righteousness is the very own righteousness of God! "Righteousness and justice are the foundation of your

(God's) throne," Psalm 89:14 declares. Satan cannot, I repeat, cannot fight against that. One of my favorite promises in the Bible is, "'No weapon formed against you shall prosper, and every tongue which rises against you in judgment You shall condemn. This is the heritage of the servants of the Lord, And their righteousness is from Me,' says the Lord" (Isaiah 54:17). The KJV says, "Their righteousness is of me." The Hebrew word for righteousness means "rightness." It refers to God being personified truth, right *all* the time. He is so right that He is never wrong, He is pure rightness. That is amazing and glorious! God will never lose a battle with the devil. But then it gets better!

Second Corinthians 5:21 says, "For He [God] made Him who knew no sin (Jesus) to be sin for us, that we might become the righteousness of God in Him." In Christ, in Jesus, *we* become the righteousness of God. Not our own human rightness but God's. And there is no higher level. Applying the blood of Jesus reminds us of that transaction. And when we stand before the enemy with all of our rightness shining out and looking just like Jesus, he gets confused. There is nothing he can do. His plans and plots fail. However, since he is a lunatic and a bully, he still tries, but we are here to remind him that the blood of Jesus beats him every time.

The devil has no legal authority over someone who has been declared forgiven by God. He knows this, but he is not sure if *you* know it. And the devil is a legalist all the way (except when it comes to himself). Remember the game children play. Someone says to his brother, "You can't wear my new sneakers." Then the brother thinks to himself, *You didn't say I couldn't wear your old sneakers.* Or your mom says, "You can't eat that candy before dinner," and you think, *She didn't say I couldn't eat this candy!* The devil plays with the words and twists them like a shady lawyer to get what he wants. If we are unaware of his tactics, we will fall victim to his nonsense every time. He might attack you with a pain in your leg, then when you command him to stop, the pain switches to your other leg because you didn't specify *that* one.

Using the blood of Jesus as a weapon works something like this. Say you are fighting an attack in some area of your life, you might pray something like this: "Lord, I thank you for the blood of Jesus! That precious blood that you gave for me on the cross has cleansed me from my sin and made me righteous. When you look at me, you see a perfect child who has never sinned. I pray now that the power of that blood will surround me and protect me from whatever the devil has planned against me. He has to pass over me when he sees the blood. I thank you and give you all the praise and all the glory for this victory!" or "Lord, I thank you for your blood that has removed my sin as far as the east is from the west. I apply that blood against the devil and his plans to destroy me now. I push him back out of this situation, and I command him to stop [whatever he's doing] in the name of Jesus!" There are no perfect words to say, just words that show that you understand what the weapon does.

Talking about the blood might sound messy, but it is the very substance that has made atonement or paid the price for our sins. The devil cringes when we talk about the blood of Jesus. Good! People are set free from every oppression of the enemy by the power of the blood of Jesus. Let's *talk about it*! When we take Communion, the bread and the wine (or juice), we remember what Jesus did and acknowledge the power of the blood of Jesus to wash away our sins. Taking Communion is very powerful and another useful tool in our arsenal.

Revelation 12:11 tells us that Christians have overcome the devil "by the blood of the Lamb and by the word of their testimony" When you pray, remember the power of the blood of Jesus. It protects us, just like the blood applied on the doorposts of the Israelites protected them from the destroyer on the first Passover. Let the destroyer pass right over you. Nothing to see here, devil, keep on movin'.

Offensive Weapon # 3 The Word of God

The Bible tells us that the Word of God (the scripture) is like a sword, which is clearly an offensive weapon (Ephesians 6:17). God has given us exceedingly great and precious promises (2 Peter 1:4) that we can use to combat the lies that the devil tries to fool us with. When a thought or situation rears its ugly head in our direction, we take one of the promises of God that fits that situation and proclaim it, declare it, meditate on it, pray it, hum it, sing it, "stand" on it by faith. We receive the promise by faith and declare it to be the truth. You speak the scripture or "the truth" out loud, but you can do it privately. It doesn't have to be said in front of anyone else. Not that it can't be, but you are speaking to the spirits behind the lie, and they are invisible. Whatever lie the devil is proposing, it eventually has to crumble in the face of the truth that we dare to believe no matter what we see in the natural. Faith pleases God. We know that because the scripture says that "without faith it is impossible to please God" (Hebrews 11:6). When we believe what He says instead of what the devil says, we are well on our way to defeating the enemy. That is just what Jesus did when He was tempted in the wilderness. He countered every attack with a scripture that plainly said the opposite. He used truth to combat lies (read Luke chapter 4).

Example: suppose the situation is one of sickness. The symptoms assert themselves such as fever or pain. This is just the same as the devil talking to you and saying, "You are so sick! This is the worst pain anyone could ever feel and probably means you will die." Your best response, even though you feel the pain or experience the fever, is to quote a scripture on healing, such as, "By His stripes [marks caused by beating] you were healed" (1 Peter 2:24)—*His* meaning Jesus, *you* meaning you, and *were* meaning it has already happened. In fact, to help you receive it for yourself, you could say, "By His stripes I was already healed." It means the same thing. If the sickness is being caused by a lie from a demon, usually what happens is, after you have quoted a scripture, believing that you receive healing, the symptoms hang on for a little while longer, testing you to see if you really mean what you say. Then they go away. During the course of the situation or trial, you keep on speaking the Word of God (don't just say it once), declaring who He is and what He said over the situation.

Think of it like taking spiritual medicine. A doctor might prescribe something to take three times a day. Do the same with the scripture. Take it three or four or ten times a day. When you say the scripture, your ears will hear it and your faith will get stronger (Romans 10:17). Either the demon will go if he caused the symptoms or the sickness will go if it's caused by something else. You win because Jesus already won. You are enforcing the victory by standing on the Word of God in the face of opposition.

That is how you take the scripture and use it as a sword to defeat the lies of the enemy. Slash! Slash! Take that, you liar! Here is another scenario. Suppose you are in a situation where someone is angry with you. Use the scripture to calm the storm. Proverbs 15:1 says, "A soft answer turns away wrath." So if this is a verbal argument, you soften your words and believe God to turn around the situation. Or if you feel physically threatened, you might use, "No weapon formed against you will prosper And every tongue which rises against you in judgment you shall condemn [or refute]" (Isaiah 54:17). You might not be able to quote it out loud at the moment, but you can say it in your mind and wrap your faith around it. Say it out loud if you can. Again, sometimes it is helpful to make the scriptures more personal to you and your situation by changing the pronoun from *you* to *me*. "No weapon formed against *me* will prosper and every tongue that rises against *me* in judgment *I* will condemn!" It doesn't change the meaning of the scripture, but it does provide a point of contact for your faith. The Amplified Bible says the scripture this way.

> But no weapon that is formed against you shall prosper, and every tongue that shall rise against you in judgment you shall show to be in the wrong. This [peace, righteousness, security, triumph over opposition] is the heritage of the servants of the Lord [those in whom the ideal Servant of the Lord is reproduced]; this is the righteousness or the vindication which they obtain from Me [this is that which I impart to them as their justification], says the Lord.

And this is a very handy scripture to have in your arsenal! Do you see why it is important to know what the scriptures say? Spending time reading the Bible is to your very real benefit! Every scripture you spend time with becomes a sword in your collection or an arrow in your quiver, ready to use to defend and protect your life and your family's lives.

Here's another scripture you can use for physical protection or any other kind of protection for that matter. Jesus said, "Behold I give you authority…over all the power of the enemy and nothing shall by any means hurt you [or say hurt me]!" (Luke 10:19). And another, "A thousand may fall at your [my] side, and ten thousand at your [my] right hand but it shall not come near you [me]" (Psalm 91:7). The Bible is filled with scriptures for protection, deliverance, healing, wisdom, and financial help. He has given us everything we need to succeed in this life, as well as the next life. His Word is eternal and will never be outdated. It is *the truth*. Remember, Jesus said, "I am the way, *the truth,* and the life."

Speak It!

Just knowing what the Bible says about something is not the same as wielding the Word of God as the sword of the Spirit. You have to speak the words, if possible. That activates the sword. Saying, "I can do all things through Christ which gives me strength!" is more powerful than just thinking it. Your spirit hears your voice speak it, and it is by hearing the Word of God that faith grows. Of course, in some cases, like severe sickness, you might not be able to say the words out loud. In that case, speak them deliberately in your mind as if you were saying them out loud. Is it okay to whisper the words? Sure, but if you really want your faith to rise up, don't be shy. When the devil hears you speaking the scriptures, he gets really nervous. When he hears that tone of voice that tells him you mean business, he flees. Let's mean what we say!

Our Armor

In addition to our offensive weapons, we have armor. That's right, armor to protect us! God has given to us everything we need to succeed against the enemy. We are not victims here. The devil should not scare us. He is afraid of *us*! He is so afraid that we will find out the truth about who he is and what Jesus has done. He is afraid that once the Church discovers the power they have, they will ruin all his plans. He's right! Every piece of armor is designed to help and protect us in a special way.

> Finally, my brethren, be strong in the Lord and in the power of His might. Put on the whole armor of God, that you may be able to stand against the wiles of the devil. For we do not wrestle against flesh and blood, but against principalities, against powers, against the rulers of the darkness of this age, against spiritual hosts of wickedness in the heavenly places. Therefore take up the whole armor of God, that you may be able to withstand in the evil day, and having done all, to stand. (Ephesians 6:10–13)

With our armor on, we are fully protected. We are strong *in the Lord* and in the power of *His* might, not ours. Isn't that good news? With that armor on, it's like there is a big tank sitting behind us with its guns aimed at the devil. However, we are told to "put on" and "take up" the armor. It is not on us automatically. You put on the armor by consciously thinking about it and how it will affect you and your situation. Think about what each piece means and how it will protect you.

Stand therefore, having girded your waist with truth [the belt of truth], having put on the breastplate of righteousness, and having shod your feet [you are wearing shoes] with the preparation of the gospel of peace; above all, taking the shield of faith with which you will be able to quench all the fiery darts of the wicked one. And take the helmet of salvation, and the sword of the Spirit, which is the word of God; praying always with all prayer and supplication in the Spirit, being watch-ful to this end with all perseverance and supplication for all the saints. (Ephesians 6:14–18)

Breaking it down, here is what our armor consists of:

1. *Belt of truth*—Truth holds our pants up! Truth exposes the lies of the enemy. There is nothing that will weaken our strength like a lie and nothing that will help to set us free more than the truth. Be brave! Dare to open yourself up to the truth. The Word of God is truth. Start there, finish there. What you see and feel are circumstantial evidence, but they are not the same as truth. Feelings can change, and seeing is colored by your point of view, but truth is solid as a rock. It doesn't change because of your feelings or even because of the culture you currently live in. God *is* truth.

   You can depend on His Word to never change. "Jesus Christ, the same yesterday, today, and forever" (Hebrews 13:8). Knowing the truth will transform you and make you beautiful like you were intended to be. Pontius Pilate, when Jesus was brought to him for judgment, asked Him, "What is truth?" (John 18:38). The correct question would have been, who is truth? The truth was standing right in front of him, and he didn't see it. That is like us sometimes. If you don't know what to look for, you might miss it. The actual truth may be completely different from what you are currently experiencing.

When I was very young, I began to believe a lie about myself. The lie was that nobody wanted to hear what I had to say. The lie took root in my heart, and soon I stopped wanting to talk to people. Everyone thought I was just shy. So did I. I believed that lie for a long time about myself. It was my experience, but it wasn't the truth. I am not the only one this kind of thing has happened to. The devil lies to us all the time. Do a self-check. Is what you have been believing about yourself really true? Think about the people around you. Are you believing the truth about them? Are you believing the truth about the situation you find yourself in? It takes courage to seek the truth because finding the truth means we may have to change the way we have been thinking about something, even ourselves, all along. We may have held on to certain beliefs for a long time, and because they have been there so long, they feel comfortable and right. But in some cases, we have been deceived, and those lies have bound us up, making us into someone we do not want to be. But the truth, Jesus said, will make you free (John 8:32). To find the truth, start with Jesus, the Word of God. Find out what He says about you. Jesus always tells the truth because

He *is* the truth! "I am the way the truth and the life" (John 14:6). If you find the way to the truth, you will find life.

2. *Breastplate of righteousness*—Our confidence in the protection and salvation of God rests in the knowledge that He has given us—just plain out given us—His very own righteousness. Not *our* righteousness but His perfect and spotless way of being right. And God is always right. "If God be for us, who can be against us?" (Romans 8:31). His righteousness is the ultimate covering for our hearts and critical organs. It protects us from the accusations of the devil that say we are not worthy of God's love and blessings. Of course, we are not worthy! Jesus has *made* us worthy. Now God's own righteousness is our legal position with God. He does not see us as the dirty, vagrant criminals that we once were. We are now, because of Jesus, restored by grace and elevated to a position of highest honor in the Kingdom of God. The devil would like to bring us back down to our previous level where he can oppress us. When he starts droning on and on about how worthless we are and how we have totally messed up this time, we need to pick up our breastplates and position them over our hearts and core. This is the part of our bodies that represent our identity and our inner self. Who are we? We are the righteousness of God in Christ! There is nothing the devil can do or say to change that reality if we dare to believe it!

3. *Shoes of the gospel of peace*—This is a readiness to witness and give our testimony of the good news,

readiness to spread the love and peace of Jesus wherever we are. This part of the armor includes the idea of preparing ourselves with the gospel, learning all we can about it to make it understandable to others. People will have questions. How will you answer? Can you explain your own relationship with God? Can you tell about your own experience or give your testimony of how the gospel (good news) took you out of the kingdom of darkness and put you in the Kingdom of Light, and how once you didn't understand but now you do? Putting on your shoes means you are ready to go and ready to share your experience with others.

For whoever calls on the name of the Lord shall be saved How then shall they call on Him in whom they have not believed? And how shall they believe in Him of whom they have not heard? And how shall they hear without a preacher? And how shall they preach unless they are sent? As it is written: How beautiful are the feet of those who preach the gospel of peace, who bring glad tidings of good things! (Romans 10:13–15)

The Bible says we overcome Satan by the blood of Jesus and the *word of our testimony*. (Revelation 12:11).

Those who are wise shall shine like the brightness of the firmament, and those who turn many to righteousness like the stars forever and ever. (Daniel 12:3)

4. *Shield of faith*—This is the piece of armor that helps you quench the fiery darts of the enemy. Fiery darts are the lies he shoots out at us. If one gets in, it can burrow down deep and cause all kinds of trouble, and sometimes it takes a long time to get rid of it. I mentioned before that I was believing a lie about myself. This is what happened. When I was in the second grade, the devil used my teacher to shoot a fiery dart at me. Children are also subject to attacks. I was a very bright and outgoing child. I raised my hand to answer every question. I was excited about learning. My mother fostered that love of learning, teaching me to read before I entered kindergarten. The first-grade teacher had encouraged me to flourish at an accelerated pace. But the second-grade teacher, probably annoyed at my enthusiasm and possibly wanting to encourage other kids, took it in a negative way. I am a teacher, too, so I can see how that could happen. But one day, she spoke these words over me. "Nobody wants to hear from you!" And I believed her. People that are in authority over you, like parents, teachers, bosses, pastors, etc., have influence when they speak things over your life. That statement entered my heart like a fiery dart. From then on, I never raised my hand, never participated in any discussions, and never gave my opinion at school. I wasn't sulking; I was living up to my teacher's expectations. All throughout elementary school, middle school, high school, and even college, this fiery dart became my identity. It was not true, but I accepted it as true, and so I acted like it was true. I became what the lie said I was. I was not naturally a shy person, but I became one.

Do you see that what you feel is not at all the same as truth? That fiery dart was unfortunate for me, to say the least. It changed my personality so that even my own family thought of me as a shy, introverted person. They felt sorry for me, but since none of us knew the Lord at that time, they were unable to understand what had happened and could not help me cast that lie out. Of course, that became part of the problem because they accepted my personality change as the new normal. They supported the lie of the enemy.

So that one fiery dart, supported by the words of those around me, shaped my youth and adulthood—needlessly, I might add. I missed out on more than one opportunity because of my so-called shyness. The poison of that fiery dart spread and created stage fright, fear of certain people and animals, and probably a bunch of other things I couldn't even name. Once one lie gets in, it invites other bits of nonsense to come in with it over time. It's a good idea to remind ourselves that the things we are believing about ourselves, about others, about our situations are vulnerable to attack. It was not until I began to see myself as God sees me that I opened one eye to what was going on. I was well into my adulthood before the lie was exposed to the light of the Word of God and eventually dispelled. The scripture tells us, "Do not conform to the pattern of this world, but be transformed by the renewing of your mind. Then you will be able to test and approve what God's will is—his good, pleasing and perfect will" (Romans 12:2). Thank God for His Word! It set me free from a debilitating lie, something that had bound me and crippled me on the inside for many years.

The shield of faith counters those lie attacks, those fiery darts from the enemy. It lifts up the Word of God like a shield, saying, "Oh no, you don't, devil! I'm going to believe the best, I'm going to believe what the Bible says, I'm going to believe what Jesus says, I'm going to believe and not doubt no matter what I see or hear or feel. Knowing what I know now, I should have said, at least to myself, "No weapon formed against me will prosper and every tongue that rises up against me shall be shown to be wrong! The righteous are bold as a lion! Even if you don't want to hear from me, my heavenly Father loves to hear the sound of my voice!" Faith rises up like a protective dome around us and counters every fiery dart the devil launches against us. We could say this is the Holy Spirit force field of faith. The devil's strategy is to get us to doubt, get us to fear, and, duh, discourage us from talking to other people so we can't share the gospel. But we are believers, not doubters, and we operate in the faith realm, not in fear territory. Glory to God! Sometimes we forget that it is by faith that we obtain our victories. These things are not automatic.

Faith is the key. Faith switches on the power button. Faith and truth work together, faith and righteousness work together, faith and sharing the good news about Jesus work together. Romans 10:17 tells us that faith comes by hearing the Word of God, and the word translated "hearing" is a continuous kind of verb—that is, we need to be hearing and hearing and continuing to hear, not just hearing once. To activate your shield (Holy Spirit force field) and keep it activated, you have to put yourself in a position where you can hear what the scriptures say. Read them, quote them (hearing yourself speak the Word is very effective), listen to someone teach about them, sing them—all of those are good.

5. *Helmet of salvation*—This part of the armor protects your mind, your thoughts. Are you getting the idea that spiritual warfare centers around your thought life? Good, you're on the right track! There are two important strands to the concept of salvation. One is salvation from final judgment. Once we are born again, we are delivered, saved from an eternity in hell, and we have assurance of an eternity with Jesus in heaven or wherever He goes. This state of being is unshakable, and we don't need to worry about it anymore. We are safe. Think about that!

The other kind of salvation has to do with living this life on earth now. It is deliverance from this world's system of operation as well as from the weaknesses of our physical earthly bodies. Just as we obtain eternal salvation of our spirits by faith in the Word of God, we can also have victory over the enemy's world system and our physical "flesh" on a daily basis by faith in the Word. The struggle is always in what we believe. Will we believe what God says, or will we believe what someone else says?

There is right thinking and wrong thinking. Right thinking agrees with God. Now that we are believers, we know we have a choice in what we think. The devil's lie about that has been exposed. We are not obligated to embrace all the random thoughts he bombards us with. As Martin Luther once said, "You cannot keep birds from flying over your head, but you can keep them from building a nest in your hair."

Your thoughts cannot possibly define you unless you let them because some of them have come from the outside and they don't represent you at all. This helmet of salvation protects our minds. The helmet "re-minds" us to think like Jesus. "But we have the mind of Christ" (1 Corinthians 2:16).

"Do not conform to the pattern of this world, but be transformed by the renewing of your mind. Then you will be able to test and approve what God's will is—His good, pleasing and perfect will" (Romans 12:2).

We renew our minds by readjusting and lining up our thinking to what God's Word says.

"Finally, brethren, whatsoever things are true, whatsoever things are honest, whatsoever things are just, whatsoever things are pure, whatsoever things are lovely, whatsoever things are of good report; if there be any virtue, and if there be any praise, think on these things" (Philippians 4:8).

As Christians, we don't just think about junk anymore. We learn to control our thought life. It's actually possible. This is not *mind control*. It is *mind self-control*. Who we are is who God says we are, not the world, not the devil, and not Aunt Suzy. What we can do is based on what God says we can do, not what the guy next door says or what our dad says, or even what the media says. Let the right thoughts, the good thoughts, God's thoughts in and throw the devil's thoughts into thought jail. Better yet, toss them right in the garbage. Keep that helmet on!

6. *Sword of the Spirit*—The only piece of the armor that is specifically used for offense is the Word of God. We discussed this one earlier. Using scripture to fight the attacks of the enemy is the way to go. The sword or swordlike objects were the most dangerous weapons of war they had back in Roman days. They didn't have tanks and machine guns back then. To get a better understanding of this weapon from our culture, try to imagine what this sword represents. This is the Living Word of the Holy Spirit of God Almighty, the second person of the Trinity, who created the universe and all things in it. All things are upheld or kept in motion—planets, the sun, the sea, all sea life, insects, protozoa, gravity, electricity, and the breath of every human being "by the Word of His power" (Hebrews 1:3). We might as well say this piece of the armor is like the tank of the Spirit, or better yet, the nuclear bomb of the Spirit! We see the power of the Word of God in John 18:6, when a detachment of troops and officers from the chief priests and Pharisees came there with lanterns, torches, and weapons to arrest Jesus. All He said was His name, "I Am," and everybody drew back and fell down. This was not a small group of people. The word used here for the soldiers refers to a Roman cohort, which according to Wikipedia means "a standard tactical military unit of a legion. Although

the standard size changed with *time* and situation, it was generally composed of 480 soldiers." The Word of God is powerful!

Now with all your armor on, all clean and shiny, you don't really have to do much. Jesus has already done all the hard stuff. We just stand there and look pretty. *"And having done all, to stand"* means that when trouble comes, we make sure our armor is on and we don't move our faith from that position. Even if the doctor's report doesn't look good, your bank statement doesn't look good, your relationship is looking rocky, the neighbor is threatening you, and the dog is growling, stand in faith and speak the Word of God over your situation. Don't back down and say to yourself that it isn't working just because things didn't change immediately.

Ephesians 6 says, "Stand therefore…" If you don't retreat, the devil will assume you are serious and eventually get tired of waiting for you to blink. He knows he is defeated. You are not stepping out of bounds here. You are just enforcing the victory that Jesus already won. You are drawing a line in the sand, setting a boundary around your life and your family and your stuff. Don't let him steal from you or push you around! Tell him to back off and take a hike! He will leave. He obeyed Jesus, he obeyed all those disciples, and he will obey you too. Stand, therefore!

Other Powerful Weapons

Here are some other weapons in the arsenal that are very powerful. God has totally equipped us for victory in this life.

It is our own lack of understanding that prevents us from accessing any of these in a time of trial.

- *Praise and Worship*—Praising and declaring who God is brings His presence and, as such, involves Him in your circumstances. You want this! His presence dispels darkness and every demon. Worshiping God puts you in a place to receive His protection, and He can give you insight and wisdom for what is going on. Worshiping God places Him in His rightful place, above all, in all and through all. He is our victory over the devil.

- *Praying in the Spirit*—Using the heavenly language God gives through the baptism in the Holy Spirit builds you up, edifies you, makes you strong. This language is the perfect prayer because it is said in words inspired by God and known only to Him so your mind can't mess them up with fear and doubt and unbelief. The devil can't understand it, and it drives him crazy.

- *Intercessory Prayer*—This kind of prayer can address the spiritual realm directly for you or someone else, for a region, a city, or a nation. It uses the Word of God to mess up the plans of principalities and powers that are devised against us. It is advisable for churches and ministries to assemble an intercessory prayer team to regularly support them in prayer. Intercessory prayer can also be used to bind the enemy from interfering in your families and neighborhoods.

- *Fasting*—Jesus recommended fasting in addition to prayer when it comes to casting out certain demons. Fasting is when you decide to deny yourself something you particularly like for a short period of time. It is saying no to your flesh. Usually people fast some type of food or whole meals, for a period of time, but other things can be fasted as well (TV, phone, social activities, etc.). The purpose for fasting is to humble your natural self, body or soul, and elevate and exult or illuminate your spiritual self. So if you were under a vicious attack of the enemy, you might spend extra time praying, reading, and meditating on scriptural, spiritual "food" while denying yourself natural food for a while. Fasting works like a catalyst to help us break through certain stubborn situations. It doesn't force God to do something, but it sharpens our own spiritual eyes and helps us to focus our faith.

Be consistent, persistent, confident, and don't fear. Stay close to God, obey Him, and don't stray away from the flock. You got this!

When Believers Are Awake

He said to them, "Go into all the world and preach the gospel to all creation. Whoever believes and is baptized will be saved, but whoever does not believe will be condemned.

And these signs will accompany those who believe: In my name they will drive out demons; they will speak in new tongues; they will pick up snakes with their hands; and when they drink deadly poison, it will not hurt them at all; they will place their hands on sick people, and they will get well."

> After the Lord Jesus had spoken to them, He was taken up into heaven and He sat at the right hand of God. Then the disciples went out and preached everywhere, and the Lord worked with them and confirmed His word by the signs that accompanied it. (Mark 16:15–20 NIV)

This scripture tells us the last things Jesus said to His disciples before He went back to heaven. Are you a believer? If so, this scripture was written to encourage you. You do have authority in His name to do the things He did. Isn't that awesome?

Ephesians 1:22–23 tells us that we are the body of Christ. He is the head, we are the body, the arms and legs and hands and feet. We are the ones now that walk around and preach the good news, healing people and casting out demons who are causing trouble for people. It not only helps those people, but it is training for us at the same time. Are we perfect at it? No, but we are learning and getting better. When you lay hands on a sick person and pray for him, you should have the expectation that he will get well, if not immediately, then he should begin to get better over time. Your job is to pray; Jesus does the actual healing. You cast out the demon with your words, and Jesus makes him go with the power of the Holy Spirit. Your only responsibility is to be the hands and feet of Jesus. Don't be discouraged if nothing happens every single time. There are other factors at work. One of those is the faith factor. We'll talk about that more in one of the next lessons.

Jesus gave us the mission and said, "Go." He said we would pick up snakes, not run away from them. A snake is a symbol for the devil, since he chose that identity back in beginning in the garden. We are not supposed to be afraid of the devil. He is afraid of us. Even a baby Christian can "pick him up" and hold him helpless in the air. "God has not given us a spirit of fear, but of power, love, and a sound mind" (2 Timothy 1:7). There is a battle going on, and if we are not fighting back, we are not completing the mission. This kingdom is for us, and we have a part to play.

Discussion Questions

1. Which of these weapons do you think you need to focus on in your own life? Why?

2. Do you know of a situation that might require you to, "having done all, to stand"?

3. What is the mission of a Christian according to Mark 16:15–20 in your own words?

LESSON 13

PRAISE AND WORSHIP—WHO'S THE BIG DEAL?

You're watching a movie called *Satan's Delight*. (Why you are watching such a dumb movie, I don't know). During the story, one of the characters stumbles upon a secret society meeting. The members of the society are chanting unintelligible words, singing, dancing, and prostrating themselves on the floor in front of a statue of the devil, while one of them takes an animal and sacrifices it on an altar, blood sprinkling everywhere. The statue seems to come to life, all ugly and gross, with a goat's head and everything. The guy who carries out the sacrifice shouts, "All hail King Lucifer!" Then all the other members begin to shout, "All hail King Lucifer!" The leader's eyes change to make it look like he is now possessed. He leads the others in a procession where each one bows before the statue comes to life. Each one pledges his own life for his master. Some of them are cutting themselves. The leader continues to shout out things like, "All hail! Bow to your king!" And the people's voices get louder as they focus on praising their god. Uh-oh, the leader spots our character who is observing this event from afar and screams to the others, "Kill him!" Hopefully, the guy gets away.

If we asked you what you had just observed in that movie, you would most likely say that the character had discovered a group of devil worshipers. You know this because the members of the society were all totally focused on the object of their affection, in this case, the devil. His assumed presence was there. They didn't seem to care how odd or ridiculous they might look to each other. They were not concerned at all about themselves. Worship is like that. These worshipers were using their whole bodies, dancing, bowing, prostrating (bowing low, lying down face-first) on the floor. They were humbling themselves and exalting their idol. He was all that was important.

Now let's think about what many Christians call worship of *their* God.

If our character would stumble into one of our Christian church services, what would he see? In some churches, the services themselves are referred to as their "worship." What are they doing during these "services"? They are sitting quietly in pews or chairs, possibly listening to a sermon, maybe singing a few songs. I say *maybe* because not everybody sings and not everybody listens. You would certainly not expect a devil worship service to look like that! Why is that? Is it just because the devil is wild and noisy, so people worship in a wild and abandoned way? And God is reserved and quiet, and to please Him, you must be quiet and respectful, not showing any emotion? Uh, no. Something seems wrong with this picture. When we contrast one against another, doesn't it make it look like devil worshipers are better at worshiping than us believers? How can that be? Maybe the problem is a difference in the definition of the word *worship*. Let's look a little deeper into what the Bible says the word *worship* means.

What Is Worship?

The word for worship in the Old Testament is *shachah* *(shaw-kaw)*, meaning to depress, i.e., prostrate in homage to royalty or God, bow oneself down, crouch, fall down (flat), humbly beseech, do (make) obeisance, do reverence, make to stoop, worship. We find this word in passages like, "Yea, he maketh a god and worshipeth it" (Isaiah 44:15), "And the host of heaven worship Thee" (Nehemiah 9:6), "I will worship toward thy holy temple" (Psalm 5:7), and "For thou shalt worship no other gods" (Exodus 34:14). *Shachah* is a physical activity, as well as mental or spiritual investment. This word *worship* is found one hundred times in the Bible. (That's a lot.) This word for worship is used to speak of worship of false gods—and *also of worship to the true God.* Hmmm, you don't say.

Well, someone might argue we are New Testament believers. We are more sophisticated.

Let's see. The New Testament has several words for worship, but the most common is *proskuneo*, meaning to kiss, like a dog licking his master's hand, fawn, or crouch, (fig. or lit.) prostrate oneself in homage to, do reverence, to adore (a person, a presence), to worship. It is very similar to the Old Testament word but with an even *more* intimate and personal relationship. This word means more than to revere; it means to adore, to love. It is, like the Old Testament word *shachah,* a physical activity. This word is found in Hebrews 1:6, "Let all the angels of God worship Him," "For we have seen His star in the east and have come to worship Him" (Matthew 2:2), "If thou will fall down and worship me, (Satan speaking to Jesus here)" (Matthew 4:9), "If any man worship the beast and his image" (Revelation 14:9), "Thou shalt worship the Lord" (Luke 4:8), "They that worship Him must worship in spirit and in truth" (John 4:24), and "The Father seeks such to worship Him" (John 4:23). It is found about sixty times in the Bible. (Notice the same word for worship is used for worship of the devil, the beast, *and* worship of God…hmmm.)

Do they *proskuneo* at your church? Probably not. Bowing our heads is about as close as it gets in some places. And in some places, we might kneel or sit or stand, depending on what they tell us to do. But this is not the same as loving God so much, we can be compared to a dog licking its master's hand, grateful to be allowed to come so close, looking up with adoring eyes, whining to get closer, wanting to jump right up into its master's lap. That is *proskuneo*, the worship of a dog for his master.

Respect vs. Worship

We may walk into a church and immediately get quiet. Respect for God is good, but it is not the same as worship of God. What we have taught in many churches, especially some denominational churches, is to have respect for God and what we consider to be holy things. This is not a bad thing. On the contrary, it is a very good thing. In some nondenominational churches, respect for holy things, or more specifically, a holy environment, seems to be missing to a certain degree, which is sad. However, we can respect someone without worshiping them. God is looking for something deeper from His people. The Father seeks *worshipers* (John 4:23), *proskuneo* worshipers.

A lot of people's attempt at worship of the God that has created them, rescued them, died in their place, and given them everything is just coming to the church building once a week. This is a sacrifice, of course, because they would have rather stayed home, and God understands and is glad you came. But that is something like the kid who only comes home for Christmas and holidays and then complains the whole time that he has to be there. What parent really wants that kind of sacrifice? Parents want the kid who can't wait to see you and leaves his or her comfortable life, dropping everything to come home for the holidays, bringing joy and a loving attitude, ready for a good time. Or better yet, the kid who bought a house on the same street just so he can drop by for coffee every morning and hang out with us. God is our parent, but not the kind where we grow up and move away and live on our own. He is the kind where He builds an addition onto His house for us and our families. He wants us to want to spend time with Him. Many of us, if we're honest, have never learned to enjoy His company. *Proskuneo worship implies that we enjoy being in the presence of God,* and He enjoys us being there. God gave us the example of a dog, not a cat! Everybody knows how dogs are. Dogs run to greet their owners, whine when they go away, stand at the window, waiting and watching for their return, and jump up, trying to lick their faces when they get home, sit at their feet or on their laps, trying to get as close as they can. This, my friends, is where we are going with the worship idea.

Somehow the definition of Christian worship has changed, while other types of worship remain the same. "He worships the ground she walks on," "Aww, that little dog worships him," "Look at all those sun worshipers on the beach." We all seem to use the word in one way for other situations, but for the Christian response to God, the word *worship* has come to mean something else. "Where do you worship?" "What time is worship?" "How long is your worship service?" Coming from an outsider looking into some of those "worship" services, like our movie character, our response to those questions might be, "What worship?" In many churches, our worship attitude toward our master is more like that of a cat. A cat thinks it is the boss. It comes to you when it feels like it. Cats do not worship anybody but themselves. That is not what God is looking for in His Church.

So if I say, like some people, that the church service itself is my "worship," do I mean the activities, the offering, the message, the singing? Let's take a closer look at the activities of the traditional Sunday church service.

The Offering

Some people like to say we are worshiping the Lord with our offerings. What they mean is that we are *honoring* God with our tithes and offerings. It is God's generosity that gives us everything we have. Out of *respect* for God, we are giving some money for the Church to use instead of keeping it all for ourselves. Best-case scenario, if you tithe (giving one-tenth of your money), it's one for Him and nine for you. I'm not trying to judge anyone's intentions, just throwing this out for discussion. If giving money is the worship, then which side gets more worship, God or us? And, really, do we all give 10 percent (a tithe) of our substance like it was established in the Old Testament? I doubt it. I'm not saying it's wrong to give an offering or that we are not honoring and respecting God when we do it. I'm just saying for us to call what little we give an act of "worship" falls far short of the definition for many of us.

> Solomon went up to the bronze altar before the Lord in the tent of meeting and offered a thousand burnt offerings on it. (2 Chronicles 1:6)
>
> And [King] Solomon offered a sacrifice of peace offerings, which he offered unto the Lord, two

and twenty thousand oxen, and a hundred and twenty thousand sheep. So the king and all the children of Israel dedicated the house of the Lord. (1 Kings 8:63)

Now that is how you use offerings as worship! Solomon learned the example from his father, King David. To worship through an offering requires a cost, a sacrifice on our part.

Araunah said, "Why has my lord the king come to his servant?" "To buy your threshing floor," David answered, "so I can build an altar to the Lord, that the plague on the people may be stopped. Now Araunah said to David, "Let my lord the king take and offer whatever seems good to him. Look, here are oxen for burnt sacrifice, and threshing implements and the yokes of the oxen for wood. Your Majesty, Araunah gives all this to the king." Araunah also said to him, "May the Lord your God accept you." But the king replied to Araunah, "No, I insist on buying it, for I will not present burnt offerings to the LORD my God that have cost me nothing." So David paid him fifty pieces of silver for the threshing floor and the oxen. (2 Samuel 24:21–24)

If the offering is to fall into the worship category, then by definition, it needs to be costly. Again, I'm not saying don't give offerings! Churches need offerings because that is how the lights stay on, the bathrooms get cleaned, the staff is paid, the phone bill and heat or air-conditioning is paid, the building insurance is paid, the maintenance of the building is paid for, etc. It's called offerings because no one is telling you how much to give or how often (aside from the 10 percent general tithe rule in the Bible). Giving offerings is voluntary. Many people, strangely enough, feel that the Church should not ask for any money at all. Think that through. These same people want a nice place to come to, they want the heat or air-conditioning to work, they want paved parking lots, clean bathrooms, etc. Who do we think pays for all of that? Sometimes people think that the pastor takes all the money, but that is like saying the president gets to keep all of our taxes. Supporting your local church is a lot like paying taxes. The taxes pay for all the services that help your community. So keep giving offerings and don't be stingy! If you're not sure where the money is going in your church, ask. Most churches are very open about their budgets and finances. But let's call offerings what they are—offerings—and let's call worshiping in the presence of the great God Jehovah—with all of our focus on Him, freely loving Him like a dog loves its master—worship.

The Sermon

Are we worshiping God through simply listening to the message that is preached or taught? The message might be motivational or exciting, or it might encourage you to dig deeper into the scriptures for yourself. It might stir up emotions toward God or others, it might be revelational, or it might be a call to action of some kind. In some churches, the congregation is allowed to make responses to the preacher, like saying, "Amen!" when he or she says something they agree with. In other churches, responses like that are frowned upon. The protocol is to be quiet. (Sleeping would seem to be more preferable than speaking out.) Hopefully, whatever the message, it draws us closer to God in some way. That is great in theory, right? Unfortunately, not everyone is listening; they are just being polite and are sitting quietly until it is over. Many people can't even tell you what the message was about fifteen minutes after the service. So should we call this worship? Let's call sitting quietly and listening politely "respect" for God, not worship.

The Singing

Being in the music ministry for many years, I have heard lots of different comments on the music/singing portion of the services. My friend Robyn and I led praise and worship services at large women's conferences, and after the conference was over, we would get together with the pastor's wife and others, who worked as a team to put on the conference, and we would read the exit surveys given to the participants in order to have a better idea of what to do for the next conference. The answers to the questions were all over the place. The singing was too long, the singing was too short, the songs were too old, the songs were too new, the food was great, the food was terrible, the building was too cold, it was too hot. We learned that if you are trying to please the people, don't hold your breath!

This is what happens in many churches where the music is concerned. People have different tastes and preferences in style. Some like country, some like rock and roll. Some like old, some like new. Musical style is a cultural thing and not necessarily a spiritual thing. If the purpose of singing in church is to express our musical talents, styles, or to experience singing in a group, we have probably hit the mark. If we are to call it worship, though, in many churches we have some work to do.

Of course, the music and the words of the songs help us to focus on God in some way, so that is the plus. But many of our words, whether old favorite hymns or the latest trendy songs, are talking about us or what God has done for us instead of the focus being on God Himself personally. If the song is really still all about us, is it actually worship by definition? If the song, even if it is contemporary and emotionally moving, is talking about what God has done for us or will do for us, *we* are still the focus of the song no matter how cool the music is. This type of song is a song of praise to God, which is wonderful, appropriate, but still not worship, not according to the Bible definition of the word. *Praise is not the same thing as worship.* More on that later.

Worship as a Lifestyle?

I have talked with different churchgoers about why some church services refer to their programs as worship, and the pat answer is that worship is a lifestyle, and everything we do is an act of worship. That is such a nice, religious sort of thing to say. But if we take a serious look, are we all living a lifestyle of *scriptural* worship, where God is our total focus, where we continually and consistently adore Him spirit, soul, and body? Look around, my friends. Can you see any evidence of God worship without changing the definition of what we're looking for? I think the confusion goes back to the definition of the word *worship*. There are other words for doing something out of a heart for God—honor, respect, politeness, service. These are all appropriate words for our church attendance. But let's challenge ourselves a bit— scriptural worship is a whole different ballgame.

As we have totally changed the definition of the word *worship*, substituting it for church attendance and man-made programs, we have fallen for a trick of the devil to get our focus off what's important to water down our relationships with God. By calling everything we do worship, we minimize the importance of the actual need to *proskuneo*. If you were the devil and you knew how powerful a believer's worship of God is, wouldn't you do everything you could to minimize its effects? We are so gullible. Remember, Lucifer knows all about what real worship in heaven is like. Some people believe he was the worship leader in heaven. His body played music when he walked. There are angels that worship God 24-7. These angels fly around the throne room, beholding the presence of God continually. They are continually overwhelmed by some new facet of God's person and cry, "Holy! Holy! Holy!" Notice, the angels are not going about their other business, calling their lifestyles worship.

Worship vs. Service

One reason for the confusion in definition could be the Bible translators themselves. Romans 12:1 is translated in the NKJ version as "I beseech you therefore, brethren, that you present your bodies a living sacrifice, holy, acceptable to God, which is your reasonable service. And do not be conformed to this world, but be transformed by the renewing of your mind, that you may prove what is that good and acceptable and perfect will of God." The NIV and some other modern versions translate the first part of this passage this way. "Therefore, I urge you, brothers and sisters, in view of God's mercy, to offer your bodies as a living sacrifice, holy and pleasing to God—this is your true and proper worship." This translation makes it sound like worship is a lifestyle, doesn't it? It makes it seem like we are to consistently, on a daily basis, offer ourselves as a worship sacrifice. But the word translated worship here is not *proskuneo*. It is *latreia*, which means to minister or do sacrificial or priestlike service to God. It is associated with performing religious rituals. This is a service-oriented word, not a love-relationship word. Serving God could be many things, and they could be lovingly done but not necessarily. Doing something out of a sense of duty is not at all the same as doing it as an expression of love.

Wuest's translation of Romans 12:1 makes it more clear. "I therefore beg you, please, brethren, through the instrumentality of the aforementioned mercies of God, by a once-for-all presentation to place your bodies at the disposal of God, a sacrifice, a living one, a holy one, well-pleasing, your rational, sacred service, [rational, in that this service is performed by the exercise of the mind]." This passage is clearly about a dedication of our bodies to ministerial service and is not the same as *proskuneo* worship, the kind our Father God is looking for. Remember, He is seeking a certain kind of worship, and it is by His definition, not ours.

Martha and Mary

There were two sisters in the Bible called Mary and Martha. We can learn from them.

> Now it happened as they went that He entered a certain village; and a certain woman named Martha welcomed him into her house. And she had a sister called Mary who also sat at Jesus' feet and heard His word. But Martha was distracted with much serving, and she approached Him and said, "Lord, do You not care that my sister has left me to serve alone? Therefore, tell her to help me." Jesus answered and said to her,

"Martha, Martha, you are worried and troubled about many things. But one thing is needed, and Mary has chosen that good part, which will not be taken away from her." (Luke 10:38–42)

Jesus said that Mary, sitting at His feet (kind of like an adoring pet dog, right?), had chosen the right response to His presence. The serving and details may be important, but they are not as important as sitting in the presence of the Lord, being close to Him, hearing what He is saying, watching His facial expressions. If you are close enough, even if He speaks softly, you will hear His voice. Mary represents *proskuneo*, Martha represents *latreia*. To bring this example into our present situation, in many churches, all of our man-made programs are of some importance, but the presence of the Holy Spirit, the Spirit of Jesus, is more important and precious, according to God. *Proskuneo* is top priority, and *latreia* should be second.

Latreia is not a bad thing; it is a very good thing. Many things we do solely because we love God. Martha was serving not because she didn't love Jesus but because she did. It is the form or the expression of that love that carries the difference between *latreia* and *proskuneo*. There is a time for *latreia*, and there is a time for *proskuneo*, even in the church service.

Another Greek word, closely associated with *latreia*, is *leitourgeo*, which means to serve or minister in an official manner. This is thought to be where we got the English term *liturgy* from. The liturgy in many denominational churches is a script, a planned-out itinerary of official church activities to be done as service to God. The minister knows exactly what to say, and the congregation knows exactly how to respond. They know when to sit and when to stand. It is repeated every Sunday in exactly the same way, reciting the same "lines," with minor variations for seasonal events like Lent and Easter. Churches using liturgies in this manner quite happily pat themselves on the back for their performance. They call it their worship. Martha, Martha…

Discussion Question

1.   If we define worship of God as the same as worship of the devil, what should our worship look like?

The Difference between Praise and Worship

Think back to the devil worship scenario. Were those participants just sitting, yawning, fanning themselves, thinking about what to make for dinner, or rather that they should have slept in or be playing golf? No, real worship is a response, a focused response of adoration to the presence of God, and requires active participation. You might say, "Well, I am worshiping God in my heart," and that is, of course, wonderful. We start there, but according to the definitions God has used in the Bible, He seems to be looking for something more than that.

If we think about it, we know people need to respond in some way in order to have worship. That's why in some services, the response is written for them. It is a script. The minister says something, and the people respond, saying their lines. Asking folks to sing is also a way to get them to respond. But we all know this is fake news. It's not the same as real worship.

We know we are not supposed to worship idols, so falling down in front of a statue is not appropriate, even if it represents Jesus. We are not worshiping the pastor or the altar. The only appropriate scenario or real legitimate setting for worship is that the *presence of the living God* has somehow shown up, and if He is there, then we should be free to worship our heads off. In some churches, they have discovered that God *will* show up in a supernatural way if you invite Him. How do we invite Him? How do we get God to come in a more concentrated and possibly tangible way?

Praise Draws God

Although they are often linked together, praise is not the same as worship. The word *praise* is found over 350 times in various forms in the Bible. That alone should cause us to sit up and take notice. Praise has been defined as expressing warm approval or admiration of something. It is exalting, lifting up, congratulating, saying nice things. We want to do that for God. He is worth it! He is worthy of all the praise we can muster up. If we praise Him, not only do we begin to see God in a bigger, better light ourselves, but the scriptures promise that God is drawn to our expressed love and admiration for Him. Wouldn't you be? He is, of course, everywhere, but He will come and manifest His presence in a more intimate, intense, special, and sometimes even tangible way in the midst of our praise. Only God could do that! Remember, He spoke to Moses out of a burning bush. He is capable of manifesting or showing His presence in a group of believers in the same way.

Psalm 22:3 (AKJV) declares, "But you are holy, O you that inhabit the praises of Israel." Some other translations say: "Yet you are holy, enthroned on the praises of Israel" (ESV) and "And thou art holy, thou that dwellest amid the praises of Israel" (DBY). When we praise God, He is drawn to it and comes to hear us, and then He pulls up a chair and stays for a while. The scripture says He lives there, right there in the middle of our praise.

God likes us to praise Him, but it isn't because He needs encouragement. It is like music to His ears to hear His children speaking or singing the truth. The truth is, He *is* great! He *is* amazing! He is all those nice things we can think of to say and declare about Him and more. *It is the truth found in praise that draws Him.* Jesus said, "I am way, the truth, and the life. No one comes to the Father except through Me" (John 14:6). Psalm 50:23 says, "Whoever offers praise glorifies Me." Declaring who God is and what He has done is declaring the truth to ourselves, to the angels, to the demons, and to all of creation. And since Jesus is "the truth," proclaiming the truth is glorifying Jesus, and our Father loves it! While we are praising and exclaiming the truth, our faith grows and is built up listening to all that. Hebrews 11:6 says, "Without faith it is impossible to please God." When our faith begins to fire up, God is well pleased! Want to make God happy?

Faith Draws God

Faith always attracts God. Jesus felt virtue leave His body through the faith of the woman with an issue of blood (Luke 8:43–48). He immediately turned and said, "Who touched Me?" He stopped in His tracks, and His attention was immediately drawn to this woman. God gets excited when people express faith in Him. We want to draw the presence of the Lord to our church services. We need His presence, His living, healing touch. We know that Jesus said in Matthew 18:20, "For where two or three are gathered together in My name, I am there in the midst of them." He has promised to be with us when we gather to acknowledge Him in some capacity. If we add our faith to that promise, believing that Jesus will do what He said He would do, His presence will begin to manifest itself more and more in our gatherings. By speaking or singing or shouting our faith in the truth of His Word and His promises through praise, we provide a throne for Him, a dwelling place, right in the center of our gathering, and His presence will be felt in an even stronger way. We will be able to sense that He is physically there, and miracles are likely to take place when Jesus shows up!

Praising God can be singing songs that talk about how He has done great things for us, how strong and mighty He is, how He died for us and set us free, how we now live in the victory He has won for us. *Praise is celebratory*, and so praise songs are usually upbeat and happy. Songs about repentance, about the sinful nature of man, or songs about our struggles of life are not praise songs. Praise focuses on the victory of a battle that has been won and a God that has done more than we asked for. Praise doesn't have to be sung; it can be spoken or shouted. Singing or shouting "Hallelujah!" is a form of praise. Could we sing a song about our struggles? Sure, but if our time is limited, we'd better not spend a lot of time on that song or songs like that. It's praise songs that start a fire in a group of believers. Their faith is ignited by praise. We become the "burning bush," so to speak, a vehicle through which God can speak and manifest Himself.

In the Old Testament, 2 Samuel 6:12–15, David organized a big procession with music and dancing and all kinds of celebration to bring the Ark of the Covenant back to Jerusalem, where the people could have better access to it. The ark represented the physical presence of God, and David knew it was super important to have God in the midst of the people. David's procession is an illustration of how our praise ushers in the ark or the presence of God.

You know, Christianity is not a club. It is not even a religion. Christian believers enjoy a relationship with the King of kings, the God of all the universe, and our own Father. We do not gather to hear ourselves talk; we gather to hear from God and to share the gifts that He gave to each of us with our brothers and sisters. Each time we gather, it is like a family reunion. It is not much of a reunion if the dad doesn't come. The thing is, God won't necessarily come if He is not invited and welcomed. In some churches, man just does his own thing. That's sad. But just because you build a building and call it a church doesn't mean God will be there. It is faith in the Word that draws Him. The scripture, "For where two or three are gathered together in My name, I am there in the midst of them" (Matthew 18:20), implies Jesus has also been invited. *Well, that's silly*, you might think. He knows we go to church because of Him. Why would He stay away? Sadly, we have produced church services that contain lots of programs and try to meet the needs of the children, the teens, the seniors, the moms, the dads, but we forget the most important person. Someone might ask, can't God take care of Himself? Why does He have to be specially invited? Because, my friend, He is worthy of the most honored attention and fussing over. He is a great King! You don't treat any king so lackadaisical, and especially the King of all the kings! If we don't know what is due His position, at least He knows it. He will wait until we figure it out.

He has given us a way to invite Him, to draw Him, if you will. It is through our praise.

Let's look at some definitions of the word that has been translated as "praise." Praise is defined through seven Hebrew words in the Bible.

- *Halal*—to boast, brag, or rave about God, make a show, shine, celebrate, even to the extent of appearing foolish (where we get the word *hallelujah* from)

- *Yadah*—to worship with extended hands, lift your hands toward heaven, often translated as giving thanks (this is why we lift our hands)

- *Barak*—to bless God (out loud), which is a privilege

- *Tehillah*—to sing or to laud

- *Zamar*—to pluck the strings of an instrument, translated into the New Testament as "psallo," "Speaking to one another with psalms, hymns, and songs from the Spirit. Sing and make music from your heart to the Lord" (Ephesians 5:19). David used many types of musical instruments in his music ministry.

- *Todah*—to shout or address with a loud voice. It includes an attitude of gratitude for God's promised deliverance even while we are still in need. This type of praise also refers to lifting of the hands in inviting God's help. Todah praise is having faith and assurance that all is well even before the victory actually comes. For example, when David was trapped by the Philistines in Gath, he gave thanks and offered "todah" praise even before God delivered him.

- *Shabach*—to shout or address in a loud tone. You might possibly be thinking by now, *Where is the word that means to keep quiet in church?*

Sorry, all these praise words are loud and have to do with excited, boisterous, flamboyant, extravagant praise about God. If you go to a church that is congratulating itself because they are the quietest on the block, think about what is happening. God is not quiet, and He has never told us to be, except when we are being polite and listening to someone else speak. The words He has defined to be used to compliment Him are mostly loud, even shouting! Where did we get the idea that being quiet in church shows that we are holy? Even Paul's criticism of the early Church didn't forbid any noise from the participants; he just tried to organize it so that everyone could be heard. If you walked into a church where people were using praise according to the biblical definition, you might see all kinds of action going on, like singing, shouting, lots of shouting, lifting hands toward heaven, clapping, perhaps swaying to the music, processions, maybe dancing! Does that sound scary and inappropriate? Only if you don't understand the biblical definition of the word *praise*.

What happens when you praise God like that? He comes! He shows up and manifests His glory. He joins in the fun. Yes, God likes a party too. And what happens when Jesus comes to the party? He touches people, heals them, gives them answers, solves their problems, delivers them from demonic activity, corrects their thinking, loves them, hugs them, ministers to them on an individual basis. Does that sound like something you would like to have happen in your church? Let's learn to praise extravagantly because our Father loves us extravagantly. And then, once the presence of the Lord is there, let us move on to worship extravagantly.

What Does Real Worship in the Church Look Like?

Worship is a response to the presence of God. If the president of the United States were to walk into the assembly with all his bodyguards, what would we do? Probably, our posture might change, and we would become more attentive to the proceedings and crane our necks to get a good look at him, hold our kids up on our shoulders, maybe even jump up and down to see better. The message might be cut short to give him time to speak to us if he wanted to, and we might not bother with an offering right then, and it would be okay with everyone if we went over the time allotted. He might sign autographs and might shake hands with some of us. It would be so exciting!

When Jesus the King shows Himself (spiritually) in the midst of the assembly and the people realize He is there, the praise begins to take on a different tone. Even though invisible to our human eyes, the presence of Jesus can still be sensed. The songs, if we are still singing, become more and more intimate, loving the person of Jesus. If the musicians are not tied rigidly to the planned song list or the instrumental tracks, we may find that the music slows down or speeds up, depending on the moving of the Holy Spirit. Sometimes the flow becomes thematic, such as the majesty of the Lord or the sweet gentleness of the healing touch of Jesus. The rhythm of the music ebbs and flows according to the Spirit of the Lord. Sometimes it rises to a driving intensity. Other times the rhythm of the music stops completely, and it seems as though the Spirit is "hovering over the waters," His creative power waiting and desiring to bless the people. The congregation may change their posture, and *everyone doesn't always have to do the same thing*. Some may bow down, some may stand

and lift their hands, some may prostrate themselves (lay face down), some may dance or twirl gracefully in a flowing manner to show the moving of the Holy Spirit. Some may just sit down in their seats, tears streaming down their faces, as they have a conversation with the God who loves them and is there to touch them.

There is a freedom to real worship that we rarely see in our churches. Second Corinthians 3:17 tells us that "the Lord is the Spirit. And wherever the Spirit of the Lord is, there is freedom." The word translated *freedom* here means "*unrestrained*." It is being free in contrast with being a slave.

If you think about it, our behavior in many churches is the opposite of freedom. The people are totally restrained from expressing themselves in any way. We go to church and sit down quietly to see the show. We may sing a few songs, stand, sit, kneel, sit again, but the script, as someone has said, has been written, and we are not allowed to deviate from it. The people on the platform are not free either. They follow the same script-like plan. There is nothing remotely reminiscent of unrestrained freedom of worship in the presence of the Spirit of Jesus in many of our beloved churches. Still, we call it worship, but it is the furthest thing from it!

Clapping

Many times we clap for the worship team at the end for their adequate performance, but this is not the same as worship. Even our attempts to focus that response into "clapping for the Lord" are shallow at best. When asked to "give the Lord some praise" or something to that effect, generally people applaud because they don't know what else to do. But there are seven words translated praise in the

Bible. Let's do one of those! "Clapping for the Lord" is like clapping for any type of worldly performance, but our Lord, the High King, is worthy of a better response. He is not there to perform. He is there to love us, to heal us, to set us free. We don't clap for His ministry, but clapping our hands with the beat of the music is fine and appropriate. Can you imagine a child clapping for his dad when he fixes a toy or swats a fly? Or clapping for your friend when she does something nice for you?

Psalm 47 says, "Clap your hands, all you peoples! Shout to God with the voice of triumph... God has gone out with a shout, the Lord with the sound of a trumpet. Sing praises to God, sing praises! Sing praises to our King, sing praises... *Sing praises with understanding.*" The word translated "clap" here also means clang an instrument, smite, thrust, or drive a nail or weapon or blow a trumpet. If we clap our hands with purpose, we are driving weapons, thrusting our swords through the enemy. We may not be able to blow a trumpet in the natural, but our clapping in the Spirit is like blowing a trumpet battle cry that will freeze the enemy in his tracks. The Word says to sing with the Spirit and sing with the understanding. Let's clap with understanding as well. It is a spiritual weapon when applied in the right way. If we're going to clap, let's clap with the understanding that it is a spiritual weapon, not praise to God. Sing your praises to God according to scripture.

Music Ministry

The music ministry in the service is there to assist us in our praise and worship. They are not there to worship for us but to lend us assistance. They are there to inspire us and lead us into a higher or deeper experience with the presence of God. Many people come to a church gathering weighed down with problems and concerns. They need help to tear their eyes from themselves and whatever crisis they are facing at home so that they can refocus their eyes on Jesus, who will minister life and healing to them and who will solve their problems. They need help to rid themselves from the chains, big and small, that are trying to bind them and prevent them from freely worshiping with abandon. The devil knows that our worship of the true God is a powerful weapon against him, and he throws every kind of obstacle in our way to prevent that from happening.

Sometimes the music ministers don't fully understand their role in the church. They think it is all about the music, but it is really more about ministry. Every musician, singer, or instrumentalist on the platform is leading worship, not just the MC. The people are watching the whole team. Music ministers who are not ministers at heart can never accomplish the mission and really should not be on the platform. Only a worshiper can inspire another to worship. Some worship teams have singers who can hold a microphone, but their faces and body language show the congregation that they are not connected. I remember one time being asked why I looked so mad while I was playing the keyboard during a worship service. I was shocked. "I'm not mad, I'm just intense! I'm trying to concentrate here," was my reflexed response. After I thought about it, I was mortified to think I had given the wrong impression to anyone in the congregation. I had to learn to purposefully relax my facial features and smile once in a while. I wanted to represent a worshiper's face, not just my own face. The congregation wants to know how to operate in the presence of the Lord. They will copy what the worship team does. For example, if the pastor would like the congregation to feel free to lift their hands during the praise and worship time, the worship team needs to model that. The worship leader is like a shepherd. He or she is leading the people in an upward direction, like going up a mountain. "Many people shall come and say, 'Come, and let us go up to the mountain of the Lord, To the house of the God of Jacob; He will teach us His ways, And we shall walk in His paths…" (Isaiah 2:3).

Praise Is a Type of Prayer

"Let my prayer be set before You as incense, The lifting up of my hands as the evening sacrifice" (Psalm 141:2).

The word used for prayer here is *tefillah*, prayer that is often sung. In fact, one of its definitions is "hymn." You could say, "Let my hymn [song] be set before you as incense…" This is from one of David's psalms, and he knew about worship. He set up the first organized praise and worship ministry. What he was showing us is that the function of our praise is similar to the function of incense. When incense is burned, its smoke rises to the sky. Our praise should have a sense of direction, a going up toward heaven. The protocol is, as we go up or our praises go up, He comes down. This is how we experience God. This is also how the rapture at the end of this age will work. We go up, and He comes down. So shall we "meet the Lord in the air and thus we shall always be with the Lord" (1 Thessalonians 4:17).

Why Are We Singing That?

In most church services, the songs are chosen for various reasons: people like them, they are easy for the musicians to play, the pastor likes them, they are short, the words talk about the theme of the day, etc. I suggest that if the mission is to assist people to experience an ever-increasing experience with the presence of God, the songs should also be carefully selected for *that* reason. Song selection can be as anointed and crucial to the church service as the sermon is.

Some hymns and songs sung in our churches have lyrics that are not even scriptural. Let's be careful about what we are saying and singing. Words are important according to the Bible. "Death and life are in the power of the tongue," Proverbs 18:21 tells us. If we are trying to get free, we don't want to be singing about how we are hopelessly lost in sin. We need to sing songs that build our faith, that prepare us to enter the presence of the Lord, and to get us ready to receive a miracle.

The lyrics are a big reason why certain songs are selected to be used in the worship service. Song lyrics addressed to the people or about people's troubles and feelings are used to transition their focus from themselves and to put their full attention onto God. Their spirits begin to rise as they focus on the goodness of God. Songs with lyrics personally directed to God move the people higher and deeper in the Spirit until they can touch Him for themselves. You wouldn't then want to do a song with lyrics all about the people and their troubles again because that would change the direction of the flow toward God. Of course, there is no hard and fast rule. Worship leaders follow the direction of the Holy Spirit. Only He knows what the people need and when they need it. If a certain part of a song is really ministering to the people, the Holy Spirit might direct the musicians to continue to play that part over and over again and not just sing the whole song through every time. It's spiritual, not natural. Our minds might rebel and think, *We already sang that, let's go to the next verse,* but surprisingly, invisible chains are broken, and victories are won when we follow the leading of the Spirit and not just follow our prepared song list.

People come to church to touch and to be touched by God, and many times that happens during the praise and worship time, long before the preacher gets up to give the message. Praise and worship breaks invisible chains or ties that are holding people back, it paves the way for spiritual deliverance, and it can free a soul from demonic interference, like in the story of David when he played his harp and the evil spirit departed from King Saul (1 Samuel 16:14–23). The praise and worship time can pave the way, or plough the way, for the sowing of the seed of the Word of God. People will be far better able to receive whatever the message is if the "ground" of their hearts has been opened up spiritually by the time spent in worship.

Corporate Worship

Worship is individual, yet it is also a group thing. God sees us as unique persons within a body of believers, a unit. Yes, you can worship at home by yourself, but there is something powerful about coming together to worship as a congregation. Romans 12:5 and 1 Corinthians 12:27 tell us that we are the body of Christ. Jesus is the head, and the Church—that's us—is the body. There is something special that happens when we get together and express the Lord's body. Worship for us is not meant to be just an individual, private matter. We are meant to also experience the coming together of the body of Christ, worshiping at the same time yet individually. This is the time when the gifts of the Spirit begin to manifest themselves, like prophecy, the gift of knowledge, and gifts of healing. You might not be operating in one of those gifts yourself right now, but someone else in the congregation could be. If you are not there in the "gathering together" and stay home that day, you would miss out on the supernatural ministry of the Holy Spirit. Remember Matthew 18:20, "Where two or three are gathered together in My name, there I am in the midst." The body is supposed to come together and manifest the unity of the Holy Spirit. It is a beautiful expression of the glory of Jesus. We will be doing a lot of that in heaven.

The Time Issue

In case you haven't noticed, a worship experience or service of this type and magnitude would require some time. This is probably the biggest factor causing the hesitancy of church leaders to move in the direction of more freedom to worship. When you let go of your control of the service and let God take over, well, you never know how long it will last. Once the presence of God is there to minister, He is in charge of the service. He decides when He is finished, not the pastor, not the worship leader, not the elders, nor the children's workers. What will we do if He goes longer than our hour and fifteen minutes service? We think that the people will never go along with lengthening the time of the service and that the people will leave the church. The trend for most churches these days is the shorter the better, right? We think, what if they get hungry? Or what if *we* get hungry? (Now that is a serious problem.) What did the multitudes do in Matthew 15 when Jesus was teaching and healing everyone? Did they go home disgruntled after an hour and a half? No, they stayed and stayed. They wanted to hear every last word that Jesus was saying and watch Him heal everyone that came to Him. It was exciting and supernatural! He was changing their thinking and changing their lives. They stayed so long that Jesus had to make them sit down and think about food. (You know, God cares about stuff like that too.)

Changing how we think about time might present a problem with the way services are currently run. Many services limit their time to an hour or an hour and a half for what they consider to be good reasons. But all of our good reasons resulting in our trend toward comfort and convenience are interfering with the mighty supernatural presence of the living God being allowed to minister to the people. And why do the people come to church anyway? Is it to see a man, meet their friends, have a cup of coffee, sing in a choir? Or is it to connect with God? Our church services, in many cases, have become poor substitutes for a real bask in the presence of the Lord. We need to be with Jesus! Acts 4:13 shows us that people can tell the difference. "Now when they saw the boldness of Peter and John, and perceived that they were uneducated and untrained men, they marveled. And they realized that they had been with Jesus." Peter and John started acting like Jesus, talking like Jesus. They had been in His presence and watched Him heal people and cast out demons, so that's what they began to do. And everybody could tell who those guys had been hanging around. Of course, we need to spend time reading the written Word and hearing anointed preaching because Jesus is the Word. But Jesus, being the wonderfully supernatural God that He is, is also able to visit His people and touch them supernaturally as they worship Him. He likes to! Why wouldn't we want to provide time for Him to do what He likes to do? Besides, we are a supernatural people because God has made us that way. We like what He likes. We should not be afraid of who we are.

Signs and Wonders

Let's not be afraid to "launch out into the deep water," like Jesus told Peter in Luke 5:4. The deep is where the fish are. It is the supernatural, the signs and wonders, that drew the multitudes to Jesus, and they should be regularly happening in our churches if we are claiming to be disciples of Jesus. The trouble is, we have gone so long without any supernatural manifestation of God's presence, especially in some denominational churches, that we actually have become suspicious of them. How crazy is that! Jesus was constantly doing miracles! He said, "Which is easier, to say to the paralytic, 'Your sins are forgiven you,' or to say, 'Arise, take up your bed and walk'? But that you may know that the Son of Man has power on earth to forgive sins," He said to the paralytic, "I say to you, arise, take up your bed, and go to your house. Immediately he arose, took up the bed, and went out in the presence of them all, so that all were amazed and glorified God, saying, "We never saw anything like this!" (Mark 2:9–12). Jesus did miracles so that the people would know He could forgive sins. Signs and wonders drew the people's attention to the real miracle of a renewed relationship with God. This is what is missing in many of our churches today. As Paul said in 2 Timothy 3:5 in the last days, "having a form of godliness but denying its power." Let's not be one of those churches. Let's not be one of those Christians! God is powerful. He is supernatural and He wants to show us what He can do if we will invite Him.

What Are We Afraid Of?

Some church leaders are worried that if we open the door to the possibility of signs and wonders happening in our church, the devil will immediately come in and imitate them, like he did when Moses came to deliver the people from slavery in Egypt. Exodus 7 tells us that Moses threw his rod (staff) down on the ground, and it became a serpent. So the magicians in Pharaoh's court threw their rods down, and they became serpents too. Many of us stop there and say, "See? The devil can do those signs and wonders too. How will we be able to tell the difference?" But when we read on, we find out that Moses's serpent ate up all the others. God is far stronger and smarter than any of the devil's tricks! The Holy Spirit in us helps us sense when something is of God, or if it is not. If we are paying attention, we can tell when the spirit behind the supernatural is "off." Let's not be so intimidated by the devil's ability to counterfeit the workings of God that we throw the real thing out the window!

What Is Our Priority?

So what are we saying? Are all those other church activities that we do wrong? No, not at all. By themselves they are fine ideas, but if we have limited time, what should our priority be? It seems likely that what we need most is not man-made programs; we need as much of God's supernatural presence as we can get! And if we really feel the need to add all those other activities, and we probably will, our time frame must be enlarged. Church services will have to be lengthened. What if people need to leave early? Let them, no problem. Just because some folks have to leave earlier doesn't necessitate the need for the rest of us to close the service. What about the children? Can they sit in a long service? We are smart people. We could come up with a great plan for the kids if we want to, if the time we spend with the Spirit of God in church is important to us.

The church I went to for many years had two-hour services, and we came Wednesday nights, Sunday morning, and Sunday nights. Church was important, or rather, being in the presence of God was important. We ordered the rest of our lives around it. If there was a special conference going on at church, we would attend three or four nights a week. We didn't want to miss a single moment. When God showed up there was life, there was joy, there was healing, there was victory. We felt that we couldn't afford *not* to go to church! These were all two-to three-hour services, and we just wished they would go on longer. And of course, if anyone needed to leave, they were free to do so. The rest of us were not affected or offended. Some church services in history have lasted all day. Demonic "church" services last for several hours at a time. Why are we so anxious to get back to our worldly lives? What does that say about us?

In defense of those churches that have not even considered the possibility that God Himself might show up to one of their services, I don't really blame the people. They don't know. They have never heard of such a thing because the pastors don't teach about it. And sadly, the seminaries and Bible colleges don't teach it either. They fill their students' heads with lofty intellectual theories and doctrinal ideologies that produce religion instead of life. There it is again. "Having a form of godliness but denying its power. From such turn away!" 2 Timothy 3:5 warns us.

Today, the Church has assimilated the culture of the world. The trouble with that is that the world has no Jesus. Jesus is not in their schedule. If we are trying to be like the world, we will not have time for Jesus either.

Discussion Questions

1. How long should a church service last?
2. Why would it be important to have God's presence in your church service?

LESSON 14

WALKING BY FAITH (PART 1)

Faith has several different definitions. We call our religious belief systems our faith. Judaism, Hinduism, Catholicism, and Christianity are examples of people's faith. Another way we talk about faith is to say that we have faith in something, that we believe that something is true or trustworthy. Sometimes we say we have faith in people, which means we trust them. We also use the word *faith* to describe how we believe or trust in invisible things. For instance, we have faith that when we sit down, our chair will hold us. Of course, we use the word *faith* when we talk about believing in God because God is both invisible and trustworthy.

For this study, we will focus on the most common Bible use of the word. The Bible says that God created the worlds by *faith in the words He spoke*. "By faith we understand that the worlds were framed by the Word of God, so that the things which are seen were not made of things which are visible" (Hebrews 11:3). Faith is used in the Bible as a *tool*. It works together with the Word of God to create the visible out of the invisible. And the Bible tells us something else that is very, very important. "Without faith, it is impossible to please God" (Hebrews 11:6). That statement alone should change our lives. The word *please* used here is from a different Greek word than the one in the scripture, "Those who are in the flesh cannot please God" (Romans 8:8). In Romans 8, the word means "to make acceptable." But in Hebrews 11, the first scripture, the word *please* means "to gratify entirely," "to satisfy" God. That is a big difference! Wouldn't we like to know how to gratify entirely and completely satisfy God? Developing unwavering faith in His Word will do that.

Jesus talked a lot about faith. He talked about using faith as a tool to accomplish tasks. He said in Matthew 17:20, "For assuredly, I say to you, if you have faith as a mustard seed, you will say to this mountain, 'Move from here to there,' and it will move; and nothing will be impossible for you." Why would you want to make a mountain move? Well, mountains can be physical, sure, but they can also represent big obstacles in your life. Jesus was saying that things that seem too big to handle for us are actually easy to manipulate when you use your faith tool. In fact, nothing shall be impossible for us. Wow, this sounds great! We all want that kind of faith. And the good news is, Jesus said it doesn't take that much faith to do the impossible. A mustard seed is very tiny.

Fear vs. Faith

Unfortunately, when we're going through a difficult situation, we tend to forget what Jesus said. Like the disciples in the boat trying to cross the sea in the midst of a storm (Luke 8:22–25), we look at the circumstances all around us, the howling winds and high waves, all that foaming, raging water, the scary lightning, and all the reasons why it must be *impossible*. That great big mountainous situation seems too much for our teeny tiny mustard seed faith. In fact, our faith seems to take wings and fly away! We allow fear to take over, and faith and fear have a hard time existing together. So Jesus, knowing us so well, gave us an example of what to do in a storm. He was not the least bit afraid. In fact, He had so much peace that He actually fell asleep in the boat. No wonder He's called the Prince of Peace! When His disciples, all filled with fear and hysterical, woke Him up, Jesus simply spoke to the storm, saying, "Peace, be still," and all that noisy howling wind stopped, and the waves became calm (Mark 4:39). Fear paralyzes us. Fear could not have calmed that storm, but faith could. Let's learn how to use our faith.

Belief or Unbelief?

When we pray or ask God for something, we are showing a certain amount of faith because we are praying to an invisible God. That is a good start. But faith for answers to prayer goes beyond that basic faith. One time, a man asked Jesus to heal his son who was possessed by a demon.

> "Whenever it seizes him, it throws him to the ground. He foams at the mouth, gnashes his teeth, and becomes rigid. I asked Your disciples to drive it out, but they were unable." "O unbelieving generation!" Jesus replied. "How long must I remain with you? How long must I put up with you? Bring the boy to Me." So they brought him, and seeing Jesus, the spirit immediately threw the boy into a convulsion. He fell to the ground and rolled around, foaming at the mouth. So He asked his father, "How long has this been happening to him?" And he said, "From childhood. It often throws him into the fire or into the water, trying to kill him. But if You can do anything, have compassion on us and help us."
>
> "If you can?" echoed Jesus. "All things are possible to him who believes." Immediately the

boy's father cried out, "I do believe; help my unbelief!" (Mark 9:22–24 BSB)

So let's analyze this scripture a little bit. Doesn't that guy in the Gospel account sound like us sometimes? His faith was all over the place. After describing all the details of the problem, he questions Jesus's ability to help, saying, "*If* you can do anything…," which basically means he didn't really trust Him to get the job done. After that, He says, "I do believe," and then confesses he really doesn't and, in desperation, asks Jesus for help. Seriously, doesn't that sound like us? We do believe…sort of… and then we don't. The trouble is, that kind of wavering back and forth between doubt and faith is not very effective according to scripture. It's like when you are trying to hammer a nail in the wall in order to hang a picture, and every time you pick up the hammer, you put it back down again. The nail will never make it into the wall if you don't use the hammer. James 1:6–7 says, "But let him ask in faith, with no doubting (nothing wavering), for the one who doubts is like a wave of the sea that is driven and tossed by the wind. That person should not expect to receive anything from the Lord."

That kind of wavering back and forth, in and out of faith, wasn't going to cut it for the man and his son that we are talking about in Mark 9, and he knew it. He cried out to Jesus, "Help my unbelief!" The same is true for us. Faith and doubt are total opposites. You can't mix doubt and unbelief in with faith and think you will see any results when you pray. Unbelief cancels out belief by nature of its definition.

Effective faith doesn't waver. Can you see why we don't always see a lot of miracles happening around us? It's because we are too much like the man in Mark 9. Faith is believing in the end result so solidly that you can see it, hear it, taste it, and smell it right now. How do we get that solid kind of faith that God will answer our prayer, the kind that will move the obstacles or mountains in our lives? Keep going and you will probably find out.

When we pray and ask God to intervene in some way in our lives, whether for healing, finances, relationships, or wisdom, we need to pray in faith, to believe that God is going to answer that prayer. God is attracted to our faith. He likes it. It pleases Him. He has given each man a measure of faith (Romans 12:3). It's not that our faith needs to grow; it's that the faith that we already have needs to become activated. The disciples asked Jesus to increase their faith. "The apostles said to the Lord, "Increase our faith!" And the Lord answered, "If you have faith the size of a mustard seed, you can say to this mulberry tree, 'Be uprooted and planted in the sea,' and it will obey you..." (Luke 17:5-6). Jesus was saying we can do a whole lot with the measure of faith we already have.

What Is Faith?

What is faith, anyway, the kind of faith Jesus was talking about? Hebrews 11:1 (KJV) defines it this way: "Now faith is the substance of things hoped for, the evidence of things not seen." Bible faith is, by itself, evidence. It is, by itself, the substance, the essence of what you are praying for. The word translated substance in the KJV is *hupostasis*, and it comes from a combination of two Greek words: *hystemi*, meaning to stand or abide or *establish*, and *hupo*, meaning underneath. Together they give the idea of setting under or being the support or the essence of a thing. In other words, *our faith is the establishment of the thing we are praying for*. Wuest's translation of Hebrews 11:1 reads, "Now faith is the title deed of things hoped for, the proof of things which are not being seen."

I like the idea of faith being evidence and substance and proof. If you have the title deed to a piece of property, you know you own it, even if you don't see it in front of you at the moment. That's how it is with faith. When you have prayed and are believing God for something, you have to see it as being yours from that moment on until it appears in your life. You have it, you own it. It belongs to you. Our struggle many times is the back-and-forth, like the guy with the son who was demon-possessed—we believe, we don't believe, we believe, we don't believe. We might believe while we are praying, but then the prayer is over, and we don't see any immediate results. So instead of continuing to believe while we wait for the answer to come, we waver and doubt. How do we overcome that doubt that screams nothing has changed? "I don't see anything changing!" Let's find out what is going on.

Unseen, Not Missing

God lives in what to us is an unseen world. The spiritual dimension does not appear to man's natural eye. However, that so-called invisible realm is not invisible at all to those that dwell there; like the angels, it is just invisible to us, who are limited by our human earth (flesh) bodies and human eyes in particular. There are things going on in the invisible realm all the time that we don't see and, therefore, don't know anything about. When Jesus came, He taught about the unseen world of the Spirit, assuring us that it is just as real, if not *more* real than the seen world of the natural. He let us know that just because we can't see it doesn't mean it isn't important. Jesus talked about the Holy Spirit's activity being like the wind. "The wind blows wherever it pleases. You hear its sound, but you cannot tell where it comes from or where it is going. So it is with everyone born of the Spirit" (John 3:8). You can't see the wind, but you can see its effects. He showed us that things that are unseen *affect* the things that are seen. And He showed us that there is a way to see what is happening without using your natural eyes.

Unseen, Not Unscientific

Some people think of faith as unscientific. What they mean is, faith is believing in things you cannot observe and, therefore, are not real. But remembering what Sir Francis Bacon said, who was the guy that founded the whole scientific method of "observation," "It is true, that a little philosophy [or way of thinking] inclineth man's mind to atheism [or as modern culture would say, "science"]; but depth in philosophy [or deeper thinking] bringeth men's minds about to religion [God's spiritual dimension—faith]." Sir Francis believed that observation was more than just seeing with your physical eyes. It is observing how it is all put together, seen and unseen, that gives you the big picture. To understand what is really going on, you need more than just your physical senses.

The Senses

We experience our physical world through our senses. The senses are there to tell us the "truth" or reality about our world. If we touch something hot, we know through our sense of touch not to go there. We perceive the truth that we will be burned if we continue to touch whatever that is. When we hear an ambulance siren, our sense of hearing tells us to look out for a fast-moving vehicle on its way to an emergency. The truth is that there is possible danger. When we smell the aroma of cookies baking in the oven, the truth, based on our previous experience, tells us those cookies would be good to eat. Our senses, from the time we are babies, continually help us relate to our physical world, teaching us new things, connecting and alerting us to truths we have already learned, and they shape the way we react to different situations. And we don't need all of the senses working at the same time to help us draw conclusions about our reality. If we smell the aroma of fresh cookies, we assume the cookies are there even if we don't see them with our sense of sight. We believe in the cookies without seeing them. If we are in the dark and we hear something buzzing near our ear, we might swat at an invisible mosquito, assuming it is there without seeing it. We believe in the presence of a mosquito without—you guessed it—seeing it. Our senses can help us, but *we are not limited by them.*

There are many things in our lives that are invisible yet valid. The force of gravity, for instance, plays a constant role in our lives. Even though we can't see it, we still have to deal with it daily. Music, the wind, heat, cold, oxygen, pain, laughter, dreams, imagination, words, thoughts—the list goes on and on of things in our reality that are invisible. In fact, if we were to only relate to things we could see, our "reality" would look like a bad science-fiction story. Faith in and of itself is actually not unusual or weird. It is not hard to believe in something you have not seen despite what the world tells us. Contrary to the narrative fed to us by the media, the so-called education system, and even religion, faith is not the opposite of science or intelligent thought. It is just a deeper understanding of what is going on around us. It is a higher level, not lower. We believe in electricity and experience its force every day without thinking about it, but it was there long before mankind discovered it and harnessed it for use. Many things in this world are unseen with the physical eye. It takes faith to relate to them, or we might say, believe in them, which basically means we trust that they are true. *Faith relates to invisible situations.* And we have all been given a certain amount of faith (Romans 12:3).

The Power of an Eyewitness

One way to look at faith is that it is believing something is true that you have not seen personally because you accept or believe the eyewitness account of someone else. We accept that heaven exists by faith, but we also have *evidence* that it exists from eyewitnesses. There are actually many people that have had death-like experiences and prophets in the scriptures that have seen visions of the world to come. You've probably heard of some of them. There are more than you may think. The Internet has lots of stories of people who have witnessed heaven and hell in this way and come back to tell us about it and not just that they "went through a tunnel" or saw "a light." Their stories and descriptions of a real place with trees and flowers and people that have gone on before us seem to match with each other pretty well, and I believe these phenomena will increase as the days grow closer to the end of the age. God wants us to get excited about coming home!

In addition to the "regular guy" witnesses, our biggest eyewitness, the most influential eyewitness to heaven's existence, was Jesus Himself. He talked about heaven and described it, and His account is accurate because He came from there and lived there. He is a very credible witness. So when we think about heaven, even though we ourselves have not seen it yet, we can believe it is a real place, the same way we believe Disneyland is a real place even if we've never been there because others have told us that *they* have seen it. We do this kind of thing all the time. In fact, our judicial system is set up that way.

In a court of law, the judge or jury has to decide which side of an argument is true. Is the defendant guilty or innocent? Did the crime happen or not? Is the accusation true or not true? Since none of the jurors or the judge were there at the time the crime was committed, or whatever the case is, to see what happened for themselves, they base their decision on the evidence brought to their attention. Both the defending attorney and the prosecuting attorney bring evidence to place before the jury as proof that their side is telling the truth about what happened. There is circumstantial evidence, and there is eyewitness evidence. Circumstantial evidence is something that suggests a fact by implication or inference. An eyewitness is considered direct evidence and requires no inference. This direct evidence alone is the proof. As Christians, we believe the eyewitness account of Jesus as direct evidence, proof in itself. Hebrews 11:1 says about faith, "Now faith is the substance of things hoped for, the evidence (proof) of things not seen." Our faith is based on the direct evidence of the eyewitness testimony of Jesus Christ.

As the juror for your personal situation, how do you perceive the evidence? Do you judge the testimony of Jesus, the Word of God to be more true or your circumstances to be more true? Jesus, the Word of God, is the eyewitness account. It is direct evidence given by God Himself and, thus, true. It is more true than your circumstantial evidence, your circumstances, if you will. Faith is the invisible hand that delivers the verdict to the situation: God's Word is true.

How to Activate Your Faith

The Bible tells us how to activate our faith. It's by hearing the Word of God. Romans 10:17 says, "So then, faith comes by hearing, and hearing by the Word of God." When you hear someone preach or pray the words from the Bible, or you quote them or read them out loud to yourself, your faith begins to wake up inside you. The more you hear the scriptures, the more your faith rises up on the inside and flexes its muscles. Then when you pray, your spirit cries out in faith, "Give me that mountain! Look out, devil, you don't want to mess with me! King Jesus is alive and well and living in me!" That's when miracles happen.

Pray the Scriptures

When we pray, the best way to link up to our faith is to find a scripture that relates to our prayer, something God has already spoken. We know that the Word of God is the expressed will of God, and we know for sure that God will always agree with Himself. So we take the scripture and turn it into a prayer. Because it is the Word of God, our faith can grab a hold of it like an anchor and hold on until we receive the answer. Let's look at some examples.

Prayer for healing. First Peter 2:24 declares that "by His stripes you were healed." We can use that scripture for our own healing or someone else's by making the pronoun personal. "By His stripes *I* was healed" or "By His stripes my *child* was healed." We are not changing the intention of the scripture but just making it personal to us in order to stir up our faith. We believe that God meant what He said. So your prayer might go something like this: "I thank you, Father, that you sent your Son Jesus to pay for my healing on the cross. You said in 1 Peter 2:24 that by His stripes I was healed. I believe your Word is true. By the stripes of Jesus I was healed, and if I was healed two thousand years ago, I am healed now. In the name of the Lord Jesus Christ, amen!"

I have had lots of opportunities to use my faith for healing. For instance, when my son was a baby, his little feet and legs didn't look normal. They were turned in the wrong direction. The pediatrician told us to put a brace on his legs, especially at night, so that the knees would turn, and hopefully the legs would grow straighter as he got older. The trouble with doing that was, to get his little feet into the shoes attached to the braces, I would have to force them in a direction that was painful to my little guy. He screamed and cried, and I couldn't stand to have him in pain. So I went to the Lord and asked Him what to do. I was a new Christian and didn't have much experience, but I believed that I could ask God and He would come up with a plan. The Lord did not speak to me audibly, but He reminded me of a scripture that said if you believe, you can have whatever you say (Mark 11:23). I knew the Holy Spirit was showing me what to do, so I declared the scripture out loud not just in my mind. I don't remember my exact words, but it was along the lines of "You said, Lord, that I can have what I say. I say that by the stripes of Jesus, my son is healed. I believe his little legs are whole and perfect. His knees are straight and his feet are straight, and he can walk normally with no complications. Therefore, he does not need these braces." I never put the braces back on, and his legs as an adult are totally fine today. I don't remember the exact moment they changed. I just spoke the Word and forgot about it. Later I saw the result. God's Word works. Faith in His Word changes things.

It is possible to find a scripture for pretty much anything you need to pray about. Many Bibles have common prayer themes or subjects with scriptures that relate to them in the back of the book, but if you're not sure where to find the one you need, try doing an Internet search like, "scriptures about finances" or "verses about wisdom," etc.

The Door to Heaven's Resources

What is faith for and how do we use it? Jesus told us we are not of this world. "If you were of the world, the world would love its own [be fond of that which came from itself]. Yet, because you are not of the world, but I chose you out of the world, therefore the world hates you" (John 15:19–20). It's true that the world does not like Christians. Why not? Because they are from *another* world. They are different. However, there is a good side to our being from another world. When we are born again, we are born into the Kingdom of Heaven, the Kingdom of Light. Being born in a place gives you the rights of citizenship. Like ambassadors from another country (heaven), we dwell in this country (earth) but we are not limited to its resources. As citizens of heaven (the Kingdom), we have access here on the earth to the spiritual embassy of heaven. Our heavenly embassy is a safe zone in which we have diplomatic immunity from the world's system and all its corruption. *We are not limited to the resources of this world's system.*

In John 16:23-24, Jesus says, "Most assuredly I say to you, whatever you ask the Father in My name He will give you… Ask, and you will receive, that your joy may be full." This is like you being in a foreign country with the threat of fires, looting, and destruction going on all around, but you and your family are safe inside the US embassy, enjoying a nice dinner, with soldiers protecting you, all because you were born in America and are a citizen of America, not the foreign country where you are currently residing. This is like you being stranded on a faraway desert island and a US government plane swoops over and a parachute drops down everything you need to survive. Because you are an American citizen, you are not limited to the resources on the island. When you are born again, you become a citizen of heaven. Heaven's resources are now available to you. It's like having a never-ending gift card, only better because it includes way more things, like healing when you get sick, restoration of relationships, wisdom, peace of mind, and so many other things.

> Therefore shall ye lay up these my words in your heart and in your soul, and bind them for a sign upon your hand, that they may be as frontlets between your eyes… That your days may be multiplied, and the days of your children, in the land which the Lord sware unto your fathers to give them, as the days of heaven upon the earth. (Deuteronomy 11:18–21 KJV)
>
> So then, pray in this manner: "Our Father in heaven, hallowed be Your name, Your kingdom come, Your will be done, on earth as it is in heaven…." (Luke 11:2)

God's resources are readily available in heaven. He wants the same for His children on the earth. The world may hate you, but God loves you. You are His own now, and He knows how to take care of His people!

The Key of Faith Opens the Door

"Because I live, you will also live," Jesus said (John 14:19). Think about that. Some people think that this is only referring to us going to heaven when we die, but it is so much more. How did Jesus live? How did He live His life on a daily basis? He lived in victory over the curse, the curse that brought sin, sickness, lack, and destruction. Because of Jesus's victory over death and destruction, we now, as the body of Christ, also have victory over death and destruction here in this life, although we don't always see or feel things that way. We have *access to a door* that is locked to unbelievers that do not know God. That door opens for us because we *do* know God. It is the door to the embassy of heaven, our future home. How do we unlock the door? With our key of faith.

We live in a natural world. God lives in a spiritual world. He has given us access to the spiritual world, like a door that opens to heaven, hidden to unbelievers. One way to think of it is like on the other side of that door is a huge warehouse of everything we need to live victorious lives here on the earth in this lifetime. Jesus is the door.

Now that the door is open, the things that we need are available to us, like new health, new body parts, financial assistance, physical things like houses and cars and food, babies, loving relationships, and nonphysical things like abilities, peace, joy, answers to questions, wisdom for all kinds of situations, patience, long life, and oh so many other things! But once you are through the door, the way you reach in and take what you need requires faith. Some things are on the low shelves, so to speak, and easy to reach. They don't take much faith. Other things are way up on the high shelves or stacked up behind other things, and it's harder to get at those. Faith is a force, like a forklift or a mechanical robot arm, that helps you attain your goals. Jesus said, "When you pray [for something], believe that you receive [it] and you shall have [it]" (Mark 11:24). We need faith to believe in God, but the faith that receives answers to prayer is on a more active level. When we believe His Word, really believe it is true for us now, today, we are in a position to receive what His Word says we can have for our lives *now*, today.

What Did Jesus's Sacrifice Win for Us?

Faith works for us. It works to obtain for us what Jesus died to give us. Everything we receive from God comes to us by faith. Just like we first have to believe that Jesus died for us and then we are born again, *everything God has for us requires us to first believe and then we receive*. We always want to do it the other way around. In Mark 15:32, the crowd shouted to Jesus, "Let the Christ, the King of Israel descend now from the cross, that we may see and believe!" And the same way in John 6:30, Jesus was asked, "What sign will you perform then, that we may see it and believe you?" The way that pleases God is the opposite.

First you believe, then you see. Believe that you receive, and then you shall have.

So what all did He provide for us through His death and resurrection? Great question! Here is a list of some of the things Jesus died to give us:

- Forgiveness of all our sins, past, present, and future

- A free pass to get into heaven (our names are now written in the Book of the Lamb)
- Healing for our bodies
- Wisdom for our minds
- Victory over every attempt of the enemy to take us down
- Salvation for our children and our descendants
- Favor wherever we go
- Prosperity and blessing on our finances (Psalm 34:10, 23:1, 84:11, Proverbs 10:22)
- Beauty for ashes
- Restoration for our souls
- Joy instead of mourning
- Peace that passes all understanding
- Renewed youth
- Strength for our bodies
- Long life should Jesus tarry (wait to come back)

The Prodigal Son Parable

The evidence that we have access now to the blessings of the future is seen in the parable Jesus told about the prodigal son and his brother. This story is found in Luke 15:11–32. A man has two sons. One of them is a diligent and responsible son who works hard for the estate, and the other is kind of a slacker. The younger son, the slacker, tells the father he wants his share of the inheritance now, not when the father dies. So his loving father divides the inheritance and gives the young man his share. He leaves home to go see the world and ends up squandering away all the money. When he comes back home in disgrace, the father is relieved and delighted to see him. In fact, he throws a big party. The elder son becomes angry when he sees his father's response, but his father tells him, "Son, all that I have is yours." The elder son could have used his inheritance anytime he wanted to. The father had already divided it up. What is Jesus showing us here? Of course, the obvious answer is that God welcomes home the sinner and rejoices that His son has made the decision to return to the family. But there is another theme in this parable—the idea of the Father's blessing to His children of *an inheritance*, one they don't have to wait for until they get to heaven, one that they can enjoy here right now in this life.

> And do not seek what you should eat or what you should drink, nor have an anxious mind. For all these things the nations of the world seek after, and your Father knows that you need these things. But seek first the kingdom of God, and all these things shall be added to you. Do not fear, little flock, for it is the Father's good pleasure to give you the kingdom. (Luke 12:29–32).

Our Inheritance—The Kingdom

Our Father God has given us a rich inheritance that we share with Jesus. We are joint heirs with Christ, the Bible tells us in Romans 8:17. What does that mean? It means that, like the two sons in the parable, the inheritance has been divided up, and we already have legal access to everything heaven has to offer. There is plenty to go around. God has everything, and if He doesn't have it, He can make it! An inheritance is normally realized or received after the person who has the wealth is dead and gone, usually some future time. In this case, our Father God will never die. But Jesus told us the story of the prodigal son and the elder brother partly to show us that we can receive our inheritance now, not just in the future when we get to heaven. Since God will never die, the only way for us to receive the inheritance the Bible talks about is to receive it in a way that time is not a factor.

God does not live with the restrictions of time like we do. He is eternally present. His name is I Am, not I was, or I will be (Exodus 3:13–14). There is no past or future with Him. He is always living in the present—the now. When we are born again, we have a glorious future ahead of us, but because God is always living in the present, our eternal life actually begins immediately, from His point of view, not some future time. Our spirits will now live forever, but our forever has already started. It is not waiting until our earthly bodies die. We are citizens of heaven now. Jesus said, "If you were of the world, the world would love its own. Yet because you are not of the world, but I chose you out of the world, therefore the world hates you" (John 15:19).

Jesus told us we are not of (or from) this world. Where are we from then? Heaven! And when did this happen? When we accepted Jesus's sacrifice as a payment for our sins and God acknowledged our decision. As soon as that transaction occurred, we were born again, and our citizenship changed. Just like those from another country who come to United States, take a test, swear their allegiance to the USA, and become new American citizens, so we are sworn in (without the test) by declaring Jesus is our Lord, and we become citizens of heaven. We are new creatures (2 Corinthians 5:17) and we come from heaven. It sometimes takes a while to get used to the idea. Our outsides still look the same, but our insides have changed drastically. Before they were black as coal, but now they are white as snow.

Jesus continued to explain, "Father…glorify your Son, that your Son also may glorify You, as You have given Him authority over all flesh, that He should give eternal life to as many as You have given Him. And this is eternal life, that they may know You, the only true God, and Jesus Christ whom You have sent" (John 17:1–3). Eternal life is not just going to heaven when we die. Eternal life is knowing God. When we are born again, we are introduced to God and from then on begin a journey to know Him better and better. Eternal life begins at the moment of our salvation decision. We become citizens of heaven in that instant transformation, translated from the kingdom of darkness into the Kingdom of Light. Imagine that!

Spirit-Filled Man

Jesus showed us how to lay hold of the resources of heaven. Philippians 2:7–8 tells us that He came to the earth as a man, laying aside His divinity. Some translations say, "He emptied himself." Others say, "He made Himself of no reputation." In other words, He put aside His God-self and became a human. Everything He did, every miracle He performed was while operating as a man, filled with the Holy Spirit, and *not* as God. That is really tough for some people to believe. To them, He did miracles because He was God. That makes sense in our minds because obviously *we* can't do miracles. But Jesus said *we* would do the same works and greater works than He did after He went back to heaven and sent the Holy Spirit (John 14:12). How is that possible? Because Jesus was acting as a Spirit-filled man, just like a born-again believer filled with the Holy Spirit. Remember when the dove came and landed on Him after He was baptized? That is when the Holy Spirit baptized and anointed Him for ministry… as a man with no sin. Jesus is called the last Adam, an Adam do-over. God was certainly involved in doing the miracles, but Jesus showed us how it would be for us when we are filled with the Holy Spirit. He wasn't operating on a God level. *Jesus was operating on a God-filled Man level.* When Jesus returned to heaven, He left us a set of keys, and those keys give us access to heaven's resources. We have the same Holy Spirit that Jesus had, and we have faith, just like Jesus did. We can open the door to our inheritance. The key is our faith.

Adam's Inheritance

Jesus operated in the earth as the second Adam or last Adam. He was born without sin, just as the first Adam was created without sin. God said to the first Adam, "'Be fruitful and multiply; fill the earth and subdue it; have dominion over the fish of the sea, over the birds of the air, and over every living thing that moves upon the earth.' And God said, 'See, I have given you every herb that yields seed which is on the face of all the earth, and every tree whose fruit yields seed; to you it shall be for food…'" (Genesis 1:28–29). This was Adam's inheritance. Jesus came to die as a sacrifice for our sins, yes, but He also came to show us how to live as Adam should have lived. Adam lived a long life, but he did not exercise his authority over the earth. He gave his authority away to the devil.

Jesus, as the last Adam, did *not* give away His authority to the devil. Instead, He exercised it. When Jesus multiplied the fish, He was operating as Adam, who had dominion over the fish of the sea, and was told to be fruitful and to multiply. When He cast out demons, He was subduing the earth. Adam was given every fruit tree for food, including the fig tree.

The Fig Tree

One day, Jesus was hungry. He saw a fig tree from a distance with leaves on it. It wasn't the season for figs yet, but some fig trees produce fruit twice, once in the spring and again in the summer or fall. The fig fruit itself is associated with the opening of the leaves on the tree.

> And seeing from afar a fig tree having leaves, He went to see if perhaps He would find something on it. He found nothing but leaves, for it was not the season for figs. In response, Jesus said to it, "Let no one eat fruit from you ever again." And His disciples heard it… Now in the morning, as they passed by, they saw the fig tree dried up from the roots. And Peter, remembering, said to Him, "Rabbi, look! The fig tree which You cursed has withered away." So Jesus answered and said to them, "Have faith in God. For assuredly I say to you, whoever says to this mountain, 'Be removed and cast into the sea' and does not doubt in his heart, but believes that those things which he says will be done, he will have whatever he says. Therefore I say to you, whatever things you ask when you pray, believe that you receive them, and you will have them." (Mark 11:13– 14, 20–24)

Jesus went to the fig tree, as if He were Adam, and expected to be given fruit, whether it was in season or not.

As ruler of the earth (like Adam), Jesus had a right to expect fruit from that tree. In the beginning, God had given Adam every tree for food. Jesus's faith expected results. When the tree did not respond to His faith, Jesus took it out. "Every tree that does not bear good fruit is cut down and thrown into the fire" (Matthew 7:19).

This tells us two things: one, that if your faith does not produce results, it is not necessarily your faith that is the problem because *this world contains elements of resistance*; and two, God supports your faith and will judge the problem, not you. God loves faith. It is His desire that faith should work for us all the time.

Faith Is a Tool, a Servant

As we said before, faith is more than a passive believing in God. Faith is, or can be, an aggressive force that opens the door to healing, to answers, to miracles, all things that would be available to us and will be available to us in heaven. But someone may ask, isn't it being presumptuous to assume heavenly blessings while we are still on the earth? No, actually. The Bible tells us that our position in God's eyes, from His perspective, is that we are *already* seated in heavenly places with Christ, as if we had already departed this earthly life. Ephesians 2:4–7 tells us,

> But God, who is rich in mercy, because of His great love with which He loved us, even when we were dead in trespasses, made us alive together with Christ (by grace are you saved), and raised us together, and made us sit together in the heavenly places in Christ Jesus, that in the ages to come He might show the exceeding riches of

His grace in His kindness toward us in Christ Jesus.

We are not trying to get a hold of something that does not belong to us or does not belong to us yet. It is not being presumptuous to believe we are saved, even now while we are still in these mortal bodies. It is God's idea. He is eternal and is not limited by time. Time was created for this earth. *Now* we are saved. The word used for "saved" in the Bible comes from the Greek word, *sozo*, which includes being saved or rescued from danger, delivered from enemies, healed of all physical diseases, restored to health, and made well or whole. These blessings are available to us now in this life, not just the next, because from *the moment we accepted Jesus as our Savior, we stepped into eternity.* We stepped into heaven on earth, or at least the potential of it. Deuteronomy 11:21 shows us that it is God's plan and purpose for us to enjoy the blessings of heaven while we are still here. "That your days may be multiplied, and the days of your children, in the land which the Lord swore unto your fathers to give them, as the days of heaven upon the earth." These blessings are available to us, yes, but they are not automatic, which is why I said the *potential* of heaven on earth. We need to believe God specifically for them and receive them by faith, in the same way we believed and received our salvation. *Our faith is the tool, the means, that will help us receive everything Jesus has purchased for us.* Hebrews 11:1 says, "Now faith is the substance of things hoped for, the evidence of things not seen." Faith is now.

There were some instances that Jesus commented on the faith of the disciples not cutting it. "'O ye of little faith,' He said, 'O faithless generation!'" But there was one time that

He actually marveled at the faith of someone. That was a Roman centurion, a Gentile, that came and asked Him to heal his servant. In Luke 7:1–10 and Matthew 8:5–13, Jesus tells us that He had not found such great faith in all of Israel. What did the centurion have that the other disciples didn't? The scripture tells us he said to Jesus, "But say the word and my servant will be healed. For I am also a man under authority, having soldiers under me. And I say to one, 'Go,' and he goes; and to another, 'Come,' and he comes; and to my servant 'Do this,' and he does it." What made Jesus sit up and take notice was this man's understanding of how faith operates. *Faith is a servant. It does what you command it to do.* You are its boss. Jesus knew how to use faith to get things done, and that centurion recognized it.

Well, you might say, that was Jesus. Of course, faith worked for Him! But Jesus told us to have the same kind of faith He had. "Have faith in God. For assuredly I say unto you whoever says to this mountain 'Be removed and be cast into the sea,' and does not doubt in his heart, but believes that those things he says will be done, he will have whatever he say" (Mark 11:22–23). The Aramaic Bible in Plain English translates "have faith in God" this way: "Yeshua [Jesus] answered and He said to them, 'May the faith of God be in you.'" Several other translations say, "And Jesus answering, said to them: Have the faith of God." What He meant was, have the kind of faith that gets results, like God does.

When Jesus gave His blood as a sacrifice for our sins, He paid once and for all for us to obtain purity and holiness. Now God sees us, through the rose-colored glasses of the blood of Jesus, as absolutely, perfectly perfect! We are heaven-ready. Of course, the Bible tells us that our flesh is not saved and, like an old dog, needs to constantly be told to go lie down so it won't drool over everything. But let's focus on our spirits for a minute.

Our spirits are the real us, the inner man, our personality, the stuff that makes us uniquely us. Before we were saved or born again, we didn't know much about who we were. But now, through the knowledge of the Word of God, we are learning that we are strangely like Him. One day, we will live in heaven (or on the earth in the millennial Kingdom) and see God as He is. Wow, how amazing is that! Let's look at some scripture to get the idea of who we really are and where we are heading.

> Beloved, now we are the children of God; and it has not yet been revealed what we shall be, but we know that when He is revealed, we shall be like Him, for we shall see Him as He is. (1 John 3:2)

> The first man [Adam] was of the earth, made of dust; the second Man is the Lord from heaven. As was the man of dust, so also are those who are made of dust; and as is the heavenly Man, so also are those who are heavenly. And as we have borne the image of the man of dust, we shall also bear the image of the heavenly Man. (1 Corinthians 15: 47–49)

The heavenly Man is Jesus. We will look like Him. Our future bodies will be amazing! They will be able to do what Jesus did after the resurrection. He walked through locked doors, ate food with His friends, appeared and disappeared, and He was recognizable when He wanted to be. We will be recognizable, only better! All our imperfections will be gone, totally healed and made whole! Perfect skin, perfect weight, perfect hair, perfect muscle tone, you name it, the perfect us!

And we know that God, "who is rich and mercy, because of His great love with which He loved us, even when we were in trespasses, made us alive together with Christ (by grace are you saved), and raised us up together, and made us sit together in the heavenly places in Christ Jesus, that in the ages to come He might show the exceeding riches of His grace in His kindness toward us in Christ Jesus" (Ephesians 2:4–7).

God did three things for us, according to this scripture, when we received Jesus as our Savior.

1. *He made us come alive with Jesus.* We are partakers of the resurrection (even though we were never there because it was in the past).

2. *He raised us up with Jesus.* We are partakers of His ascension into heaven (even though it already happened, and we were yet to be born).

3. *He made us sit with Jesus.* Jesus is sitting on a throne next to His Father in heaven. We are sitting with Him. For us it is a future event, but for God, it has already happened. God is living in the eternal present. There is no past or future with Him.

Jesus is sitting on a throne, and we are sitting with Him. We are ruling with Him (2 Timothy 2:12, Romans 5:17, Revelation 22:5).

In God's eyes, we are bundled up in His Son forever. What God has done for Jesus, He also did for you. "In

Him (Christ) also we have obtained an inheritance, being predestined according to the purpose of Him who works all things according to the counsel of His will" (Ephesians 1:11). We are joint heirs with Christ to the riches of God, our Father.

> The Spirit himself bears witness with our spirit that we are children of God, and if children, then heirs—heirs of God and joint heirs with Christ, if indeed we suffer with Him that we may also be glorified together, For I consider that the sufferings of this present time are not worthy to be compared with the glory which shall be revealed in us. For the earnest expectation of the creation eagerly waits for the revealing of the sons of God. (Romans 8:16–19)

These are important truths that are foundational for us to understand when we talk about faith. When we pray and ask God to intervene in our lives, we are not pleading and begging. He already said He would give us anything we ask for. In Mark 11:22, the account of the fig tree, Jesus tells his disciples to "have faith in God." We know now this has been also interpreted to say, "Have the faith of God," or "Have the God kind of faith." Let's talk about God's faith.

God's Faith

The amazing ability of God to create things is astounding! He makes things out of nothing, can you believe that? One minute you can't see it, the next it's there. "By faith we understand that the worlds were framed by the word of God, so that the things which are seen were not made of things which are visible" (Hebrews 11:3). As it says in Genesis, "In the beginning God created the heavens and the earth. The earth was without form and void; and darkness was on the face of the deep. And the Spirit of God was hovering over the face of the waters. Then God said, Let there be light; and there was light" (Genesis 1:1–3).

God saw that there was darkness, but He imagined something else. Then He spoke out His thought into words and said…let there be light, as if it was there already, just as He'd imagined it would be. The Holy Spirit took those words and, by the vehicle of faith, created light, and there it was. By God's faith! That's the force or means by which the Holy Spirit made it happen. We all know that God can make anything. This is how He does it. Hebrews 11:1 says, "Now faith is the substance of things hoped for, the evidence of things not seen." Mind-boggling, isn't it? Hebrews 11 goes on to say, "By faith we understand that the worlds were framed by the word of God, so that the things which are seen were not made of things which are visible."

God created the worlds using His Word, and the vehicle that transported His Word to get the job done, to move it from imagination to reality, was His faith. Romans 4:16– 17 tells us that the promise of God came to us through faith.

> Therefore it is of faith that it might be according to grace, so that the promise might be sure to all the seed [descendants], not only to those who are of the law [the Jews], but also to those who are of the faith of Abraham [that believe the Word of God—Christians], who is the father of us all, [as it is written, 'I have made you a father of many nations'] in the presence of Him whom he believe—God who gives life to the dead and calls

those things which do not exist as though they did…

The promise of God that sin would be vanquished and that we should be made righteous comes to us through faith. Every other promise comes to us in this way, too, although we rarely hear it preached like the forgiveness of sins is preached. But this is how it all works. We see it in the Word, believe it in our hearts, speak it out, and receive it into our lives.

Jesus said, "For assuredly I say to you, whoever says to this mountain, Be removed and cast into the sea, and does not doubt in his heart, but believes that those things which he says will be done, he will have whatever he says. Therefore, I say to you, whatever things you ask when you pray, believe that you receive them, and you will have them," (Mark 11:23–24). There is a creative element in Jesus's statement about faith. He used the word *whatever*. There are no limitations on the word *whatever*. It is whatever you can imagine and whatever you can believe. This is exactly what God did. *He imagined, then He believed, then He spoke, and then He received.* If there is any formula to understanding God's faith, this is it.

Discussion Questions

1. What is our inheritance?
2. Why is it important for us to believe the Word of God before we see the results of our prayers?
3. How do we use faith as a tool?

LESSON 15

Scientists have been searching for one unified theory to explain everything—all the laws, forces, and systems of nature. They believe they have found it in string theory or its newer version, M-theory. Scientists believe that the basic foundation for everything in the universe comes down to teeny, teeny, tiny one-dimensional strings that vibrate continually. This bears repeating. Scientists are now saying that the smallest particles of matter, smaller than the atom, are strings that vibrate. They say *everything is really made up of a response to sound.* What causes a string on a guitar to vibrate? Someone has to pluck it. What causes sound waves to vibrate and produce sounds that we hear? Someone or something has to cause the energy to move. When you speak, the sound waves begin to vibrate, and our ears interpret the waves as sound or words.

So who is the instrument maker? Who has created the strings of the universe and caused them to vibrate? Who has spoken such powerful words that the whole universe vibrates in tune with itself? Who has composed such a symphony? God the Father has spoken! It was the voice of God saying, *"Let there be light…"* *The universe was created with the sound of words*, spoken words, not thoughts. God used words mixed with faith to make it all. And if that wasn't awesome enough, we—that's right, little ol' me and you— are created in the image of God, and therefore, our words are also creative if we mix them with faith. I know this sounds incredible but keep going.

Here is an excerpt from "Exploring the Sound of String Theory" by Queen Mary University of London. It is a little technical, but it's talking about the science behind music and, conversely, the music of science.

String theory encourages us to think of the vibrating strings not only as dictating the properties of the particles, but as "being" the particles. The same string harmonics idea of a violin, where one string sounds like an F and another string sounds like a G, applies to the four forces of nature (gravity, electromagnetism, the weak nuclear force and the strong nuclear force), as well as the particles. Different harmonics determine different particles and forces so that all matter and forces are united in one elementary theory. The characteristic patterns of vibrating, oscillating strings provide the music of science, "String Theories") particlecentral.com

Dr Berman explains: "The cutting edge of science has always impacted the music and art world; Einstein's relativity and the world of quantum mechanics has been influencing artists for 100 years. Now string theory is at the cutting edge of physics and the interest by artists in the challenging concepts of theoretical physics continues. We have been exploring the relationship between the cutting edge of science and that of sound art." phys.org

The universe was created by the sound of words spoken by God. God said the way He created everything was by speaking words and believing that what He said would come to pass. Romans 4:17 says, "God who gives life to the dead and calls into being what does not yet exist." Or as the NKJV says it, "…God, who gives life to the dead and calls those things which do not exist as though they did."

"As though they did" shows us where the faith part comes in. This is calling into being from the invisible realm into the visible. *In God's invisible imagination, everything exists. He just calls it forth, like Jesus called Lazarus from the tomb.* Jesus said, "Lazarus, come forth!" And Lazarus, who had been dead for four days, walked out of the tomb alive and well (John 11:43–44).

We are talking here about the force of faith that God used, and that Jesus showed us *we* are able to use when He said, "Have the God kind of faith." This idea goes way beyond believing in God. We are assuming that we believe in God as a foundational truth. When you begin to learn about God's ways and His preferences, His laws, His vision for the future, His faith will undoubtedly pop up. Faith is a big deal to God. It is how He operates. "But without faith it is impossible to please Him (God), for he who comes to God must believe that He is, and that He is a rewarder of those who diligently seek Him" (Hebrews 11:6). You could look at that scripture this way. He who comes to God or he *who desires to connect with God* must believe not only that God exists but also that He is a rewarder of those who diligently seek Him.

When you reach out to God by faith, you receive a reward. The best reward, of course, is a relationship with Him. But there are additional rewards as you come to know

God. God is a giver, a blesser. He has said to ask Him for whatever we desire. This is a foundational way of thinking about faith. Faith apart from your relationship to God is nothing, but faith because of your relationship to God is the way we receive everything from Him. Without faith, it is impossible to please God (gratify Him entirely). But when you please God, He turns around and pleases or rewards you! He is a rewarder of those that diligently seek Him. You receive the reward—what you are believing for. God is all about faith. It's how the universe operates. And God wants us to know about it and to be able to use it.

Jesus expected people to have more faith than they did.

> "Where is your faith?" He [Jesus] asked His disciples. In fear and amazement, they asked one another, "Who is this? He commands even the winds and the water, and they obey Him." (Luke 8:25)

> "Why are you so afraid?" He asked. "Do you still have no faith?" (Mark 4:40)

> If that is how God clothes the grass of the field, which is here today and tomorrow is thrown into the fire, will He not much more clothe you—you of little faith? (Matthew 6:30)

> But Jesus, being aware of it, said to them, "O you of little faith, why do you reason among yourselves because you have brought no bread? Do you not yet understand, or remember the five loaves of the five thousand and how many baskets you took up?" (Matthew 16:8–9)

It was not that the disciples didn't believe *in* Jesus. He was standing right there! That wasn't what Jesus was talking about. Jesus was disappointed (*not* pleased) that they didn't believe that they had access to heaven's resources! He had shown them the open door, but they didn't comprehend it. However, they did later.

The Robe of Righteousness

Some people may object to this interpretation of scripture, that God wants us to use our faith like He does. They may feel that it is man usurping authority from God or trying to make himself into God, which was Satan's sin. Let me clarify. God is the ultimate authority. He alone is God, not us. But because of what Jesus did for us, our position has changed. We are no longer just the descendants of Adam and Eve. We are now new creatures, born of the Holy Spirit, God's own offspring. Jesus is called the first-born of many brethren. "For whom He foreknew, He also predestined to be conformed to the image of His Son, that He might be the firstborn among many brethren" (Romans 8:29). If we were merely the sons of Adam, wouldn't Adam be the firstborn? But no, Jesus is the firstborn of a new race. We no longer are just restored to our position on the earth, but we are seated in heaven with Him now. That is our heavenly or spiritual position with God. It is not us who are grasping at a spiritual identity. It is God who made us this way. This is why the devil hates us. He wanted that position.

It pleases God to have a family made in His image. Yes, He will always be the Father, and we will always be His children. We are not trying to be Him. We are trying to be us, the us who He has said we now have become. All agreed, we are not worthy of this honor and have done nothing to deserve it, but this is how royalty is passed down from father to son, by birth. The throne is not passed to a servant.

> Just as He chose us in Him before the foundation of the world, that we should be holy, and without blame before Him in love…according to the good pleasure of His will, to the praise and glory of His grace, by which He made us accepted in the Beloved…having made known to us the mystery of His will, according to His good pleasure, which He purposed in Himself… In Him we also have an inheritance, having believed, you were sealed with the Holy Spirit of promise, who is the guarantee of our inheritance…made us alive together with Christ (by grace you have been saved) and raised us up together, and made us sit together in the heavenly places in Christ Jesus… (Ephesians 1:4-2:6)

Continuing to see ourselves as wretched sinners and lowly worms, who are separated from a holy God, is the opposite of the gospel. That is sin consciousness, and we need to fight against that, for the Word of God declares this:

> For the law, having a shadow of the good things to come, and not the very image of the things, can never with these same sacrifices, which they offer continually year by year, make those who approach perfect. For then would they not have ceased to be offered? For the worshipers, once purified, would have had no more consciousness of sins… But this Man [Jesus], after He had

offered one sacrifice for sins forever, sat down at the right hand of God...for by one offering He has perfected forever those who are being sanctified [made holy]. (Hebrews 10:1–14)

Let us draw near with a true heart in full assurance of faith, with our hearts sprinkled clean from an evil conscience [sin consciousness] and our bodies washed with pure water. (Hebrews 10:22)

After we are born again, the Word of God tells us we have been made righteous (holy) by the blood of Jesus. In order to see ourselves as God sees us, we need to become righteousness-conscious! This truth is so contrary to religious thinking that it's not even funny. The devil uses religion, the idea of working to earn God's favor, to keep us from living in the victory that Jesus won for us on the cross. As sinners, the cross is before us, but after we become Christians, the cross is behind us. Isaiah 61:10 says, "For He has clothed me with the garments of salvation; He has covered me with the robe of righteousness." Contrary to religious thinking, it does not please God when we refuse to wear our beautiful robe of righteousness.

And if that weren't amazing enough, in John 17, Jesus prays this prayer about us, They are not of the world, just as I am not of the world. Sanctify [purify, make holy] them by Your truth. Your word is truth. As you sent Me into the world, I also have sent them into the world, and for their sakes, I sanctify Myself, that they also may be sanctified by the truth. I do not pray for these alone, but also for those who will believe in Me through their word, that they all may be one, as You, Father, are in Me, and I in You; that they also may be one in Us, that the world may believe that You sent Me. And the glory which You gave Me I have given them, that they may be one just as We are one; I in them, and You in Me; that they may be made perfect [complete, finished] in one...

It is through the Word—knowing the truth about God, about what Jesus did for us, His finished work—that we are made complete and why we are able to wear that robe of righteousness that our Father has given to us. This is the foundation of our faith for answers to prayer. We are not pleading to God to have mercy on us. He has already had mercy and transformed us. We don't pray for everything by saying, "If it be thy will." The Word of God *is* His will. We already know what He said and, therefore, how He feels about a lot of things. He desires all men to be saved. We don't have to ask if it is His will that we witness to someone or pray for them to be saved. It is the same for other things. By getting familiar with what He already said in the Bible, we don't have to wonder when we pray if we should apply our faith to something or not. We find a scripture that supports the direction of our prayer and use it as a platform to shoot out our faith like a rocket!

Believing and Speaking, Faith's Dynamic Duo

In the operation of faith, believing and speaking go together. They are faith's dynamic duo. Believing is the first side of the dynamic duo.

Assuredly I say to you, whoever says to this mountain, "Be removed and be cast into the sea," and does not doubt in his heart, but *believes* that those things which he says will be done, he will have whatever he says. Therefore, I say to you, whatever things you ask when you pray, *believe* that you receive them, and you shall have them. (Mark 11:23–24, emphasis mine)

If we believe it will come to pass, then it will, Jesus said. Faith *is* the reality. It is the evidence of things not seen. If we believe what we say, our faith carries the unseen into the realm of the seen.

Speaking is the other side of the dynamic duo. Remember, everything is made of sound and will respond to the spoken Word of God. Here is the same scripture we just read, with the emphasis on the speaking side.

Assuredly I say to you, whoever *says* to this mountain, "Be removed and be cast into the sea," and does not doubt in his heart, but believes that those things which he *says* will be done, he will have whatever he *says*. Therefore, I say to you, whatever things you ask when you pray, believe that you receive them, and you shall have them. (Mark 11:23–24, emphasis mine)

In the natural world, molecules, consisting of atoms that are made of strings of sound, make up everything we see. These molecules, rearranged in different combinations, make different things. We know that the spiritual realm is a higher realm than the natural and that the spiritual world affects the natural world. When we speak words of faith, in the name of Jesus, the creation responds to the authority of the name of Jesus and rearranges itself to produce what we have spoken by faith into existence. The basics are already there. God has seen to that.

Faith is activated by the sound of your voice speaking the Word(s) of God and believing that what you are saying will come to pass. To operate in the faith realm, we need to believe what God has said, *and* we need to speak those powerful God-words with our own mouths.

The promises of God are more true, more "basic" than what we can see with our natural senses. The spiritual world came first. Its laws supersede the natural laws of earth and the natural laws of this fallen world. When we believe what God has said over what someone else says, or even what we actually see or feel, weird as that may seem, the circumstances will change to match the Word of God. God has already spoken His will (His Word) into existence. Our faith just links up to what He already said. And we are not limited to what God said in Genesis. He has given us hundreds of promises in the Bible. Jesus spoke many words into existence during His ministry on the earth. Those words are waiting for us to link up with, to use, to call them into existence in our own lives by our faith. He said, "My words are spirit, and they are life" (John 6:63).

The word translated "life" here is the Greek word *zoe*, which is many times found together with the word eternal as in "eternal life." John 1:4 says, describing Jesus, "In Him was life, and the life was the light of men." "Fight the good fight of faith; take hold of the eternal life to which you were called..." (1 Timothy 6:12) This word *zoe* life is talking about God's own kind of life, not our limited human existence. God wants us to share in His life, to live eternally with Him. "My words are spirit, and they are life." Every word of scripture has this life of God already inside it, waiting to be released in our lives (2 Timothy 3:16).

That life should be bubbling up inside of us like a fountain of youth, a continual renewal of everlasting life. Jesus said, "Out of your belly (heart) shall flow rivers of living water (life)" (John 7:38). The Church has been living far beneath her great potential! It is time to move into the destiny to which the Father has called us. Let's start speaking life to our situations and to the world, which desperately needs it. Let's start calling things that "be not" as though they were, like God has shown us, so that we defeat the devil in every place he considers his domain. Let the rivers flow!

God is listening to what we say. The devil is listening to what we say. And the universe, the whole creation, is listening to what we say. "Out of the abundance of the heart, the mouth speaks" (Matthew 12:34). Proverbs 18:21, "Death and life are in the power of the tongue." *What we say proves what we believe!*

The Day of Pentecost

On the Day of Pentecost, the Holy Spirit sat on each of the disciples in the form of tongues of fire. Tongues? The first time I heard that, I thought someone had made a mistake. Why would God appear like a tongue? It seems so random, but the more I come to understand how God feels about the spoken word, the more I see where He appears to be going with this. Words are super important, spoken words, not just thinking words in our minds. You don't need a tongue to think words. And words are more important than feelings. God has feelings, which is why He gave them to us, but He is not all about feelings. Sure, emotions and feelings have a place, but the Bible is quite clear that we should keep our emotions under control and not let them rule our behavior. Words, spoken words, are more important and can subdue feelings.

God created many different kinds of animals. Many of them have a form of communication, but none of them, with the exception of a few birds who mimic sounds, can speak words like humans can, who are created in the image of God. He reserved the gift of the spoken word for humanity alone. Evolutionists get all excited about the similarities between monkeys and humans, but monkeys can't talk. Sorry, guys, they fall way short of being human.

> When the Day of Pentecost had fully come, they were all with one accord in one place. And suddenly, they heard a sound from heaven, as of a rushing mighty wind, and it filled the whole house where they were sitting. Then there appeared to them divided tongues, as of fire, and one sat upon each of them. And they were all filled with the Holy Ghost and began to speak with other tongues, as the Spirit gave them utterance. (Acts 2:1–4)

On the Day of Pentecost, the disciples were all together in one place. They were all talking about Jesus. The Bible says they were all of one accord. How would anyone know that? By their conversation, what they were saying. Thoughts are important, but it is thoughts expressed out loud that can create unity with another person. When we pray together, if we are all praying silently, how will we know we are in agreement? How can we say "Amen," which means we agree?

Those disciples had seen Jesus back from the dead. He had been with them for forty days after His resurrection, teaching them, encouraging them, preparing them for ministry. And then He ascended into heaven and was gone. Now they were alone and yet not alone because they had each other. They were drawn to each other. They wanted to talk to each other about Him, remember things He said and what He had done in their midst. And then... they heard a sound like a mighty rushing wind.

The Holy Spirit was rushing to come to them, filling them with the Spirit of Jesus. He was back! Tongues of fire showed up and sat on each of them. Why tongues? What was the significance of tongues? It was like a big neon sign flashing, "It's in the speaking of words, folks! Say the words! Speak to the mountains and see them move! And these tongues were made of fire. Fire stands for boldness and passion. The Holy Spirit was saying, don't be afraid to speak the words of Jesus. The words of Jesus, the spoken scriptures, can change your situation. They can heal sick bodies and cast out demons. They can even raise the dead. Yes, Jesus was back, only spread out among all the believers this time. *They* had become His body to represent His presence in the earth now. And this is still where we are today.

Let's dissect some of this scripture that tells us about the coming of the Holy Spirit. You can read a scripture at face value and get a picture of the history, and then you can look closer to find a deeper meaning by the words that were used to tell the story. Every word in scripture is important.

- *Sound—"Suddenly they heard a sound from heaven..."* The word used here is like an echoing sound. The sound they heard was not a particular word, but the sound of many words echoing each other like a waterfall of water drops, overlapping each other. Ezekiel 43:2 says, "His voice was like a noise of many waters and the earth shone with His glory." Revelation 14:2 adds, "And I heard a voice from heaven, like the voice of many waters, and as the voice of mighty thunderings…". The Christian Standard Version translates this passage as the "sound of cascading waters and like the rumbling of loud thunder." The Good News translation describes the voice of God as sounding "like a roaring waterfall."

Picture turning on a water faucet full blast to fill the bathtub. What does that sound like? Picture a fire hydrant with water pouring out onto the street. What does that sound like? Picture the sound of a river with a strong current that develops rapids as it moves over rocks. Picture the sound of a large waterfall like Niagara Falls. The voice of God is like that—the voice of many waters—and it sounds like rolling thunder, words falling upon words, words overlapping words.

- *Wind*—"A sound from heaven as of a rushing mighty wind" In John 3:8, Jesus compared the Holy Spirit to the wind. "The wind blows where it wishes, and you hear the sound of it, but cannot tell where it comes from and where it goes. So is everyone who is born of the Spirit." In that scripture, He was saying you can't see the Holy Spirit, but you can see the effects of the Spirit by what He has done. The scripture is also showing us that though we can't see the Holy Spirit, we can hear Him. He is in the Word of God that we speak out loud. The word used here for "wind" also means "breath." On the Day of Pentecost, the Holy Spirit came to breathe life into the Church and get it started. The word used for "rushing" mighty wind means to bear or carry something. The wind or breath of the Holy Spirit was carrying the tongues of fire, representing the precious Word of God. When we speak the Word of God, we are breathing life into our situation, the breath or wind of the Holy Spirit.

- *Sat upon them*—"Then there appeared to them divided tongues, as of fire, and one sat upon each of them." There were 120 disciples in that place, including Jesus's mother and His brothers. The tongues sat on them. The word *sat* means to be seated, sit down, settle on, dwell, continue, tarry. Wuest's translation says the tongues *"took up a position on each of them."* It is the same word used for the scripture in Hebrews 1:3, "[Jesus] Who being the brightness of His [the Father's] glory and the express image of His person and upholding all things by the word of His power, when He had by Himself purged our sins, sat down at the right hand of the Majesty on High." The Holy Spirit came to stay, to dwell on and in each of them, and He brought the fire of the Word of God with Him. We should be confident that the Holy Spirit is with us, in us, and for us, and He is not leaving us.

God is a threefold being: the Father, the Son or Word, and the Holy Spirit. Jesus said, "Don't you know Me, Philip, even after I have been among you such a long time? Anyone who has seen Me has seen the Father. How can you say, 'Show us the Father'?" (John 14:9). So when you see Jesus, you see the Father, and when you hear Jesus, who is the Word of God, you hear the Father and you hear what the Father is saying. Likewise, when you hear the Holy Spirit, you hear Jesus. When someone hears us, they should be able to hear Jesus in what we say. People ought to be able to say of us, "When you've seen them, you've seen Jesus."

We are the body of Christ, made in the image of God, and we must learn not only to act like Him but also to talk like Him, to *sound* like Him. When we say or quote His own words, we sound like Him. The devil gets very confused.

Some Principles of Faith

Here are some important things to know about faith:

1. The Word of God is the basis for everything.

2. Heaven's resources are made available to us by, or through, faith in the Word.

3. We operate in faith by speaking the Word of God out loud, agreeing with God.

4. Everything is made of sound and will respond to the spoken Word of God. The visible world can be rearranged by speaking the Word of God in faith.

5. We continue (not just saying it once) to speak faith-filled words that align with the scripture. As we hear our own mouths speaking the Word, our faith is strengthened.

6. A double-minded man (faith mixed with unbelief) does not receive anything.

7. Through faith and patience, we inherit the promises. Sometimes patience is required.

8. Man's free will cannot be overcome by the faith of someone else.

9. Faith works through love.

10. Nothing is impossible with God.

Connecting With Jesus

For three and a half years, Jesus was with us, showing us how to live, how to act as children of the Father. He did amazing miracles and spoke with an authority that was strange to His disciples. "The people were amazed at His teaching, because He taught them as one who had authority, not as the teachers of the law" (Mark 1:22). He got this authority from God the Father. John 5:19 says, "Jesus gave them this answer: 'Very truly I tell you, the Son can do nothing by Himself; He can do only what He sees His Father doing, because whatever the Father does the Son also does.'" The scriptures in John continue, "For the Father loves the Son and shows Him all He does. Yes, and He will show Him even greater works than these, so that you will be amazed."

Jesus goes on to tell us that our faith can connect us with Him, and as we are plugged into Him, we will be able to do what He did. "Most assuredly I say to you, He who believes in Me, the works that I do He will do also; and greater works than these will He do, because I go to My Father. And whatever you ask in My name, that I will do, that the Father may be glorified in the Son. If you ask anything in My name, I will do it..." (John 14:12-14).

Then He lets us know that it is His words, not feelings, that help make the connection. "If anyone loves Me, he will keep My word; and My Father will love him, and we will come to him and make our abode with him. He who does not love Me does not keep My words; and the word which you hear is not Mine but the Father's, who sent Me" (John 14:23-24).

Keeping the words of Jesus is how we stay connected to Him. *Keeping His word means doing what He says to do.* The power is not in knowing the words, but it is in doing them. And if we keep His words, it is like He is still living His life on earth through us.

> Abide in Me, and I in you. As the branch cannot bear fruit of itself, unless it abides in the vine, neither can you, unless you abide in Me…for without Me you can do nothing… If you abide in Me, and My words abide in you, you will ask what you desire, and it shall be done for you. By this My Father is glorified, that you bear much fruit; so will you be My disciples… (John 15:4–8)

If we keep the words of Jesus, allowing Him to live through us, the Father will respond to us just like He responded to Jesus. He loves Jesus and He loves us. If Jesus asked Him to do something, the Father would do it. Now, as believers, if we ask the Father to do something for us, Jesus said He will do it.

> And in that day, you will ask Me nothing. Most assuredly, I say to you, whatever you ask the Father in My name, He will give you. Until now you have asked nothing in My name. Ask, and you will receive, that your joy may be full… For the Father Himself loves you, because you have loved Me and have believed that I came forth

from God. I came forth from the Father and have come into the world. Again, I leave the world and go to the Father. (John 16:23–28)

This is a huge deal! Look at how many times Jesus tells us to ask in these two chapters of John:

- "<u>Whatever you ask</u> in My name, I will do."
- "If you <u>ask anything</u> in My name, I will do it."
- "You will <u>ask what you desire</u>, and it shall be done for you."
- "In that day you will <u>ask Me</u> nothing (because)…"
- "<u>Whatever you ask</u> the Father in My name, He will give you."
- "<u>Ask</u> and you will receive, that your joy may be full."

Some people read those scriptures and think Jesus can't possibly mean what He said. That would be too crazy! I mean, He's saying "whatever" and "anything." What if I asked for a million dollars? What if I asked for something bad? Can I be trusted?

Okay, balance is good. Part of the scripture mentions us connecting to Jesus. What would Jesus ask for? Jesus was a minister during His time on the earth, thinking of the welfare of others. He cared about whether or not other people knew the truth, if they were fed, if they were lonely, if they were well, if they were happy. He cared about their needs, always giving to the poor. So we can certainly ask for things for other people. And here we have to take a step back for a minute, lest we fall over in the super-spiritual ditch on the other side. Jesus was (and is) a real guy. He lived in a house, had parents and siblings, worked as a carpenter (some people say stone mason) or craftsman, hung out with friends, maybe went fishing from time to time. He knows what real situations and problems are. Being a craftsman, He probably had to make choices, like, which tool to use. He had life choices. "What should I eat for dinner? Should I put on my right shoe first or my left shoe? Should I wear sandals or go barefoot?" He had desires and preferences that were not all necessarily ministry-related while He lived on the earth. When the scripture offers us a choice, saying whatever things you desire, it is not referring only to ministerial things. John 15:11 says, "These things have I spoken to you, that My joy may remain in you, and that your joy may be full." "You will ask what you desire… (John 15:7). "Ask and you will receive, that your joy may be full" (John 16:24). Of course, when we pray, we are usually thinking about solving problems for other people, but we are also allowed to ask God for things that would make us happy personally. The Father loves us! Ask that your joy may be full!

Sometimes we are hesitant to ask for something big. We might ask God to help with the little things in our lives, but when it comes to something super big or important, we are afraid to stretch our faith out that far. But Jesus told His disciples in the boat to "launch out into the deep" (Luke 5:4). God is pleased when we stretch our faith for something larger than we have done before. One time, I was asking God for some property to build a house. He told me that I needed to be more specific. What kind of property? What location? He wanted details. So I wrote down a list of characteristics that I thought would be good for my family. I wanted waterfront, near a town, but with a country feel. I wanted lots of trees and a good view of the water. It would be nice to have a place for a firepit and room for the kids to play games in the yard. You get the idea. God wanted details, so I gave Him details. I prayed about the property and believed God to find it. It was a stretch for me to believe for all those things together. I struggled with thinking that it was too much to ask, but God continually assured me that it was not. A few weeks later, we found the property. God had provided every detail. Don't be afraid to think bigger. Stretch your faith for the impossible! Have radical faith. God is a radical God. "He is able to do exceedingly above all that we can ask or think!" (Ephesians 3:20).

Trials Purify Our Faith

All praise to God, the Father of our Lord Jesus Christ. It is by his great mercy that we have been born again, because God raised Jesus Christ from the dead. Now we live with great expectation, and we have a priceless inheritance—an inheritance that is kept in heaven for you, pure and undefiled, beyond the reach of change and decay. And through your faith, God is protecting you by his power until you receive this salvation, which is ready to be revealed on the last day for all to see. So be truly glad. There is wonderful joy ahead, even though you must endure many trials for a little while. These trials will show that your faith is genuine. It is being tested as fire tests and purifies gold—though your faith is far more precious than mere gold. So when your faith remains strong through many trials, it will bring you much praise and glory and honor on the day

when Jesus Christ is revealed to the whole world.
(1 Peter 1: 3–7 NLT)

Everybody goes through things. There is a devil running around causing trouble. But Christians have a promise that the trials or struggles we go through are not wasted time. They are being used by God to help us look good. When our faith remains strong, it will bring us praise and glory and honor in the future. How great is that! Don't lose heart and get discouraged if what you are believing for doesn't happen right away. Hebrews 6:11–12 says, "And we desire that each one of you show the same diligence to the full assurance of hope until the end, that you do not become sluggish, but imitate those who through faith and patience inherit the promises." We will inherit or receive the promises of God sooner or later. Of course, we want it to be sooner, but this scripture tells us that patience is sometimes needed to complete the answer to prayer.

This reminds me of when I applied for the government's teacher loan forgiveness program. I filled out all the paperwork, and if you have any dealings with the government, you know there is always a lot of paperwork. But the potential was a loan cancellation of $17,000. I submitted all of the identification, names, addresses, proof of employment in a Title 1 school for more than five years, etc. Then I waited for a response. Patience…I finally received a communication saying I did not fill out one of the items to their satisfaction, so I called the government office, and after waiting a long time on the phone, you know how that is—I spoke to a representative that told me about some little thing I should have added. It was minor. Patience. So I resubmitted all the paperwork, prayed, and waited for the debt to show that it was $17,000 less in my account. After two or three weeks, I received a letter saying there was just one thing I needed to change on my application before it would go through. I called and again waited a long time to get through to someone who could tell me what was going on. Finally, I got to speak with a person who said, "Oh yes, apparently you need to send in…" some piece of information, whatever it was. I tried to say very nicely, "Why didn't anyone tell me I needed to send in something else when I called before? And why didn't they include that in the instructions?" The representative didn't know but assured me I was all set. "Are you sure there isn't anything else I need?" "No, you seem to have everything, we need to process your application." Patience. Two or three weeks later, I received a third letter requesting yet another minor change. By this time, I was really frustrated. I called again and spoke to a man, and he was not that sympathetic. After hearing about my three letters and less than satisfactory phone calls, He said something that stuck with me. He said, "Well, it's a lot of money. So what if you have to do a few extra steps? Isn't it worth it?" He was right! I did finally get the money. This is like it is for us sometimes receiving by faith. It takes patience, consistent confession, speaking what we want to see change, thanking and praising God for the answer, and not canceling out our faith with doubt and unbelief while we wait. The answer is on its way. Wait for it. It will be worth the wait.

Bible Precedence

"God is no respecter of persons," the scripture tells us. If He has done something for one, He can do it for you. If something has happened one time, it is possible to do it again. This is the rule of Bible precedence. If Jesus healed a blind man, that means He can heal the blind. Your faith can stand on that word that if He did it once, He can do it again. If Jesus multiplied the loaves and fishes, we can believe He is able to multiply the pasta on your stove for a surprise guest. If God stopped the rain, started the rain, made the sun stand still, calmed the storm, then He can change the path of the hurricane or the weather pattern for you. If God prospered Abraham, Isaac, Jacob, Joseph, David, Solomon, etc., He can also do it for us. If God provided a husband for Ruth and a wife for Isaac, He can do it for us. If God supernaturally brought children to barren women, He can do it for us. If He gave David victory over all his enemies, He can do that for us too. If you find a precedence in the Bible that God did it for one, you can, in a general sense, use your faith to believe that God will do the same for you.

Obstacles to Faith

Here are some things that block our faith from being effective:

- Limited hearing of the Word of God
- Not diligently seeking God
- Prayer life slacking
- Fear
- Filling our minds with worldly thinking (doubt and unbelief)
- Strange doctrine

The things listed here are basically all related to not reading or hearing the Word of God.

How do we hear the message of the Word of God? We can hear it in a church sermon—that is, if we attend a faith-believing church; we can hear it at a Bible study; we can hear it from a recorded message; we can hear it while talking to Christian friends; or we can hear it from our own mouths as we say it out loud. Reading the Word is also good, of course, but the scripture makes it plain that the hearing of the Word is how faith comes, so we want to be sure we are doing it God's way.

When the things of this world become so distracting that we are spending all of our time on them and not enough on the things of the Kingdom, our faith will lack the strength to believe for impossible things. God promises a reward to those that diligently seek Him. He knows it takes effort. If we miss church, have no time for a Bible study, don't read the Word ourselves very often, it will soon become evident in our faith walk. Nothing will happen. If we are not feeding ourselves daily with the Word, our prayer life will show it. We are told to pray without ceasing. That's how crucial our communication with the Father is. Jesus said that He is the vine, and we are the branches. If we never connect to the vine, our fruit will either be shriveled or nonexistent.

Fear slips in when we're not paying attention. Things we watch on TV, hear on the news, hear from another person, experiences we have in the world like accidents, people getting laid off from their jobs, death in the family, all can open a door for fear to get a toe in the door. We need to be diligent to watch out for fear, kick it back out when we spot it sneaking in. Fear can paralyze faith. What's the quickest way to get rid of fear? Cuddle up to the love of God. Perfect love casts out fear, the Bible tells us. There is no fear in love, and faith works by love.

Besides fear, all kinds of worldly thinking can seep in while we are mindlessly watching TV or reading the newspaper or enjoying social media. There are so many people who do not know God, and they broadcast their opinions about everything on social media as if they are the ones we should listen to. A lot of that thinking is aggressively ungodly. It is filled with doubt and unbelief about everything to do with God. That's what the people in Noah's day were doing, minus the technology. That's what the people in Sodom and Gomorrah were doing. It was not helpful. They never figured it out until the judgment fell, and by then it was too late. The Bible says, "There is a way that seems right to a man, but the end thereof is the way of death" (Proverbs 14:12). Let's not follow *that* path. If you are drenched in the world's way of thinking and doing, you will never develop enough faith to move mountains. Faith is how we access the Kingdom. It is the connection by which we get from this world to that one. Remember, this Kingdom was made for us.

Discussion Questions

1. How would your faith be affected if you didn't think God wanted you to have what you were praying for?

2. How would your faith be affected if you were sure God wanted to grant your request?

LESSON 16

THE TIMELINE (PART 1)

Although the Bible is much more than a history book, the timeline it portrays is important to know. If we are to understand God and His plans, we need to understand the times we now find ourselves in, what has occurred before and what is to occur next.

God is eternal. There is no time frame for Him. The Bible says that to the Lord, "one day is as a thousand years and a thousand years as one day" (2 Peter 3:8). We, His creation, on the other hand, do have a beginning. Time was created for us. Sun and moon, day and night, seasons and years, time itself was set up when the world began (Genesis 1:14).

The timeline of this age began at creation and continues until the millennium (thousand-year reign of Jesus as King on the earth), and after the millennium age, God will create a new heaven and a new earth (Revelation 21:1). It is important for us to have an understanding of the beginning, what happened, what was said, and also of the end, what will happen and what has been said about it, so that we will be able to discern where we are in time.

Here is a simple version of the Bible timeline. (Not to scale)

Creation	Israel Born	Kings/Prophets	Jesus' Ministry	Rapture	New Earth-
__/_____	/_____	/_____	/_____	/_____	/ Heaven
	/	/	/	/	/
Fall of Man	10 Commandments Given	Fall of Israel	Church Age	7 years Tribulation	Jesus Reigns Millennium

Here is another way of looking at it:

Creation		Jesus'	**Church Age**	Tribulation	Millennium
7 Days	4000 years	Ministry	2000 years	7 years	1000 years

/_____/_____/_____/

If you look at the numbers in this timeline, you find that there is recurring theme of 7. Numbers in the Bible are significant. The number *7* means complete. God created the heavens and the earth in six days and rested on the seventh. With the number *7*, it was complete. The last few years of this premillennial age (before Jesus comes back) are the *seven* years of tribulation, which are *seven* years to complete the judgment of this world. If we add up the four thousand years before Jesus and the approximately two thousand years that have gone by since, we get six thousand years. Add the one thousand years planned for the millennium kingdom, and we total seven thousand. Remember, "a thousand years is as one day" with the Lord. Seven thousand years is as the *seven* days of creation. Whether or not we use that "thousand days" scripture to explain it, *seven* remains the significant number, and seven thousand years makes a complete end of God's Earth project. It is very interesting how the number *7* keeps showing up throughout the scriptures. Noah was in the ark *seven* days before the rain fell, the tribulation period lasts *seven* years, etc.

Being Ready

Many people believe that we are in the very last days of the Church age. They look at those numbers and many other signs happening currently to come to that conclusion. We will look at some of those other signs later, but for now, let's assume these people are correct. The Bible tells us many times to "be ready." Ready for what? Ready for the imminent return of the Lord!

And if I go and prepare a place for you, I will come again and receive you to Myself, that where I am you may be also. (John 14:3)

Now may the God of peace Himself sanctify you entirely; and may your spirit and soul and body be preserved complete, without blame at the coming of our Lord Jesus Christ. (1 Thessalonians 5:23)

Therefore be patient, brethren, until the coming of the Lord. The farmer waits for the precious produce of the soil, being patient about it, until it gets the early and late rains. You also be patient. Establish your hearts, for the coming of the Lord is at hand. (James 5:7–8)

Now as to the times and the seasons, brethren, you have no need of anything to be written to you. For you yourselves know full well that the day of the Lord will come just like a thief in the night. While they are saying, "Peace and safety!" then destruction will come upon them suddenly like labor pains upon a woman with child, and they will not escape. (1 Thessalonians 5:3)

And to wait for His Son from heaven, whom He raised from the dead, that is Jesus, who rescues us from the wrath to come. (1 Thessalonians 1:10)

So that you come short in no gift, eagerly awaiting for the revelation of our Lord Jesus Christ, who will also confirm you to the end, that you may be blameless in the day of our Lord Jesus Christ. (1 Corinthians 1:7)

Let your gentle spirit be known to all men. The Lord is near. (Philippians 4:5)

Behold, He is coming with the clouds, and every eye will see Him, even those who pierced Him; and all the tribes of the earth will mourn over Him. So it is to be. Amen. (Revelation 1:7)

Looking for the blessed hope and the appearing of the glory of our great God and Savior, Christ Jesus. (Titus 2:13)

Watch therefore [be on the alert], for you do not know which day your Lord is coming. But understand this: If the owner of the house had known at what time of night the thief was coming, he would have kept watch and would not have let his house be broken into. Therefore you also be ready, for the Son of Man is coming at an hour you do not expect. (Matthew 24:42–44)

The return of Jesus is one of the main things Christians believe. You can see why. There are lots of scriptures that talk about it. According to scripture, Jesus's return will be a surprise.

We are to be ready to receive Him, kind of like when you get ready to receive a visitor that is coming sometime in the middle of the night. (Maybe he had to take a late flight.) You get the room ready, a blanket, a pillow, towels, maybe a late-night snack, and leave the lights on. You don't go to bed, you stay up, because you know someone special is coming and you want to be there to open the door and welcome him. Being ready to meet the Lord means being watchful for His return, believing what He said, and seeing that we are doing what He said to do. Jesus taught this parable in Matthew 24:45–51.

> Who then is the faithful and wise servant, whom the master has put in charge of the servants in his household to give them their food at the proper time? It will be good for that servant whose master finds him doing so when he returns. Truly I tell you, he will put him in charge of all his possessions. But suppose that servant is wicked and says to himself, "My master is staying away a long time," and he then begins to beat his fellow servants and to eat and drink with drunkards. The master of that servant will come on a day when he does not expect him and at an hour he is not aware of. He will cut him to pieces and assign him a place with the hypocrites, where there will be weeping and gnashing of teeth.

Even in the beginning days of the Church, believers were expecting Jesus to return any day. However, if you look at the timeline, as we can see now, God was planning a more long-term Church age.

Why is He taking so long to return? We learn why from the scriptures that say that God is longsuffering (patient) and is waiting for people to make decisions to turn to Him (Romans 2:4). During these two thousand years of the Church age, as we wait, thousands and thousands of people have become believers. He doesn't want to leave anybody out that has a desire to be with Him, all our families, all our friends. After all, if He had come back when the Church was just getting started, we never would have had the chance to become believers. All along, He has been helping us and our loved ones to make the right choice, doing miracles for us, sending people to tell us about the good news, using television, radio, billboards. But once Jesus returns, the time is up. Whatever choice you think you might have made later is irrelevant. God is going with the choices that have been made up until then. You are either for Him or against Him, there is no middle ground or such a thing as sitting on the fence. There is a judgment coming on the world and its system, and the Bible tells us it will be a big surprise to those who are not prepared.

This is the time to get ready, to choose your side, and to be safe. If you have chosen to have Jesus as your Savior, then you are safe for all eternity.

Parable of the Ten Bridesmaids (Virgins)

Jesus taught this parable concerning being ready for His return. We are the bridesmaids in this parable. Jesus is the bridegroom. It is found in Matthew 25:1–13 (NLT).

Then the Kingdom of Heaven will be like ten bridesmaids who took their lamps and went to meet the bridegroom. Five of them were foolish, and five were wise. The five who were foolish didn't take enough olive oil for their lamps, but the other five were wise enough to take along extra oil. When the bridegroom was delayed, they all became drowsy and fell asleep.

At midnight they were roused by the shout, "Look, the bridegroom is coming! Come out and meet him!" All the bridesmaids got up and prepared their lamps. Then the five foolish ones asked the others, "Please give us some of your oil because our lamps are going out."

But the others replied, "We don't have enough for all of us. Go to a shop and buy some for yourselves." But while they were gone to buy oil, the bridegroom came. Then those who were ready went in with him to the marriage feast, and the door was locked. Later, when the other five bridesmaids returned, they stood outside, calling, "Lord! Lord! Open the door for us!"

But he called back, "Believe me, I don't know you!"

So you, too, must keep watch! For you do not know the day or hour of My return.

Jesus pretty much let us know there was going to be a long wait, but He didn't excuse us from being prepared and ready to receive Him when He comes. Isn't it rather shocking that the five bridesmaids with no oil thought they had the same relationship with the bridegroom as the five who had extra oil? And isn't it interesting that the bridegroom said he didn't even know them? Is it possible to think you are safe when you are not? Getting into heaven is all about whom you know and who knows you. It is not intellectual knowing but relationship, intimately knowing. It's critically important that we not only know about God, but that we get to know Him on a personal level. Reading and studying the Bible is the best way to do that. The Bible is the Word of God, and the Word of God is Jesus.

Discussion Question

1. Why do you think it is important for us to know where we are in time?

Okay, so we are in the Church age. When we talk about the end times, many people are referring to the end of the Church age. If you look back at the timeline, there is quite a bit more that happens after that. We're not really talking about the end of the end. Actually, there is no real end. At the end of the timeline is a new heaven and a new earth… and then eternity, infinity and beyond. The Bible tells us quite a bit about what is to happen before Jesus returns to set up His Kingdom on this earth. One thing is clear: when Jesus returns, it will be a day just like any other normal day. Maybe today?

Jesus said this in Matthew 24:36–39:

> But of that day and hour no one knows, not even
> the angels of heaven, but my Father only. But as

the days of Noah were, so also will the coming of the Son of Man be. For as in the days before the flood, they were eating and drinking, marrying and giving in marriage, until the day that Noah entered into the ark. And did not know until the flood came and took them all away, so also will the coming of the Son of Man be.

Luke 17:28–30 adds:

Likewise as it was also in the days of Lot: They ate, they drank, they bought, they sold, they planted, they built; but in the day that Lot went out of Sodom it rained fire and brimstone from heaven and destroyed them all. Even so will it be in the day when the Son of Man is revealed.

Jesus is prophesying in these two scriptural examples and using the past to show us the future. He was saying that at these two historical events, most of the people were taken by surprise. But two people were not: Noah and Lot. Noah had been building an ark. He knew what was coming. Lot was escorted out of the city by angels. He knew what was coming. They were watching, and they were ready. How did they know, and the others didn't? They were listening to what God was saying. That's what we need to do because our historical event is right around the corner.

Here are just some of the signs of the end of the age according to the Bible. "So likewise you, when you shall see all these things, know that it (the end of the age) is near, even at the doors" (Matthew 24:33).

- Dramatic increase in wars, famines, and pestilences, which include viruses and plagues (Matthew 24:7)

- Great earthquakes and natural disasters in various places (Matthew 24:7)

- Men will be lovers of themselves and lovers of money (2 Timothy 3:2)

- Increase in violence and brutality (2 Timothy 3:3)

- Increase in sexual immorality and perversity (Jude 1:7, Romans 1:18, 24–27)

- Increase in blasphemy, cursing, using the Lord's name in a disrespectful way, calling things that are holy as if they are common, lack of respect toward God on a variety of levels (2 Timothy 3:2)

- Families breaking up, children being disobedient and disrespectful to parents (Romans 1:30, Luke 21:16)

- Persecution of Jews and Christians (Matthew 24:9, Revelation 12:17)

- Rise of occultic practices, demonic influence, and demon worship (1 Timothy 4:1)

- False christs, false prophets rising up (Matthew 24:24)

- The gospel of the kingdom will be preached in all the world (Mark 13:10)

- Fearful sights and great signs from heaven (Luke 21:25–26)

- Knowledge will increase (Daniel 12:4)

- There will be signs in the heavens (Revelation 6:12–14)

You can see that most of these signs are not new to us. Just read the news headlines. Jesus said they would come like labor pains—far apart at first and then closer together. Every one of those signs has become more intense in our lifetime. Think about knowledge increasing. During our lifetime, knowledge has super-increased! Technology, science, medicine, mathematics, education, sports, inventions! If ever there was a time to say knowledge was increasing…we are certainly in a generation that looks like that.

Now here are some signs that have not happened yet but are not so far-fetched that they couldn't take place in a very short amount of time:

- *A global confederacy will be established consisting of ten nations*—Revelation 13:1 says, "Then I saw a [vicious] beast (antichrist) coming up out of the sea with ten horns and seven heads, and on his horns were ten royal crowns (diadems), and on his heads were blasphemous names." Don't panic when you read about beasts and horns. These images are just symbols, like the stars and stripes of the flag represent the states and early colonies of America. In this case, ten horns represent ten nations or kingdoms. Heads represents authorities. "Now the beast which I saw was like a leopard, his feet were like the feet of a bear, and his mouth like the mouth of a lion" (Revelation 13:2) This is a reference to the previous historical and expansive (world) kingdoms of Persia, Greece, and Rome. The Antichrist's short-lived kingdom will be like all of these put together. "The dragon gave him his power, his throne, and great authority" (Revelation 13:2) The dragon, or devil, is, of course, behind the whole idea of an Antichrist and a global leader. He is backing it, totally supporting it, and will be extremely involved in the whole business. This is his last move in the chess game, world domination, and, with it, universal domination. He is still after God's throne. "And all the world marveled and followed the beast (antichrist). So they worshiped the dragon who gave authority to the beast; and they worshiped the beast saying, Who is like the beast? Who is able to make war with him?" (Revelation 13:3–4). People are always looking for something to worship because we have been made with a desire to worship God. So if the object of their worship is not the real God, then it will be someone or something else, perhaps even themselves.

Think of how the world is becoming more and more globally conscious. Climate change has become a global discussion. The recent viral pandemic caused nations to be locked down, a drastic and never-before-seen response, which meant that hard-fought-for freedoms were easily suspended for the "safety and security" of the people. The result of this unfortunate circumstance, for lack of a better term, is that the governments now know that most people will obey whatever rules they set in place, even free democracies and world powers like the United States, for the right reason. Nations are forming alliances, like NATO and the United Arab Emirates, in order to gain a competitive advantage in the world. The European Union, which formed a few years ago, at one time contained ten European nations. Nationalism is quickly fading out of style. Globalism is the new trend. This all may seem like a good thing and harmless, but if you read and understand the scriptures, you know that one-world global order and economy is exactly the environment predicted that will welcome in the Antichrist.

- *There will be a seven-year peace treaty made between Israel and her enemies*—Daniel 9:27 says, "And he will enter into a binding and irrevocable covenant with the many for one week (seven years), but in the middle of the week he will stop the sacrifice and grain offering [for the remaining three and one-half years]; and on the wing of abominations will come one who makes desolate, (the antichrist) even until the complete destruction, one that is decreed, is poured out on the one who causes the horror."

Israel has not had true peace since being reestablished in 1948. In fact, before then, this prophecy would have been impossible to fulfill. The land of Israel, once a flourishing territory with boundaries set by God Himself, was ravaged by the Romans, starting with the destruction of the temple in Jerusalem in AD 70. In an attempt to completely erase Jewish history from the land, the Roman Emperor Hadrian renamed the province of Judea as Syria Palaestina. This was the beginning of the region being called Palestine. The Jewish people were scattered around the world as a judgment from God, and their land was made desolate. But the Jews are still God's chosen people, and He always had a plan for them to return to their own land, as evidenced by the many prophecies in the Old Testament. Those prophecies were fulfilled in 1948, when miraculously at the end of World War II the nation of Israel was reestablished with her own land boundaries again. But after becoming a nation, Israel has been attacked continually by her Arab neighbors, who feel they have a right to the land. Now we anticipate, because of Bible prophecy, in the midst of seemingly impossible odds, a future peace treaty with the Muslim Arab groups. Although some leaders, including our presidents, have tried to negotiate a treaty, real peace has so far eluded them due to the Arab nations' insistence that Israel should not exist and must be annihilated. However, in 1979, Egypt agreed to normalize its relationship with Israel, and in 1994, Jordan agreed to peace with Israel. In 2020, President Trump's administration negotiated a peace treaty between Israel and the United Arab Emirates, and this tells us that the time is ripe for the coming end-time peace treaty between Israel and *all* of her enemies for seven years. The signing of the seven-year treaty is the starting point of the seven-year tribulation period.

* * * * *

- *A charismatic leader will come on the scene* (Daniel 11:21)—The coming united global government will be run by someone who is anti-Christ, an antithesis, or opposite of everything Jesus Christ is and stands for. People are always looking for someone to follow, someone with answers to world problems, especially these days. The Bible says this leader will gain power through flatteries and deception. His real agenda is to set himself up as the Jewish Messiah, an Antichrist, king of the world, but his success will be short-lived. He is like a copycat criminal copying Jesus, the true Messiah and King of the world during the millennium. This Antichrist will even have a sidekick, a false prophet who follows him around like John the Baptist who came before Jesus and witnessed that He was the Lamb of God. The Bible says the Antichrist will be mortally wounded and then miraculously recover, kind of like being raised from the dead. Copycat! Do you remember the story of the beginning and how Lucifer wanted to set himself up as God's replacement? Well, guess who still wants to be ruler of the world and worshiped as a god? Nothing's changed. In fact, after three and a half years, midway through the peace treaty, the devil gets tired of waiting for the Antichrist to follow his plan and completely possesses the Antichrist's body. He can't stand the suspense any longer and assumes all the worship to himself. Then, true to form, he immediately begins to steal, kill, and destroy (John 10:10). The peace treaty is broken, and great violence breaks loose against the Jews and anyone else who supports them. Any people who may have become believers after the rapture will have to go into hiding or be arrested and beheaded. This practice makes it look like the Antichrist's administration will be sympathetic to or have a connection to the Muslim culture, where the use of beheading for capital punishment has recently made a comeback. Revelation 20:4 says, "And I saw thrones, and they sat on them, and judgment was committed to them. Then I saw the souls of those who had been beheaded for their witness to Jesus and for the word of God, who had not worshiped the beast or his image, and had not received his mark on their foreheads or on their hands. And they lived and reigned with Christ for a thousand years."

- *The false prophet, the image, and the mark of the beast—* We know the goal of the devil is to be worshiped like God. At the end of the age, he influences and empowers the Antichrist and his sidekick, the false prophet, to arrange things so that it will be impossible for people *not* to worship him.

  - *The Beast*

    When reading the scripture from the Book of Revelation, don't let the term *beast* stress you out. It's God's descriptive word for the Antichrist. It is a term that means animal and was used before in the Old Testament as a contrast with a human being made in the image of God. The Bible's use of the word *beast* to refer to the Antichrist gives you the idea of what God thinks of him. In the Book of Daniel, Daniel (the lion's den survivor) interpreted the Babylonian king's dream in which an angel prophesied that King Nebuchadnezzar would lose his mind and have to leave his palace to live in the wild. "Let his heart be changed from that of a man, Let him be given the heart of a beast…" The prophecy came to pass, and for seven years—there's that number 7 again—the king lived outside like a wild beast, eating grass like an ox (Daniel 4:16). This predicament came on the king because he had lifted himself (obnoxiously) up in pride, making a big statue of gold, an image of himself that all his subjects were required to worship or be killed. "Then a herald cried aloud: To you it is commanded, O peoples, nations, and languages, that at the time you hear the sound of the horn, flute, lyre, and psaltery, in symphony with all kinds of music, you shall fall down and worship the gold image the King Nebuchadnezzar has set up; and whoever does not fall down, and worship shall be cast immediately into the midst of a burning fiery furnace" (Daniel 3:4–6).

• The term *beast* used for King Nebuchadnezzar means wild animal. The word *beast* used for the Antichrist and his false prophet in the Book of Revelation, in contrast to the term *beast* here, means *dangerous*, wild animal. It is also found in the New Testament when referring to a venomous snake. Whoever these guys are in the endtime prophecy, they have definitely been demoted in God's eyes, and we have been warned against them.

So they worshiped the dragon (Satan) who gave authority to the beast (antichrist) and they worshiped the beast, saying, "Who is like the beast? Who is able to make war with him?… All that dwell on the earth will worship him, whose names have not been written in the Book of Life of the Lamb slain from the foundation of the world. If anyone has an ear let him hear… Then I saw another beast (false prophet)… And he exercises all the authority of the first beast in his presence, and causes the earth and those who

dwell in it to worship the first beast (antichrist)…
He performs great signs, so that he even makes
fire come down from heaven on the earth in the
sight of men [copying Elijah the prophet]. And
he deceives those who dwell on the earth by those
signs which he was granted to do in the sight of
the beast, telling those who dwell on the earth to
make an image to the beast who was wounded
by the sword and lived. He was granted power
to give breath to the image of the beast, that the
image of the beast should both speak and cause
as many as would not worship the image of the
beast to be killed.

He causes all, both small and great, rich and
poor, free and slave, to receive a mark on their
right hand or on their foreheads, and that no one
may buy or sell except one who has the mark or
the name of the beast or the number of his name.
Here is wisdom: Let him who has understanding
calculate the number of the beast, for it is the
number of a man: his number is 666.
(Revelation 13:4, 8–9, 11–18)

• *The False Prophet*

The false prophet is a guy who, like John the
Baptist's ministry for Jesus, points people to
the beast (Antichrist) and encourages them
to worship him as a god. He will probably be
a pseudo-religious character, accepting of all
non-Christian religions, including New Age,
humanism, the occult, and witchcraft, which
will lead to the establishing of a one-world
religion. He has power to impress everyone by

doing miracles, as long as he is in the presence of the demonic Antichrist, and comes up with the great idea to make a big statue of the Antichrist just like Nebuchadnezzar did. This statue, or *image of the beast*, can speak like a robot and can spot nonworshipers in the crowd. Although this has been a mystery to people in the past, we can easily see how the technology available in this generation could certainly produce such a thing.

•   *The Mark of the Beast*

The mark is a sign of identification with the beast and could be a tattoo or a stamp or anything that says you belong to the beast (Antichrist). All the people in the world will be required to receive some kind of mark on their right hands or foreheads that relates in some way to the number of the beast or Antichrist, which is 666. This number will allow them to buy and sell (Revelation 13:16–18). The number 6 in the Bible usually refers to man. The number 3 represents the Trinity of God. The significance of 666 is wrapped around the idea of man trying to make himself God. It will most likely be a political strategy to begin with, perhaps "safety"-related, but it will become almost impossible to ignore because the prophecy concerning the mark is global and signifies global allegiance to the Antichrist. Why would everyone, or almost everyone, do that? Up until now, this prophecy would have been crazy to imagine. Now, not so much.

Many Christians now believe the mark to be some kind of ID chip that will be implanted and read on the hand or forehead. The technology is here and already being used on animals, babies, and the military and is pretty much showing up all over. The prophecy tells us that no one will be able to buy or sell anything without the mark. You can imagine the sales pitch of such an idea. We went from a cash society to one that extensively uses credit and debit cards. But credit and debit cards can be lost or stolen, identities can be hacked, causing all kinds of problems. Wouldn't it be better to have your identification on a chip right inside your own body so no one could ever steal your information? And these end-time ID chips will be connected in some way to that charismatic leader known as the Antichrist. The mark (chip) will be a sign that you identify with him and support him, and people will probably feel quite patriotic when they have it implanted. But the scripture also warns us that to take the mark makes you an enemy of God, so don't do it! I would be very cautious about receiving any type of ID chip in your hand or forehead, even if you don't know who the Antichrist is yet. It's too close to what the prophecy in Revelation describes. And after living through this pandemic of the COVID-19 virus, see how easily we all, globally, have been coaxed into wearing masks for the good of society's safety. During the tribulation time, the societal pressure to display the mark on yourself will be intensely strong. And interestingly, the location of the chip or mark that is currently being hailed as cutting-edge technology goes right along with the Bible's prediction of being placed in the hand or forehead, not an arm, an ankle, or shoulder. In Revelation 7:3, God places a seal on the foreheads of his servants. The devil has no original ideas.

- *The temple will be rebuilt in Jerusalem with its daily sacrificial system reinstated* (Daniel 11:31, 12:11)— The daily sacrifice means the sacrificing of animals to God in order to temporarily cover the general sins of the people. Christians believe that Jesus fulfilled that requirement with the sacrifice of His own blood, but the Jews as a whole, at this point, do not. The Jewish temple was destroyed in AD 70 and has not been rebuilt since. This has made it impossible for them to offer a daily sacrifice. However, the Book of Daniel says,

Then he [the antichrist] shall confirm a covenant (peace treaty) for one week [seven years]; But in the middle of the week [three and a half years], he shall bring an end to sacrifice and offering... And they shall defile the sanctuary fortress; then they shall take away the daily sacrifices, and place there the abomination of desolation... And from the time that the daily sacrifice is taken away and the abomination of desolation is set up, there shall be 1290 days...(Daniel 8:11-12,9:27,11:31, and 12:11)

A forerunner of this event happened in 175 – 165 BC, when Antiochus IV, the Syrian king, ruled Palestine as a surrogate of the Greek empire. This man took to himself the title Theos Epiphanes, which means "manifest god," and he set himself up as the supreme ruler over the Jews. Making a covenant with them but later breaking it, he stopped the daily sacrifices in the temple, sacrificed a pig on the altar, which was an extremely sacrilegious and desolating act to the Jews, since the pig is considered an unclean animal to them, and set up a statue, an image of the pagan god Zeus in the midst of the temple, a gross abomination. Does this sound faintly reminiscent of King Nebuchadnezzar? You know, the I-am-a-god delusion and the psycho image necessity making one larger than life? The future Antichrist will make both Nebuchadnezzar and Antiochus IV look like amateurs.

Some people say that because the prophecy in Daniel was fulfilled with Antiochus Epiphanes, it no longer applies to the future lawless Antichrist. But don't fall for that thinking. There are other prophecies that God has given to us that have had more than one fulfillment. The coming of Jesus, for instance, was fulfilled two thousand years ago, but that doesn't mean He is not coming again. The first coming fulfilled some of the prophecies, but when He comes the second time, He will complete the whole picture. The spirit of the Antichrist is not new either. It has been around for a while. John said, "For many deceivers have gone out into the world who do not confess Jesus Christ as coming in the flesh. This is a deceiver and an antichrist" (2 John 7).

"And this is the spirit of the antichrist, which you have heard was coming, and is now already in the world" (1 John 4:3).

Besides, Jesus prophesied in AD 33, more than one hundred years after Antiochus Epiphanes, quoting Daniel's words. He said, "Therefore, when you see the abomination of desolation, spoken of by Daniel the prophet, standing in the holy place, then let those who are in Judea flee to the mountains" (Matthew 24:15). So if Jesus believed the Antichrist prophecies are still for future end-time fulfillment, then we should too. Paul in 2 Thessalonians 2:3–4 also talks about the Antichrist and the temple. "Let no one deceive you by any means; for that Day will not come unless the falling away comes first, and the man of sin is revealed, the son of perdition [the antichrist], who opposes and exalts himself above all that is called God or that is worshiped, so that he sits as God in the temple of God, showing himself that he is God."

So because of all this scripture talking about the temple and the daily sacrifices, it is pretty difficult to consider an end-times scenario without including the rebuilding of the Jewish temple. Obviously, in order for the Antichrist to *take away* the daily sacrifice from the temple, as prophesied, there would have to be a daily sacrifice system up and running. And for the daily sacrificial system to be in operation, there would have to be a physical temple. For a long time, this has seemed literally impossible. For one thing, Israel has only come back to official existence since 1948. And for another thing, the grounds on which their temple has been built and rebuilt in the past, the Temple Mount, is the same ground on which, unfortunately, now stands the Muslim Dome of the Rock. The Jews want to rebuild their temple on the Temple Mount, the site of Abraham's sacrifice of his son Isaac and the site where the previous other two temples have stood. Muslims have no plans to tear down their sacred building to build a Jewish temple. But some people believe that the future covenant of peace signed with Israel will contain the element of access and permission for rebuilding the third temple. There are actually plans in progress now for the rebuilding of the temple.

- *Jerusalem will be surrounded by armies (as usual)* (Luke 21:20)—The land of Israel, once a desert wilderness like its surrounding neighbors, has blossomed into a fruitful, beautiful garden of a country since 1948. It contains rich natural resources that others would love to get their hands on. The bordering Arab nations have been in constant conflict with Israel since the time of Abraham and now more than ever. What is the problem? One answer is that Abraham had two sons, Ishmael, whose mother was Hagar, a servant, and Isaac, whose mother was Sarah, Abraham's wife. Abraham sent away his son Ishmael and Hagar, his mother, settling his inheritance solely on Isaac. Ishmael's descendants, basically the Islamic Arab nations, have rewritten history so that in their view, the Muslim's view, Ishmael was the heir to the land of Abraham. Their hatred and jealousy of Israel goes back thousands of years. They deny Israel's right to exist and want the land's resources for themselves. Their final conflict will culminate in the Battle of Armageddon, which includes nations like Iran, Libya, and Ethiopia, following the orders of the Antichrist. Other players that are named in the end-time drama are Russia and China. These two communist countries have been plotting and scheming for world domination, and their desire to overthrow the Antichrist will engage them all in one final battle. Some people dispute the idea of Russia, the "land to the north" of Israel, and believe the end-time conflict to include Turkey. But either way, the Battle of Armageddon is the final war at the end of the age. It starts with a focus to annihilate the land of Israel but culminates in an all-out rebellion against God Himself. But be of good cheer, God is not worried! In the midst of the battle, Jesus returns with a huge army of believers and saves the day!

- *The Church will be glorious*
  The previous signs we talked about are the usual ones that most Christians think about, but there is one other sign that is not discussed all that much. It is the most important sign of all, in my opinion, and is found in Ephesians 5:25–27: "Husbands, love your wives, just as Christ also loved the church and gave Himself for her, that He might sanctify and cleanse her with the washing of water by the Word, that He might present to Himself *a glorious church*, not having spot or wrinkle or any such thing, but that she should be holy and

without blemish." Jesus will be coming back for His bride, the Church. He is not looking for a sad, insipid, weak, and powerless group of people. The Church Jesus is referring to is without spot. Some translations use the word *stain*. In other words, she is without sin, and she doesn't live a worldly lifestyle. She is separated and holy. The end-time Church is also without wrinkle. Think about what that means. There is nothing to mar the perfection of the bride. Sickness, poverty, foolishness, and insecurity are all things that present the bride in an unfavorable light. The Song of Solomon, speaking of the bride, says, "You are all fair, my love, and there is no spot in you." The NASB says, "You are altogether beautiful, my darling, And there is no blemish on you." Jesus is returning, not just to bring judgment on the earth but to carry away His bride—the unified Church, the one that looks and sounds like Him, His mate. The end-time rapture will not happen until the Church begins to look and sound like Jesus, her bridegroom. We'll talk about the rapture in the next lesson. I can't wait!

Discussion Questions

1. What are some signs that stand out to you as being significant to this generation? Why?

2. Do you think people in America would follow a world charismatic leader? Why or why not?

LESSON 17

THE TIMELINE (PART 2) THE LEASE IS UP

In the world's eyes, God is like an absentee landlord. We know He's out there somewhere, but we think we have lots of time before He comes to collect the rent. In the meantime, we have been ignoring His rules and terms of the lease agreement and doing whatever we felt like doing. We've been partying and breaking windows, the carpets are stained, the garage door doesn't close right, and weeds have taken over the lawn due to our negligence. We have let animals come and live there as if it's a barn. There've been fights and loud music and screaming arguments. The police have been called a number of times, and we've been warned. The landlord is not going to be happy. And He's coming soon.

God originally gave Adam dominion over the earth, and then, of course, Adam gave it to the devil, complicating things. But the good news is that God didn't give the *earth* to Adam. The Bible says that God owns the earth and everything in it (Psalm 24:1). He is still the legitimate owner. What God did was give Adam the authority to rule here temporarily. It was a training ground, not the end game. So when God has decided that the time for Adam's tenancy is over, He will take it back and rule over the earth Himself. Jesus will reign as King right here on the earth, not just in heaven, as some people imagine. The scriptures call Jesus the second or last Adam. So what does it mean for the devil when Jesus takes over? He will be out. Thank goodness!

In Mark 12, Jesus tells a parable of a landlord who leases out his vineyard to people who were supposed to take care of it. At vintage time, he sent a servant to receive some of the fruit from his vineyard. Instead of giving the servant some of the crop, as per the lease, the renters beat up the servant and sent him away. Other servants were sent, and they were all treated terribly by the renters. Finally, the landlord sent his own son, thinking they would respect his son. But they killed him and cast him out of the vineyard, thinking that the inheritance would now be theirs. Lots of people think the earth belongs to them. They are misinformed. Jesus said, "Therefore what will the owner of the vineyard do? He will come and destroy the vinedressers [renters], and give the vineyard to others." The lease on this earth is almost up, and the renters are about to be evicted by the owner.

Worship, Fear, and Wisdom

The devil is not like God. God loves people and looks for those who voluntarily desire to worship Him. He cares for them like a shepherd cares for his sheep and blesses them with kindness. The devil *forces* people to worship him through fear, like a mob boss who threatens to break your legs if you don't pay him for "protection." He is not nice. He gives the illusion of power or "caring" for a short time but then takes everything away from those who serve him, including their freedom. His goal is to destroy them. Unfortunately, people tend to worship what they fear. Think about the idol worshipers of the past. People needed rain and were afraid of drought, so they imagined rain gods and sun gods. They were afraid of war with neighboring tribes, so they made up gods of war. People imagined sea gods, hunting gods, fertility gods, you name it. Because of the fear of displeasing idols, people did all kinds of crazy things. People are afraid of the devil. If they actually realized how much destruction he's caused, that fear could turn into worship pretty fast. That's why in the Old Testament, God did not reveal the devil's involvement very much. He took the responsibility for the bad that happened along with the good. The so-called destructive "acts of God" on insurance forms are really acts of demons. Thankfully, when Jesus came, He exposed the devil's activity all over the place and cast him out. Jesus gave the Church power and authority over the devil, so there is no reason to fear him anymore.

On the other hand, the Bible teaches us that to fear the Lord is a good thing.

> The fear of the Lord is the beginning of knowledge, but fools despise wisdom and instruction. (Proverbs 1:7)
>
> My son, if you receive My words, and treasure My commands within you, so that you incline your ear to wisdom, and apply your heart to understanding; Yes, if you cry out for discernment, and lift up your voice for understanding, if you seek her as silver, and search for her as for hidden treasures, then you will understand the fear of the Lord, and find the knowledge of God. For the Lord gives wisdom; from His mouth come knowledge and understanding… (Proverbs 2:1–6)

The fear of the Lord is not like being afraid of someone who will randomly hurt us. We know God loves us and has our best interests at heart. But He does have rules and they have been made plain. He is not deceived, He sees everything.

Some people treat the things of God lightly, disrespectfully, inappropriately. They think of God as a nonplayer, like He's not in the game, but they are wrong. He is the referee. There is a judgment coming. The fear of the Lord is the beginning of wisdom (Proverbs 9:10). If you fear God, you will respect Him and His ways. You will take what He says seriously. Jesus said, "And do not fear those who kill the body but cannot kill the soul. But rather fear Him who is able to destroy both soul and body in hell" (Matthew 10:28).

God is very, very powerful. Good thing for us He is also very, very patient. The Bible calls it longsuffering. But finally, a day will come when the time is up. He will say enough is enough! Enough sickness, enough pain, enough sorrow, enough idolatry, enough perversion, enough selfishness, enough destruction, enough violence, enough darkness in men's lives, enough sin! He will come to collect the rent that is due. His wrath will be poured out on the earth and anyone who happens to live here at that time. When God is angry, we don't want to be anywhere close by. Thank goodness it's only seven years! And Jesus said if He didn't shorten the time, no one would be left standing on the earth (Matthew 24:22).

70 Prophetic Weeks

The Book of Daniel was written about 165 BC, before Jesus was ever around. Besides telling some historical events, like Daniel in the lion's den, it speaks prophetically about what will happen in the end-times. God tells us He has purposed seventy weeks until the end of the age.

That's right. He already told us how it's going to be.

> Seventy weeks are determined for your people [the Jews] and the holy city [Jerusalem], to finish the transgression, to make an end of sins, to make reconciliation for iniquity, to bring in everlasting righteousness, [the Kingdom], to seal up vision and prophecy, and to anoint the Most Holy [Jesus].
>
> Know therefore and understand, that from the going forth of the command to restore and build Jerusalem until Messiah the Prince, there shall be seven weeks and sixty-two weeks [sixty-nine weeks]: The street shall be built again, even in troublesome times. (Daniel 9:24–25)

Prophecy is sometimes cryptic. It's not always meant to be clear, especially when it isn't meant to come to pass for many years. This prophecy tells us there will be seventy weeks until the wrap-up of everything. It has been analyzed by every generation in the light of events happening within their own lifetimes. The same is true for us now. But after so much time has gone by, we now have the benefit of looking back at history to help us decipher the code, so to speak. Even so, there are many different ways scholars have interpreted this prophecy. But come on, seventy weeks! How hard could it be? He said it would be seventy weeks. Um…what does that mean? Seven days to a week? Seven days times seven? Forty-nine days? Well, that doesn't seem to make sense. Let's keep going.

The prophecy separates the weeks into two phases. It says there will be sixty-nine weeks until the coming of the Messiah. So where is the seventieth week? We'll get to that. Back to the prophecy.

> Know therefore and understand, that from the going forth of the command to restore and build Jerusalem until Messiah the Prince, there shall be seven weeks and sixty-two weeks [sixty-nine weeks]: The street shall be built again, even in troublesome times.

There were three different commands or decrees concerning the rebuilding of the city, and specifically, the temple. Interestingly, no matter how we look at it, which decree we start with, we get pretty much the same results: Jesus has to be the Messiah, the Prince. Here is an example of one way of interpretation using the third command to rebuild the temple and also rebuild the city (Ezra 7:12–26). The decree or permission was sent out by King Artaxerxes of Persia in 458 BC (Some historians use the year 457 BC). So from that date until the Messiah (Jesus) was to come was sixty-nine weeks, which actually means weeks of years. What?

Hold on here! Don't panic.

We learned earlier that in 2 Peter 3:8, it says, "With the Lord, one day is as a thousand years, and a thousand years as one day." But there is another scripture that says, "I have appointed thee each day for a year" (Ezekiel 4:6). One day equals one year. Yes, God likes to mix it up and sometimes refers to years as days and days as years. Remember, with God, there is no past or future. It is always present. He made time for us and reserves the right to use it or mess with it, however He sees fit. It keeps us on our toes. The word translated as *weeks* really just literally means *sevens*.

Let's do a little math. The scripture separates 7 sevens and 62 sevens.

Seven weeks of seven years = 49 years (or 7 x 7). History tells us it took forty-nine years to rebuild Jerusalem after the decree was sent out from King Artaxerxes. So that's the first part. That matches perfectly with the prophecy about seven weeks.

Sixty-two weeks of seven years = 434 years (7 x 62)— This is the time of waiting for the Messiah to come after the city was rebuilt. The total number of years for that 69 weeks adds up to 483.

"*From the going forth of the command to restore and build Jerusalem until Messiah the Prince, there shall be seven weeks and sixty-two weeks…*" So *were* there 69 weeks of years before Jesus came? Did anyone come 483 years after the decree to rebuild the temple and the city of Jerusalem? If you were a Jewish scholar or a Pharisee or scribe, you would have been diligently counting down the days till somebody would come to save you, especially during the days of the Roman occupation. They were waiting for a deliverer.

So let's calculate it ourselves.

The decree went out in the year 458 BC. Adding 69 weeks, or 483 years to that, which is really subtracting, since we are dealing with BC and AD, we get the year AD 25. The year 0 is the year Jesus was born, so Jesus would have been twenty-five years old. But most theologians say Jesus was born in the year 4 or 5 BC, which would make Him really around thirty years old at this time and exactly the age when He was baptized and began His earthly ministry as the sacrificial Messiah. Perfect fulfillment!

Other interpretations or computations using the Jewish calendar year of 360 days come up with the actual day Jesus rode into Jerusalem on a donkey with everyone shouting,

"Hosanna to the Son of David!" which was a reference to Him being the Messiah, the King. Scholars place this event on April 6, AD 32.

The Jewish religious leaders certainly knew Daniel's prophecy and must have known the times, but because Jesus didn't come on a white horse, swinging a sword, with armies behind Him, they dismissed Him as their Messiah. They were looking for a physical deliverer, and Jesus came as a spiritual deliverer. However, the next time He comes, the Bible says it will be on a white horse, with armies following Him, and He will most definitely have a sword!

So the prophecy in Daniel concerning the 69 weeks (7 weeks + 62 weeks) has been fulfilled by Jesus. There was no one else it could possibly have been.

Now for that seventieth week…

The prophecy continues, *"And after the sixty-two weeks,* ***Messiah shall be cut off****, but not for Himself; and the people of the prince who is to come shall destroy the city and the sanctuary…"*

The Messiah shall be cut off. That was phase one. Most New Testament Bible scholars agree that the Messiah is Jesus and that this "cutting off" is referring to Jesus's death, resurrection, and ascension back into heaven. He was not cut off for Himself but for the sins of the world.

Phase two of the scripture is about the prince (ruler) who is to come, which refers to the Antichrist. Was this guy going to destroy the city and the temple that had just been rebuilt? No, as it turns out, there is a huge gap in time here between the Messiah being cut off and the coming of the Antichrist. This is the tricky part with prophecy. The previous scripture is so specific as to the time down to the exact year! And now we have no reference to when the Antichrist will come at all. The early Church thought Jesus would be coming back right away. You can see why. The prophecy makes it look like the Antichrist will come right away. Many early Christians thought the Roman emperor Nero was the Antichrist. However, no one knew then that the Church age would last over two thousand years. And no one knew during the time of Daniel and the Old Testament that there would even *be* a Church! The Jewish rabbis only knew God as the God of Israel. It wasn't until the Book of Acts (New Testament) that Gentiles or non Jews were accepted into the group of believers in Jesus, who later became known as Christians (the Church).

Fast-forward two thousand years later. We are now nearing the end of the Gentile Church age and we are preparing for the remaining week of years for the Jewish people, the seventieth and last week where it all comes to the grand finale. Remember, from the timeline, there have been six thousand years since the creation of Adam according to biblical calculations. It is getting close to a very symbolic time for God to establish the Kingdom and the thousand-year millennium, finishing a seven-thousand-year earth project.

So the sixty-nine weeks refers to Israel, God's chosen Jewish people, then there is a big break in time, which, as it turns out, is the approximately two thousand years of the Church age, made up of some Jews but mainly Gentiles because the Jews rejected Jesus as their Messiah the first time He came. With the seventieth and last week of fulfillment of the prophecy, the focus is finally back on the Jews and on Israel. It is during this week that the Jews will come to realize that Jesus is their Messiah, their true anointed King, a descendant of King David, and He will come to save them from total annihilation by the armies of the Antichrist at the Battle of Armageddon.

The prophecy goes on to say, "And till the end of the war desolations are determined. Then he shall confirm a covenant with many for one week; but in the middle of the week, he shall bring an end to sacrifice and offering…"

The final week of Daniel's prophecy, set off by the signing of a covenant with Israel, is the seven years of the tribulation period.

7 weeks + 62 weeks + 1 week = 70 weeks

> Then he [the Antichrist] shall confirm a covenant [peace treaty] with many [between Israel and all her surrounding enemies] for one week [seven years of tribulation]; but in the middle of the week [after three and a half years], he shall bring an end to sacrifice and offering [he will break the treaty with Israel, preventing their worship of God in their temple]… And on the wing of abominations [horrible things he does] shall be one who makes desolate [the Antichrist], even until the consummation [the end], which is determined, is poured out on the desolate [followers of the Antichrist]. (Daniel 9:27)

The word for "desolate" or desolation in the Hebrew means to stun, grow numb—that is, devastate, stupefy, make amazed, astonish, be astonished, lay waste, destroy, wonder.

The scripture here is talking about a person, the one who makes desolate, the Antichrist and his followers, those on whom the consummation of the wrath of God is poured out. The destruction of that time will be so devastating that people will be astonished and horrified to the point of being numb. They are physically in shock. You have probably heard people joke about the end of the world as if it's going to be a big party. Songs have been written, comedy sketches have been performed about it, but those that think of this time lightly are highly misinformed. Jesus said, "Then there will be great tribulation, such as has not been since the beginning of the world until this time, no, nor ever shall be. And unless those days were shortened, no flesh will be saved" (Matthew 24:21—22).

Tribulation Defined

Tribulation (*thlipsis*) is a word used in the Bible that is translated from a word meaning "pressure," (what constricts or rubs together), used of a narrow place that "hems someone in," especially *internal pressure* that causes someone to feel confined (restricted, "without options"). The word for tribulation (or compression) carries the challenge of coping with the internal pressure of a *tribulation*, especially when feeling there is "no way of escape" ("hemmed in"), as opposed to external pressure exerted by circumstances (Strong's Concordance Online).

Luke 21:26 describes that time as "men's hearts failing them [or fainting] from fear and the expectation of those things which are coming on the earth, for the powers of the heavens will be shaken." There will be so many different and converging impending disasters and threatening circumstances that men will feel there is no way out, no way of escape, and they will collapse in fear. "And the kings of the earth, the great men, the rich men, the commanders, the mighty men, every slave and every free man, hid themselves in the caves and in the rocks of the mountains, and said to the mountains and rocks, 'Fall on us and hide us from the face of Him who sits on the throne and from the wrath of the Lamb!'" (Revelation 6:15–16).

Judgment and the Tribulation Period—One Last Chance

Jesus said,

> Now when these things begin to happen, look up and lift up your heads, because your redemption draws near… Look at the fig tree [symbol for Israel], and all the trees. When they are already budding, you see and know for yourselves that summer is now near. So you also, when you see these things happening, know that the kingdom of God is near. Assuredly I say to you, this generation will by no means pass away till all these things take place [meaning that all these signs will happen in one generation]. Heaven and earth will pass away, but My words will by no means pass away. But take heed to yourselves lest your hearts be weighed down with carousing, drunkenness, and cares of this life, and that Day come on you unexpectantly. For it will come as a snare on all those who dwell on the face of the whole earth. Watch therefore, and pray always that you may be counted worthy to escape all these things that will come to pass, and to stand before the Son of Man. (Luke 21:28–36)

The end of the age is a time of judgment. The nations (people, races, tribes) will be divided based on their relationship with Jesus.

> When the Son of Man comes in His glory, and all the holy angels with Him, then He will sit on the throne of His glory. All the nations will be gathered before Him, and He will separate them one from another, as a shepherd divides his sheep from the goats. And He will set the sheep on His right hand, but the goats on the left.
>
> Then the King will say to those on His right hand, "Come, you blessed of My Father, inherit the kingdom prepared for you from the foundation of the world…" Then He will also say to those on His left hand, "Depart from Me, you cursed, into the everlasting fire prepared for the devil and his angels…and these will go away into everlasting punishment, but the righteous into eternal life." (Matthew 25:31– 32, 41, 46)

Judgment Is Coming

The impending doom of judgment has been hanging over our heads all our lives. We know we are not living up to our moral potential. The fact that we have morals tells us there is a true right and there is a true wrong. Our morality tells us there is a standard to live up to. Morality is so much a part of us that, Ten Commandments aside, we will tend to follow a moral code of our own making. It is said there is honor among thieves. Thieves, though acting immorally to others, have their own moral code toward each other. Even the mafia has a code toward each other. Morals are a part of what makes us human, as animals and plants have no morality. Instinctively, we know what is fair and unfair. If someone tries to take your place in line, your moral compass will rise up inside you and cry, "Hey, unfair!" But though we have this sense of morality, we do not always follow it, and we sin, all of us. The Bible shows us that whether it's against our own code or whether it's against the Ten Commandments (the law of God), our sin is a treasonous rebellion against the God who made us. In fact, we have been building up quite a rap sheet, filling up those bowls of wrath (Revelation 15:7). Romans 2:5, 11–12 tells us, "But because you are stubborn and refuse to turn from your sin, you are storing up terrible punishment for yourself. For a day of anger is coming, when God's righteous judgment will be revealed... For there is no favortism with God. For all who have sinned without the law will also perish without the law, and all who have sinned under the law will be judged by the law."

Already Judged

However, judgment is only scary when you are guilty and are awaiting sentencing. Those of us who have been born again have already been judged. We have admitted to ourselves and to God that we are guilty. He then immediately stepped in to offer the payment for our sins Himself, and we received the free gift of forgiveness and eternal life. Our sentence was carried out on Jesus, and we are free to go. Romans 5:8–10 says,

> But God demonstrates His love toward us, in that while we were still sinners, Christ died for us. Much more then, having now been justified by His blood, we shall be saved from wrath

through Him. For if when we were enemies we were reconciled to God through the death of His Son, much more, having been reconciled, we shall be saved by His life.

There is no more scary judgment for us. But to those who have not accepted Jesus's death as the payment for their sins, judgment is *very* scary. They will have to pay for their sins with their own lives and for eternity. Judgment for us has already come and gone, but judgment remains for those who reject the only way out.

The tribulation time is not for us. It is for the ones who have not chosen God's Kingdom and have clung to the devil's kingdom. It is the devil's kingdom, dredged in darkness, seeped in sin—that is being judged. You don't want to go down with that ship. Now is the time to make the right choice. You may have one last chance during the tribulation period, but you will probably have to give your physical life. However, if you do lay down your physical life for Jesus's sake, during the tribulation period, you will gain an eternal reward with the rest of the saints (believers). The tribulation period is one last chance to take His side against the devil, but it will not be easy. God is gracious, so gracious, to give one more chance.

We are able to choose Jesus willingly now, in this time period of grace, and please our Father in heaven, but the scripture tells us that will change. Everyone, even His enemies, will bow before Jesus the King, willingly or unwillingly, and acknowledge that He is Lord!

Therefore God exalted Him to the highest place and gave Him the name above all names, that at the name of Jesus every knee should bow, in heaven and on earth, and under the earth, and every tongue confess that Jesus Christ is Lord, to the glory of God the Father… (Philippians 2:10)

By Myself I have sworn; truth has gone out from My mouth, a word that will not be revoked: Every knee will bow before Me, every tongue will swear allegiance. (Isaiah 45:23)

It is written: "As surely as I live, says the Lord, every knee will bow before Me; every tongue will confess to God." (Romans 14:11)

God is not willing that any should perish. "For God so loved the world that He gave His only begotten Son, that whosoever believes in Him should not perish but have everlasting life" (John 3: 16). However, He will not stop anyone from choosing to serve His enemy. God gives man the privilege of choosing whom he will serve…for a while. But in the end, there will not be a choice. Even the devil will bow his knee and confess that Jesus is his Lord and Master, and we know where he's going. Anyone on the devil's team is going down with him, just saying. If I were you, I wouldn't wait until then. It would not be very comfortable, to say the least. It is so much easier now. Make that everlasting life choice before it is too late! And tell your friends.

The Judgment Seat of Christ

That said, there *is* a time of celebration of the saints called the judgment seat of Christ. Second Corinthians 5:10 says, "For we must all appear before the judgment seat of Christ, that each one may receive the things done in the body, according to what he has done, whether good or bad." This is not the same as the judgment of the sinners in the world. It refers to the critique and judgment of what we have done to become like Jesus and to further the gospel *after* we are born again. It has to do with rewards, not punishment.

First Corinthians 3:12–15 says, "Now if anyone builds on this foundation with gold, silver, precious stones, wood, hay, straw, each one's work will become clear; for the Day will declare it, because it will be revealed by fire, and the fire will test each one's work, of what sort it is. If anyone's work which he has built on it endures, he will receive a reward. If anyone's work is burned, he will suffer loss; but he himself will be saved, yet so as through fire." This is telling us that Jesus is holding us accountable for our time spent on the earth. We have a part to play. We are supposed to produce fruit and get our own lives in order, renewing our minds and changing them to line them up with what the Word says. We are supposed to become like Him, talk like Him, and act like Him. We are supposed to fulfill the Great Commission, to be witnesses of this new life that is in us, to bring people to the Lord, and to make disciples. If we do that, we will receive a reward. If we don't, we won't— simple as that. No one is getting away with anything. God sees and knows it all. Hebrews 11:6 says, "He is a rewarder of those that diligently seek Him." Let's do our best to glorify God and to run the race and obtain the prize! Amen!

The Rapture of the Church

One of the more controversial subjects in the Bible is the concept of the rapture or catching away of the Church. This doctrine concerns those believers that will be on the earth at the time of the seven years of tribulation judgment or Day of the Lord or the end of the age. The reason it is so controversial is that the scriptures are vague as to when during the tribulation this will happen. Some people think the rapture will happen at the beginning of the seven years, some in the middle of the seven years, and still some think it will happen at the end of the seven years. In order to support the various theories, students of the Bible go back to other events and prophecies to make connections and inferences that support their points of view. This is a perfectly legitimate way to help us understand scripture and is done all the time. There are supporting arguments for all the different theories.

> Come, my people, enter your chambers, and shut your doors behind you; Hide yourself, as it were, for a little moment, until the indignation is past. For behold, the Lord comes out of His place to punish the inhabitants of the earth for their iniquity... (Isaiah 26:20–21)

The basic idea of the rapture is that Christians, who are alive at the time of the tribulation judgment, will not die, but their bodies will be changed in an instant from mortal to immortal.

This is an amazing miracle and has had the Church buzzing since day one! The believers (the bride of Christ) in their new eternal bodies will rise up in the air like Jesus did when He ascended into heaven (Acts 1:9) to be with their bridegroom. God has promised that His people would not have to go through the time of His wrath or judgment, like Noah, who was saved from the flood, and Lot, who was saved from the destruction of Sodom and Gomorrah (2 Peter 2:5–9). Here are some of the scriptures that promise us that we believers won't have to go through the wrath that God will pour out during the tribulation time. Interestingly, Noah was in the ark *seven* days before the rain fell.

For it [that Day] will come as a snare on all those who dwell on the face of the whole earth. Watch therefore, and pray always that you may be counted worthy to escape all these things that will come to pass, and to stand before the Son of Man. (Luke 21:35–36)

For God did not appoint us to wrath, but to obtain salvation through our Lord Jesus Christ. (1 Thessalonians 5: 9)

And to wait for His Son from heaven, whom He raised from the dead, even Jesus who delivers us from the wrath to come. (1 Thessalonians 1:10)

Come into the ark, you and all your household, because I have seen that you are righteous before Me in this generation... So Noah, with his sons, his wife, and his sons' wives, went into the ark... and it came to pass after seven days that the waters of the flood were on the earth. (Genesis 7:1, 7, 10)

The Rapture Described

The rapture is described by Paul in 1 Thessalonians 4:13–18:

Brothers and sisters, we do not want you to be uninformed about those who sleep in death, so that you do not grieve like the rest of mankind, who have no hope. For we believe that Jesus died and rose again, and so we believe that God will bring with Jesus those who have fallen asleep in Him. According to the Lord's word, we tell you that we who are still alive, who are left until the coming of the Lord, will certainly not precede those who have fallen asleep. For the Lord Himself will come down from heaven, with a loud command, with the voice of the archangel and with the trumpet call of God, and the dead in Christ will rise first. After that, we who are still alive and are left will be caught up together with them in the clouds to meet the Lord in the air. And so we will be with the Lord forever. Therefore encourage one another with these words.

Paul is comforting the people of Thessalonica, who were worried that their fellow believers who had already died would miss out on this fantastic moment, but he assures them that the dead in Christ (believers) will rise first, then the rest of us will follow.

1 Corinthians 15: 51–55 also mentions the event.

I declare to you, brothers and sisters, that flesh and blood cannot inherit the kingdom of God, nor does the perishable inherit the imperishable. Listen, I tell you a mystery: We will not all sleep, but we will all be changed— in a flash, in the twinkling of an eye, at the last trumpet. For the trumpet will sound, the dead will be raised imperishable, and we will be changed. For the perishable must clothe itself with the imperishable, and the mortal with immortality. When the perishable has been clothed with the imperishable, and the mortal with immortality, then the saying that is written will come true: "Death has been swallowed up in victory."

So the rapture is a miraculous event when the believers who are alive during the last days are changed from their natural bodies directly into supernatural spiritual bodies without the experience of dying. In a twinkling of an eye, Paul says mortality will "put on" immortality. None of us can enter heaven with mortal, earthly bodies. When we die, our flesh bodies decay and go back to dust, but our spirits, which are eternal, do not decay. God gives our spirits new immortal bodies to live in. For the last generation of believers, they don't have to die in order for that to happen. Pretty cool! Come, Lord Jesus!

The rapture of the Church is not the only event where people are taken directly to heaven without the experience of dying. There are at least seven "raptures" or rapture-type experiences mentioned in the Bible.

1. Enoch—Genesis 5:24, Hebrews 11:5

2. Elijah—2 Kings 2:11

3. Jesus—Acts 1:9

4. Paul—2 Corinthians 12:2

5. John—Revelation 4: 1–2

6. The Church—1 Thessalonians 4:15–17

7. Two witnesses (in the middle of the tribulation period)—Revelation 11:3–12

So the idea of a rapture, although it is usually presented as an end-time thing, is not a random doctrine. It's been around since Genesis. And although people have differing opinions as to when exactly during those seven years the rapture of the Church takes place, we all agree there's going to be one. As the T-shirt reads, "Heaven—don't miss it for the world."

Discussion Question

1. How would you live your life differently if you thought Jesus would return this year?

Now learn this lesson from the fig tree: As soon as its twigs get tender and its leaves come out, you know that summer is near. Even so, when you see all these things, you know that it is near, right at the door. Truly I tell you, this generation will certainly not pass away until all these things have happened. (Matthew 24: 32–34)

Jesus said,

Watch therefore, for you do not know what hour your Lord is coming. But know this, that if the master of the house had known what hour the thief would come, he would have watched and not allowed his house to be broken into. Therefore, you also be ready, for the Son of Man is coming at an hour you do not expect. (Matthew 24:42–44)

It may look like this is the end, but for born-again believers, it really is just the beginning. The kingdom of heaven is a kingdom created for us. Our future is glorious because we get to live with the King forever. Be blessed!

ABOUT THE AUTHOR

Kathy Zuziak has been a Bible teacher and has worked in ministry, especially the music ministry, for many years. She has a degree in music composition, a master's in divinity, and a doctorate in theology. She is an ordained minister and is currently involved in a home church ministry. She has written many Christian choruses and composed classical works, some of which were performed with symphony orchestras. She taught general music in public schools for twenty years. She has four wonderful children and six grandchildren. She loves to read, write, hike in the woods, do jigsaw puzzles, spend time with her family and friends, and talk about Jesus.